The Great Field

Soul at Play in a Conscious Universe

John James, Ph.D.

The Great Field

Library of Congress Cataloging-in-Publication Data

James, John
  The great field : soul at play in a conscious universe / John James. — 1st ed.
    p. cm.
  Includes bibliographical references.
  ISBN: 978-1-60415-015-5 (pbk.)
  1. Transpersonal psychology. 2. Consciousness. 3. Energy psychology.
I. Title.
  BF204.7.J36 2007
  110—dc22
                    2007034485
Copyright © 2007, John James

Typeset in Cochin

Printed in USA

First Edition

Typeset by Karin Kinsey

Cover design by Victoria Valentine

10 9 8 7 6 5 4 3 2 1

An investigation into the nature of the universe

and

its implications for the human soul

The concept of a Great Field inherent in every aspect of the universe provides a framework to enrich our understanding of particles and stellar systems, of our brains and our beliefs. It is capable of forming a conceptual basis for a unified cosmology that would help to clarify all creation and give meaning to the conflicts that so damage our species. The theory of the Great Field is a theory for our times.

ACKNOWLEDGMENTS

In a book of this breadth and complexity one cannot possibly acknowledge all the people who have influenced one's life or the gradual growth of this the book. What began as a thesis for a Graduate Diploma in Transpersonal Psychology grew over the next five years into a book. I would like to thank my two partners at the Crucible Centre for their involvement in every aspect of its evolution, my wife Hilary James, and our partner Marg Garvan. Also, Dr. David Wright, Ron Perry, Prof. Tony Baker, and Prof. David Russell, who supported and advised us at the Centre while the clinical research and writing was in progress. Many friends and students have given their feedback and comments. It should be said that some parts of this book are extremely dense and not always easily read. The choice was mine whether to write a very large book with full descriptions of experiments and client processes, or to keep it short, relying on the imagination and good sense of the reader to re-imagine and skim and skip as they need. So much information is now available on the Web that not everything needs to be spelled out in full. Among the many readers I would particularly like to thank are Lloyd Fell, Jane Warnock, Liz Taverner, Brian Johnson, and Norman Franklin. In particular, I thank Ruth Ammann for introducing me to Dawson Church, my publisher.

In the ocean of the Heart love opens its mouth
And gulps down the two worlds like a whale.
Heart from the Heart's wordless mysteries!
Understand what cannot be understood!
In man's stone-dark heart there burns a fire
That burns all veils to their root and foundation.
When the veils are burned away, the heart will understand completely.
                                        —Jalal-ud-Din Rumi[1]

Contents

ILLUSTRATIONS

She sat on the hill looking over the sea and breathed in the world around her. Things moved in and out of her known reality and mingled in colors and vibrations. The clouds poured into the bay and out again, repeating in a second all the complex movements of the day. Impressions of the entire past and present of the valley flowed through her consciousness, the language of the trees as they spoke to each other, where the tribes had moved and sung their dances, the changing levels of the sea. She was in the now, while immersed in all the forces that had ever flowed through this speck of consciousness, and yet deep within her there was no movement. She was utterly still and attentive. It felt that there was no time, no space and yet every sense was exquisitely attuned to each subtle nuance of the physical place where she sat. She was within everything, and without, simultaneously, and flooded with such knowing and compassion of that perfection that there was nowhere else to be but now. This was the realization of samadhi, of the pure bliss of the saints and the gurus of every denomination. She had crossed the veil within herself and had united the material world of time and the desires of the senses with the Great Field. There was no distinction any more, but only pure bliss and an unbearable compassion.

❀ ❀ ❀

---- 1 ----

INTRODUCTION

The entire cosmos, at every plane and in every form, is energy.
— Baba Ram Dass

Most of us have at some time, perhaps only when young, experienced the timeless wonder and bliss that heralds our introduction to the greater world beyond our everyday reality. Carl Jung said, "I felt I was in ecstasy, as though I were floating in space, as though I were safe in the womb of the universe — in a tremendous void but filled with the highest possible feeling of happiness. This is bliss, I thought, this cannot be described: it is too beautiful."[2] To be able to live in this space forever is one of the deepest dreams of mankind. For Christians it is being in the Grace of the Holy Spirit, for Hindus it is Samadhi, and for Zen practitioners it is Satori.

This state is real, as real as the everyday world for the rest of us. We naturally ask: what is this state, why is it hidden from us, where is it, how does it affect us, and how do we get there? It is the purpose of this book to explore these questions through the eyes of the human psyche.

For many people it is becoming clear that everything in the universe is both solid matter and fields of energy. Fields like gravity, electricity, and magnetism can be measured if not yet fully understood, and beyond them lie further fields that permeate everything. What we see and touch is where the wave functions are most dense. Beyond that lie invisible quanta that spread from and through each of us and everything. They permeate all that is.

No object or living being is truly separate. We only appear so because we cannot sense the fullness that is everywhere. We sense only empty space between us and between objects, whereas this space is in fact dense with action. Space is filled with a huge spectrum of waves: radio, ultraviolet, and so on. But beyond those that can be measured there are realms that encompass them and form further constituencies of fields. They exist without form, without dimension, and most importantly, without time. These realms contain an infinite number of possible fields, all regions of influence that extend infinitely everywhere. In this realm all is interconnected instantaneously: space itself has no meaning and time does not exist. Being instantaneous, connections move faster than the speed of light.

As fields of vibration are everywhere, each bit of creation, each human organism has the waves of every other entangled within it. We are field and matter, wave, and mass. As matter we affect things through physical contact, such as picking up a chair and moving it, or less directly through telephone and radio. But as field we affect at any distance without needing a medium in between. We are all doing this with each other all the time, participating intimately in the creation drama that is constantly unfolding. All beings are in an endless dance with each other that is inexhaustibly co-creating and re-creating the entire universe.

For a long time it was thought that such realms could not exist, and that no thing could be both particle and wave — it could be one or the other but not both at the same time. A hundred years ago it was proven that light could be simultaneously mass and energy, and shortly afterwards the theory of the quantum provided a model for understanding how this could be. From it came the revolutionary concept that it was the observer and not the particle that would determine whether light was to be experienced as mass or energy.

As Ram Dass points out above, this is not a new understanding. The intimate union of mass and vibration has been part of pre-scientific lore for thousands of years. It is a cherished part of sacred human wisdom. While our scientific knowledge is based on verifiable testing of the material side using material tools, the older knowledge is based on something altogether different: direct and substantive human experience. This understanding is gradually being integrated into modern science; it poses that the universe is an ecology in which, in Barry Commoner's classic definition made over thirty years ago, "everything is connected to everything else."[3]

The deeper implications of knowing that we are both field and matter have slowly seeped in to a wider Western consciousness, first through the scientific communities' attempts to come to grips with quantum, relativity, zero-point, and uncertainty theories, and then through the excitement some of us felt about morphic fields, holographic universes, and parapsychic phenomena. In the past twenty years there has been an accelerating scientific investigation into these things. Yet, much of this research has not yet been accepted nor integrated into significant sections of the scientific community, let alone the general populace. Many scientists continue to oppose the concept of an energy-based universe on philosophic and, at times, religious grounds, even though these grounds are not themselves subject to scientific proof. It is an odd situation.

The current scientific model is founded on the assumptions of 300 years ago that the world is made of separate entities moving in manners that can be predicted within an empty space. To this is added the view that the body is separate from both soul and mind. Nothing in this model is able to accurately explain the enormous complexity of human beings, of their relationship with the world, or, most particularly, their consciousness — though it has managed with much diligence to explain the bits in between. In a simplistic way we could say that we and our world are still being defined by educators, doctors, and scientists as if they are pieces of machinery.[4] Thus, in classical medicine the body is usually assumed to be only a bundle of matter stimulated by electrical impulses in predicable ways.

In its original promulgation, the mechanical model saw that "the entire universe was literally inanimate and soulless, and so was everything within it, except for the human intellect. Animals and plants became soulless machines, as did the human body with an unbridgeable gap between the realms of mind and matter."[5]

But in the emerging paradigm our bodies, like the whole universe, are awash with vibrations and signals that connect us within and without. Ancient religious views and the latest science are now coming together. They have met through the painstaking research of many people in biology, physics, neurology, and even astronomy, who have established that fields permeate every single thing, from the miniscule photons at the quantum level to the peptides and genes in our own bodies. The research leads to two inescapable conclusions: that everything in the universe is simultaneously physical and energetic, including the human psyche, and that every movement — *every* movement — in one realm affects every part of the other.

The implications are hard to take in at first reading, but would have staggering consequences if they were to be integrated into our lives.

I come to this story as a transpersonal psychologist. It is here, in the realm of the individual psyche, that I have had to face this issue in the most personal way. Conventional therapy is, like conventional physics and medicine, interested almost exclusively in the visible aspect of the psyche — behavior, neuroses, habits, and beliefs — with only notional concern for the larger presence of the non-tangible and the invisible. This domain is usually referred to as the transpersonal — it is the energetic body and includes the soul.

For fifteen years we have worked our way into this problem. With my wife Hilary and our partner, Margaret Garvan, I have been investigating how the psyche operates on the energetic and soul levels, while making some extraordinary discoveries of the depth and wonder of all that we are. The further we entered into the inner experiences of our clients and ourselves, the further we traveled from the orthodox theories and counseling modalities found in nearly all the professional literature. We increasingly found entire continents of issues that could not be explained in any accepted way.

As our own sensitivity increased we found we were entering new territory without fully understanding what we were doing. As the outcome for each client's well-being was beneficial we had to drop our preconceived theories and training, and allow our client's self-investigations into their own inner worlds to take us wherever they needed to. We discovered that the most effective clinical work presented us, often to our great surprise, with an entirely new and unexpected view of the human experience. This book is the outcome of that search, and we hope it will form a theoretical basis for further energetic and soul-based self-knowing.

In therapy we take it as fundamental that our private experiences are as important for our worldview as the information gained by verifiable experiment. In practice, it means that the psyche is as tangible as any object. The feelings and understandings that come from deep meditation are as vital a component of the psychic life as any scientifically analyzable data. We have found that the way in which we evolve our personalities follows the same process and stages as does every part of the universe, and shows us that we are structured just like everything else, and no differently.

This is not the place to tell you how we work, or anything of the modalities of transpersonal therapy. We cannot establish the ground for a new understanding of reality if we become distracted by methods and techniques. For this we need another book. It is enough to launch the nature of the Great Field, and our place and the place of our souls within it.

There is a distinct difference between work on the body's energy systems and work with soul and karma. The former include healing of the subtle energy paths through acupuncture, tapping, ch'i gong, and other techniques. The clinical efficacy of these methods has been under scientific analysis for some time, with considerable success.[6] This work addresses imbalances in the energy fields that affect moods such as depression and anxiety, and health issues such as cancer and psoriasis.[7]

We use some of these techniques at the Centre, but they do not form the substance of our discoveries, as you will see as you read further. Humans emit a number of energy fields, and we believe that the most important is the formative core of our being that created us that we call soul, for want of a better word.

In soul work experiences that lead to understanding are purely subjective. I doubt whether it would be possible to set up experiments that would validate this understanding. Though the outward manifestation of soul and karma in our daily behavior can be measured and analyzed, the inner forces that propel that behavior are too personal and ethereal to be quantified. Behavior is on the surface, while soul is the observable interface between our bodies and the universe of fields.

We have had to conclude that there is no place where transpersonal therapy can meet those in our discipline who rely exclusively on a scientific and statistical approach. There has been a trend among behavioral psychologists to justify themselves by being as rigorous as the other sciences, for they desire that the soft art of psychology be given a seat at the same table as the hard sciences. To this end, they have taken the view that only solid data and repeatable experimental evidence can reliably display the reality of the psyche. Our students have found that as the results cannot be independently verified, proposed research into energy systems has been refused by university ethics committees.

Psychologists are increasingly being blamed for reducing "interior states and feelings to objects, quality to quantity, levels of significance to size. Gone the eye of contemplation and gone the eye of mind — only data from the eye of flesh is being accorded primary reality."[8] It is fortunate that some in the profession have declined this view and have placed the reality described by their clients before their prior theories and agendas.

The evidence presented here will show that these psychologists have set themselves an impossible task, and that to obtain a realistic view of ourselves, we need to include research over the past century that shows there is no distinction between observer and observed, that behavior and beliefs are holistic and therefore not measurable by modern techniques.

The sum of our experiences in therapy and the discoveries of science show that the human energetic system is not an abstract idea, but is powerfully available to our five senses, even though most of us have been desensitized to its presence. Our experience shows that all existence is energy, bathed in vibrations that are connected to everything in the universe, and that our senses in daily life are just one aspect of a universe of fields. Ever since Einstein wrote, "the field is the only reality," we have increasingly come to realize that the universe embodies both these realms, and that though they may appear contradictory, they are in fact mutually enfolding.

To attempt to bring this together, the investigation that has produced this book has spread very wide, even to the furthest reaches of our knowledge of the universe. It includes research in particle physics, astronomy, biology, and the great theoreticians who have struggled to make sense of it all. Quotations will be sprinkled liberally to enfold these arguments and to give them as much veracity as the words of learned experts can give us.

I shall discuss what we perceive outside ourselves in the next chapter on the "organic view," followed by the "physical," and then our tools of perception in the brain and heart. This primes us to the nature of the Great Field, its inherent purposelessness, and the way we project our beliefs onto the Field while it projects just as powerfully back to us. The section on human energies and the holistic and transcendental qualities of the psyche come next. The more subtle understanding of the Field comes from actual clinical therapeutic experience, both from individual sessions and from group workshops. Naturally, details have been altered to maintain client anonymity. This prefaces two chapters on the primary connecting link between us and the Field: the soul, its nature and how it incarnates. The book concludes with a discussion on how knowledge of the Field may support a more intimate connection with the wholeness of the universe. In this way, soul and those collective energies that are most accessible to human consciousness have become the real subjects of this work.

If you feel uncomfortable with the first chapters, which are admittedly pretty dense though I have simplified the jargon wherever possible, I suggest you skip them and turn to sections you find more interesting. In this case, you may consider starting at the section "The Great Field" toward the end of Chapter 3.

2

THE ORGANIC VIEW

The book of nature is written in mathematical language.
—Galileo Galilei

Biological science has, until recently, presumed that each item and event in the universe can be separated from the others and studied in isolation. It has been assumed that solutions to any isolated part have meaning for the whole. Study peptides and genes, and there will be one-to-one, cause-and-effect outcomes that can be detached and understood; but seldom have these conclusions been brought into more complex experiments that would have established their interactions on a holistic basis. For example, individual insecticides have been tested for toxicity in foods, but almost never in combination. We know that each of the dozen or more chemicals that come into contact with milk from the farm to the bottle are used in safe quantities, but where are the tests on when these chemicals have been amalgamated, or heated together, or altered in any other combination?

Over 20,000 new chemicals are considered to pose no risk to health in regulated individual doses, but no one understands the long-term consequences of taking them together. Is there one that when combined with another triggers some of those conditions that are now on the increase, such as fatigue, declining sperm count, asthma, and so on? Science is skilled at testing each one in isolation, but has developed few mechanisms for assessing the whole. We can build an airplane, but have no idea why the atoms in its wings stay where they are.

It has been hard to come to a holistic view as long as it has been thought that biological interactions could occur only through physical contact, rather than through fields of energy. This shortcoming applies to all the allied sciences, to the medical drug culture, to surgery, and to psychology. This chapter presents some of the new evidence that signals, often bearing complex information, may be transmitted between and within organisms of all sizes, holistically and virtually instantaneously. Though fresh concepts are hurtling into view after the consternation that followed the "unsatisfactory" completion of the Genome Project, the giant sea-change that is now seeping through the biological sciences really began fifty years ago with monkeys.

The Hundredth Monkey

Science must provide a mechanism for the universe to come into being.

—John Wheeler

Most of us have heard the possibly apocryphal story of the hundredth monkey.[9] What is seldom remembered is what followed. In 1952 a number of tribes of monkeys in Japan, all of one species but on different islands, were provided with sweet potatoes dipped in sand. They liked the potatoes, but not the grit on them. After some months one monkey on the island of Koshima discovered she could wash off the sand in the stream. Over the next six years a few friends and siblings learned the skill. The other adults kept eating the dirty potatoes. Then there came a moment when a certain critical number was reached, and suddenly every monkey in the group was washing their potatoes.

However, this was only a small part of the story. As soon as the monkeys on Koshima took up washing, the monkeys on the other islands, which were physically out of contact with the first group, began to spontaneously wash their own potatoes. The monkey field had been augmented to the level where it was able to move into a larger group consciousness that could be spread to the whole species, no matter where they were. When a certain critical number achieved awareness, this awareness was, without any direct contact, communicated by some means other than speech or example, and was done precisely and instantaneously.

Without a verifiable connection between one tribe and another there was no scientific way to explain the phenomenon, and as no scientifically acceptable theory was available, the observations were ignored. The tantalizing questions opened by the Koshima monkeys have been dismissed as "mere correlations" or even "passion at a distance" — whatever that might mean — but no attempt has been made until recently to go further than that. Many scientists and doctors remain uncomfortable with the unanswered issues the experiment raised.

It was about the same time that Carl Jung proposed the concept of synchronicity to explain how connections could be made without direct contact, so that "coincidences" which lacked any true relational cause could sit within some theoretical framework.[10] Almost forty years later Rupert Sheldrake expanded this hypothesis to provide a universal medium of communication that he called morphic fields. These include the simplest on-off signals, as in protein receptors, as well as the more complex fields of information in emotions and reproduction.

The argument that follows sets out to establish that events may be connected even when there is no apparent causal connection. It is the holistic premise that all organisms partake in a universe of information, that molecules carry signals that may include feelings and thoughts, that genes are part of the same global empire of signals as cells and proteins, and that every living thing is capable of adapting to every other. Together these ideas show that the vast complex of information being ceaselessly traded throughout all things, especially demonstrated in the human body, is not fully explicable through the conventional notions of biology. It is my purpose to offer another approach.

Morphic fields and synchronicity

The conditions in our universe seem to be uniquely suitable for life forms like ourselves.

—John Gribbin

Sheldrake defined morphic fields as precisely as he could — though the greatest precision is not always the easiest to understand — as "non-material regions of influence extending in space and continuing in time. They are localized within and around the systems they organize...and contain the memory of their previous physical existences."[11] He postulated that these fields were as physically real as gravitation or electromagnetism and not "a bland background abstraction [but] a structure, which actively shapes and includes everything that exists or happens within the physical universe."[12] He showed that non-material vibrations had the same capacity to affect matter as any solid object, and that it could do so without direct contact.

By providing a coherent theory for the concept of communication at a distance, he opened the gate for a widespread search for fields, for signals, and for memories, and intelligence within fields. One aspect of the theory was quite startling, especially for the 1980s: It was that "memory within morphic fields is cumulative, and that is why all sorts of things become increasingly habitual through repetition. When this repetition has occurred on an astronomical scale over billions of years, as it has in the case of atoms, molecules, and crystals, the nature of these things has become so deeply habitual that it is effectively changeless, or seemingly eternal."[13]

This extraordinary yet simple statement opens up an entirely new attitude to the laws of nature. Sheldrake proposed that the laws are not necessarily permanent or immutable. Laws, in this theory, were determined by the sheer numbers of events and their repetition over eons of time, and remained permanent out of inertia. Lacking anything as huge or as ancient that could in any way alter them, they have spent the past 12 billion years getting used to each other. In fact, the most recent developments in optical clocks using a single strontium ion is suggesting that "the fundamental physical constants — numbers that help define the laws of physics, such as Newton's constant of gravitation — may change over infinitesimally short times," suggesting that Sheldrake is right, and that usage modifies the laws, if only by amounts that are so small that they are only now capable of being traced.[14]

The resulting complexity is beyond any simplistic understanding, as fields would overlap and merge into each other without end. A single bee has its own field, which partakes of the field of all bees creating the resonance of bee-ness. This in turn is part of the morphic resonance of all insects, and so on *ad infinitum.* So field overlaps field, each existing within other fields that are themselves vibrating within greater ones while having an effect on all those smaller ones that are in tune with it.

The major aspect of Sheldrake's thesis was to define fields as "the medium of 'action at a distance,' and that through them objects can affect each other even though they are not in material contact."[15] Though this provided the theoretical foundation required for understanding the action at a distance that occurred in the Koshima monkey experiment, it is an astounding notion. It seriously conflicts with our common sense view that there is a gap between subjective and objective reality. Yet in the past dozen years there has been a gradual shift in views, and the idea no longer seems so outrageous.

An example (see page 30) of connections that have no apparent significance, but are utterly fascinating when they occur and bring awareness to the possibilities for powerful correlations in our own lives can be seen with Abraham Lincoln and John F. Kennedy.

In another cogent story, there was a Russian experiment with eight little rabbits. It showed that when one of the baby rabbits was killed at random in Leningrad, the mother rabbit that was traveling in a submarine thousands of miles away reacted in a measurable way. Being on an atomic submarine that spent months under water without coming to the surface, there was no way the experimenters in Leningrad could have known where the mother rabbit was. Upon the submarine's return, instruments attached to the mother showed that it had registered a unique response to her babies' deaths. Though her behavior did not alter — she continued to

Abraham Lincoln and John F. Kennedy

President Lincoln was elected in 1860, Kennedy in 1960.

Their successors were both named Johnson.

Andrew Johnson was born in 1808. Lyndon Johnson was born in 1908.

John Wilkes Booth, Lincoln's killer, was born in 1839; Lee Harvey Oswald in 1939.

Both killers were assassinated before their trials.

Both assassins were known by their three names. Both names are composed of fifteen letters.

Lincoln's secretary, whose name was Kennedy, advised him not to go to the theater.

Kennedy's secretary, whose name was Lincoln, advised him not to go to Dallas.

Lincoln was shot at the Ford Theater, Kennedy was shot in a Lincoln made by Ford.

A week before Lincoln was shot, he was in Monroe, Maryland.

A week before Kennedy was shot, he was with Marilyn Monroe.

John Wilkes Booth shot Lincoln in a theater and ran into a warehouse.

Oswald shot Kennedy from a warehouse and ran to the local theater.

The funeral cortege for both presidents was pulled by seven grey horses, the only times in American history.

President Lincoln, it is reported, dreamed of his death a week before it happened. Had Kennedy? We do not know.

nibble and sleep — there were changes in her brain wave patterns that coincided exactly with the time of her little bunnies' execution.

The theory of morphic fields also applies to issues inherited from our ancestors. One of my clients came from Texas. She described her life as living behind a skin that shielded her from feeling anything deeply. In process she felt this skin clinging to her, wet and cold, and on inquiry recognized that it was fastened down her back with straps. The memory returned of being an Aztec priest putting on the skin of a man she had ritually killed so she could wear it to pluck the hearts out of a long line of prisoners. She carried the imprint of that religious killing in her skin. When she energetically 'took off' the skin, she found she was freed from the constrictive feeling. It later turned out that a remote ancestor had been Mexican, and the extreme trauma of slaying hundreds dressed in a clammy skin may have been passed down through the centuries.

Since Sheldrake has opened the door by providing a theoretical context, people have discovered a wide range of events that are connected without any apparent cause. It is like being given permission to think differently when a lot of effort has been put into saying it was impossible. When Roger Bannister ran the first under four-minute mile in 1954 he broke a belief that had prevented hundreds of people who came to within seconds of getting there from achieving the goal. It was a cathartic moment that I remember well. We had waited for years for this breakthrough, with runners coming to within parts of a second of crossing this barrier without doing so.

Discussion in the papers had concentrated on the 'obvious' physical impossibility of going beyond this limit, arbitrary as that limit was. And as everyone believed it, so it was. The resistance became so hardened that two Olympic games came and went in which the winners were just seconds from achieving this goal before Bannister did it. Then within weeks of him doing so the Australian John Landy had also broken the same psychological barrier. There may have been other factors, such as better lace-up shoes and so on. But the fact remains that runners hesitated for years and years before an unseen arbitrary resistance before breaking through.

Opening the door to a resistance can be very liberating. Over the past fifteen years it has become common to see the world as being filled with signals of information that influence our lives. Many people quite automatically see daily events as 'reflections' of their moods. A common example is the car with a run-down battery, of which the owner will say, "I suppose it is telling me that I am really tired." As with the monkeys in Japan, when an unconventional idea is accepted by enough people it has a rippling effect and is more readily accepted by the majority. This is the stage that Sheldrake's morphic fields theory has reached after twenty-five years.

Scientists prefer physical contact

Verification depends on intelligence and not vice-versa.

— Isaiah Berlin

It has been understood for years that cells are gatherers of information. Their surfaces are covered in receptors waiting to garner signals from their surroundings. This is awareness at the root biological level. I was taught that cells are the mere building blocks of an organic system, organized like the troops in an army. It has turned out that they are among the most complex and well-organized miniature creations on earth.

Bruce Lipton has described it this way: "The cell is a carbon-based 'computer chip' that reads the environment. Its 'keyboard' is comprised of receptors. Environmental information is entered via its protein 'keys.' The data is transduced into biological behavior by effector proteins...that serve as switches that regulate cell functions and gene expression. The nucleus represents a 'hard disk' with DNA-coded software. Recent advances in molecular biology emphasize the read/write nature of this hard drive."[16] It could be said that each cell represents a self-powered micro-processor.

Cellular activity has turned out to be far more intricate than was expected. Each cell takes part in many thousands of chemical reactions each *second*, and this is occurring in every cell in the body. Billions of signals and reactions are occurring all the time. They can read not only chemical signals (the conventional view) but also vibrational energy such as light, sound, and radio. Further, as the environment resonates with the receptors it will alter the protein's electric charge, and this causes the receptors to change shape, and hence their function.[17]

How do they keep in step? What directs this enormous activity toward harmony and survival, without wobbling out of control? There are feedback loops within the system that are too precise and too all encompassing and, more significantly, too rapid to be described purely as the action of molecules bumping into one another. Is there another way they could be acting?

Fig. 1 — The swirl and movement in vast galactic clusters is a massive expression of pure energy.

Conventional biomedical sciences hold that environmental information can *only* be passed on through direct contact, and has little time for synchronicity or morphic fields.[18] According to this notion, receptors only recognize signals that *physically* complement their surface features, which is when their structures match and one bit contacts and fits into another. From the physicality of this notion comes the belief that signals can only be transferred chemically and only when objects actually touch. It is called the key-lock interaction because the physical form in one has to match the physical shape of the receptor in the other. It is a model of the interaction between separate entities. In other words, there can only be a reaction after there has been contact. Signals at a distance, it is argued, can only be accepted when it is called gravity or electromagnetism, as in radios and mobile phones.

A world restricted to physical contact offers a lonely, if intellectually satisfying, picture of interacting bits and pieces without any feelings. This Newtonian world may be clearly defined and full of hopeful intentions for the betterment of mankind, but it nevertheless leads one to an arid, if not desolate, place. As Daniel Dennett so charmingly described this reductionist philosophy: "We are merely organic robots created by a research and development process called natural selection."[19]

Thus every effect needs a cause, and on the whole scientists are happiest when all the extraneous inputs can be eliminated so that there is only one measurable cause for each outcome. This paradigm is by now so well entrenched in the training of students at school and university that it takes a courageous mental shift to dislodge it.

Defenders of the prevailing attitude may develop a great deal of emotional heat when attacking the more fluid views to be described here. Words like "bunkum" and "complete nonsense" are used as arguments in scholarly journals, and the proponents may even be referred to as ""scoundrels."[20] There were cases where men with scientific training have employed conjurers and magicians as "experts" to disprove theories of fields and holographs.[21] Can we take hope from the impression that such invective has the flavor of a rearguard action?

From personal experience in my medieval studies I know how such paradigms drive the academic world. One cause is that basic beliefs are seldom subject to re-examination once adopted, and the other, as Susanne Langer wrote, is that most human beings are afraid "of a collapse into chaos should our ideas fail us."[22] They are also, once we reach the mortgage belt, the foundation for the way we make a living. One can understand how entrenched beliefs come to be maintained in the face of overwhelming evidence to the contrary.

"The central problem with the current theory is that it is too dependent on chance and requires a good deal of time. It can't begin to account for the speed of biological processes. [But when] the vibration of one body is reinforced by another at or near its frequency, [they create] in Jacques Benveniste's words, a 'cascade' of electromagnetic impulses traveling at the speed of light. This, rather than accidental collision, would better explain how you initi- ate a virtually instantaneous chain reaction in biochemistry."[23] As Fritz-Albert Popp has argued, molecules speak to each other in a field that is nonlocal and virtually instantaneous,[24] which describes a world that communicates beyond anything that could be envisioned in a Newtonian system.

This is where the issues are being most strenuously fought. The most important questions on which gradual progress is being made are how does thinking occur; what is knowing and consciousness; why do cells replicate as they do; how is it possible for molecular processes to occur instantaneously; and how does the fetus organize some cells into becoming arms and others into legs even though they have the same genes and proteins? What is missing is some sense of an underlying organizing principle, such as an architect brings to the design for a building without which the pile of timber and bricks gets nowhere.

How we observe determines what we observe. If our only tool is a hammer, then everything looks like a nail. Mechanistic biology is like a hammer, so everything looks dead as nails. However, were we to observe with the holistic sensitivity of organisms, we might see organisms.[25]

A universe of signals: nothing is ever alone

Reality is merely an illusion, albeit a very persistent one.

—Albert Einstein

The workings at every scale of the universe, from our bodies to individual molecules and photons, are bathed in a sea of signals. Everything is sending and receiving in a constant stream. Space, if we can call it that, is awash with more information than there is matter. Every bit sends out messages and receives them and, when congruent, acts on them. Ours is an information universe. There is nothing — not even granite — that can be called truly inert.

The cell is now being seen as an element of intelligence. This is a powerful word, yet how else can we describe something that is not only able to accept and reject signals, but to change behavior in response to these signals, and to alter its own maintenance system so that it can redesign itself and its offspring into new shapes and functions.

Every cell has the potential to be a completely autonomous system within an intelligent community of fellow systems able to adapt and animate themselves toward a communicable goal. In short, one might call each cell a small-scale version of any individual in human society — maybe less complex or powerful because it is smaller, yet still more than a relatively passive unit. This is why our bodies may be conceived as social communities with similar interactions between its members as a society presents between people.

Cells are largely made up of water, as are our bodies. The quality of our lives is intimately connected to the nature of water. There are 10,000 water molecules in the human body for every molecule of protein. When Lipton wrote "biological awareness is a measurable property,"[26] he was thinking of the experiments of French scientist Jacques Benveniste. In some impeccable yet controversial experiments he made it clear that molecules of water are "able to record previous contact with other kinds of molecules."[27] This means that molecules of water, which are the basic building blocks of nature, can hold a memory without in any way changing their nature. Water remains water, even when it is carrying a message.[28] If a molecule can carry a signal-cum-message, how can it do so without leaving any evidence that the message has in any way modified the molecule itself? What is it *in the molecule* that is the carrier of that message?[29]

"Information resides in molecules, cells, tissues, and the environment, often allowing these entities to recognize, select, and instruct each other, to construct each other and themselves, to regulate, control, induce, direct, and determine events of all kinds."[30] This is a description of an interactive universe at every level of existence from the smallest photon packets of light to the largest galaxy. In this universe none of us are immune from influence and counterinfluence of and from every molecule in our vicinity.

In tests Benveniste has shown that electromagnetic signals are as powerful as the chemical that produced them, and that they acted in exactly the same way as the chemicals would have.[31] Without any direct contact between the original substance and the organ, the organ still responded. This is the basis for homeopathy that is one form of vibrational medicine that is being successfully used every day by countless numbers of people. It works purely by resonance, for the original ingredients have been so diluted that they have left no measurable molecules in the medium. After their substance had been extracted all that remained was a 'memory' that had the power to affect our bodies.

In homeopathy vibration modifies structure in much the same way as an army marching in step will affect and ultimately modify a bridge.[32] Unlike the tramp across the bridge, molecular vibrations seem to leave a permanent record. This record remains even after the molecules themselves that were the initial source of the vibration have been removed. It is as if the bridge would 'remember' the marchers for years after they had gone, and that we could connect with that memory to find out whom they were.

Benveniste received a great deal of criticism from many scientists as well as the pharmaceutical industry. The opposition was not always disinterested, for an editorial in one of the most prestigious medical journals, *The Lancet*, rejected his experimental evidence with the words: "What could be more absurd than the notion that a substance is therapeutically active in dilutions so great that the patient is unlikely to receive a single molecule of it."[33]

To deal with the opposition, he arranged for his work to be tested in five independent laboratories in four countries. It involved some thirteen senior scientists, all of whom replicated his earlier results. For the next four years they continued to collaborate and jointly published their results showing that if solutions of antibodies were repeatedly diluted in the homeopathic way until the solution no longer contained any physical trace of the antibody, they would still get a response from the immune cells. They concluded that "specific information must have been transmitted during the dilution/shaking process" without the transfer of any material substance.[34] They are implying the core subject of this book: that fields of energy remain after dilution, and that this energy has a measurable impact on material things.

Benveniste established that a signal could take the place of a chemical. The vibration in the signal is the transferable signature of the molecule. Not contact, but resonance, is the music of the molecule. In fact, his most recent work has concentrated on showing that the messages contained in molecules may be recorded on digital tape as if they were sound waves, and transmitted across the world by e-mail so accurately that the molecule can be analyzed in any other place. Carrying actual samples to laboratories is no longer necessary. He writes, "we are confident in our belief that we have elucidated the physical nature of the molecular signal. The principle is as simple as exploding a mixture of air and gasoline, but the consequences are more enormous."[35]

This, and many other experiments that followed, have shown that modern pharmaceutical medicine is not the only way to approach healing. The core of the issue for those of us who have experienced the effectiveness of homeopathy and who have read even a little of the literature, is that signals, resonance, and memory are essential characteristics of matter. These are present whether the matter is the simplest particle or the most complex brain, and are retained without in any way changing the matter that holds them.

Chemical information can be transferred without having to connect to or pass through anything. Chemicals transmit independently, like a thought. The connection is not being made in the material realm, but in the other realm of fields.

There has been considerable opposition to this concept, in part because "what disturbs scientists is a [perceived] threat to their own image of themselves and to their relationship to knowledge, [for] the revolution would not simply be scientific, it could also become cultural, and homoeopathic doctors and their clients who use such 'folk remedies' would be vindicated and the scientific authorities who have frequently discounted them would look a little foolish. The idea of so disastrous a situation is enough to make scientists shudder."[36]

This is where the work of Masaru Emoto is having an impact.[37] He has illustrated the way that water can be affected by thought and has what we can only call a memory to retain that effect after the thought has passed. Water is not a trivial substance; it is the very foundation of life.

His work exhibits Benveniste's experimental work. It shows that human vibrational energy in thoughts, words, ideas, and music can affect the crystalline structure of water. He recorded the crystals that formed when water was frozen. Water from clear springs show brilliant, complex, and colorful snowflake patterns, while polluted water forms incomplete, asymmetrical patterns with dull colors. When exposed to negative thoughts, such as 'I hate you,' the crystalline structure broke down completely, while the same water exposed to loving words reformed in perfection. This work has never been repeated in double-blind experiments, and the choice of photos he presents is more aesthetic than rigorous. Nevertheless, the general idea is so appealing that his work became an instant success.

It contradicts the cultural belief that change only happens when objects impact on other objects, and that if there is interaction it only occurs on the chemical level. Signals have no substance, yet Emoto's photographs show that a substance may redesign itself when in the presence of the nonsubstantial. That is, water changes with message, and can absorb and hold human feelings and emotions. As water is able to imprint and store information from molecules, this enlarges our "understanding of molecules and how they 'talk' to one another in our bodies."[38] Since every cell in the human body has 10,000 molecules of water to each protein, the ability of the signals in water to affect proteins skyrockets.

Water held in the hands of a depressed man will restrict the growth of plants and even diminish the germination of seeds, the opposite of what we call green thumbs. Over forty years ago experiments confirmed that energy radiating from the body could affect the health of plants.[39] Day to day practical farming experience tells us of the influence plants have on one another.[40] Called companion planting, there are subtle symbiotic connections that are carried between plants, often underground, so that were we to place carrots next to tomatoes, both will grow better.[41]

It is the same with people. More is being discovered every day about how we radiate an influence far beyond our physical structure. Many health professionals subscribe to the notion that attitudes, especially around self-worth, can be triggers for disease. It makes sense that constant feelings of, say, unworthiness, would disorient our own cells, even to the point of mutation.

By defining learning as 'acquired characteristics' and signals as 'information' our whole worldview could be examined from a fresh point of view.[42] It means that information transcends the material realm. Unlike matter and energy, which the First Law of Thermodynamics assures us can be neither increased nor decreased, the amount of information in the universe is rapidly increasing.[43] It is not kept in books nor hard disks, but in the signal senders and receivers themselves. So the question is: how and where is all this information held?

In 1984 Francis Schmitt was one of the first to call chemicals *information substances*. The word 'information' implies intelligence. Intelligence therefore resides not only in the mind and the nervous system, but also throughout the body to include every cell and every molecule. "It is not a matter of energy acting on matter to create behavior, but intelligence in the form of information running all the systems and creating behavior."[44] It is not mind that rules the body, but mind and body as parts of the team that *become* the dynamic network of information that maintains and activates us.

Signals interact at all levels with each other, affecting moods and feelings, joy and sorrow. As the same chemicals are produced everywhere in the body, and these same chemicals control and are affected by mood, we can see that positive moods and thoughts rest at the core to our ability to heal ourselves. This is why emotional therapy lies at the heart of so many body-healing processes. In 1984 Candace Pert and Michael Ruff confirmed that "the same peptides found in the brain were also to be found in the immune system,"[45] and that "the immune system has memory and the capacity to learn...Thus intelligence is located not only in the brain but in the cells that are distributed throughout the body...The traditional separation of mental processes, including emotions, from the body is no longer valid."[46] In short, molecules, cells, and the messengers between have ways of acquiring and holding new information and passing it on to anything that is able to listen.

Information exchange is instantaneous

Mastery over the senses is brought about through concentrated meditation upon their nature.

—Patanjali Sutra

In biological systems signals are sent and received in both *physical and energetic* ways that initiate a tumble of cellular processes and changes.[47] Through a process known as electro-conformational coupling, vibrational energy fields can alter the charge in a protein, and may do so over great distances.[48]

For instance, our responses to stress have been exquisitely honed over millennia of evolution. 'Fight-or-flight' reactions to life-threatening situations include shunting blood away from the gut to serve the large muscles of our extremities in order to provide greater strength in combat or speed to get away from peril. This includes increased blood flow to the brain to improve decision-making, dilation of the pupils to provide better vision, quicker clotting of the blood to reduce loss from lacerations or internal hemorrhage, and a host of other reactions that occur not only automatically, but also instantaneously. These responses are too immediate from one end of the body to another, and too varied to be explicable in the usual way.

The usual explanation is that a protein is created by the appropriate gene in a chosen cell, which then moves off, carrying the key to unlock the required response in another cell. As a model of communication involving at least four sets of instructions and quite a bit of physical movement throughout the body's nervous and tubular systems, it would be far from the virtually instantaneous reaction we experience. Remember how quickly we pull back, shift on our toes and concentrate our attention when surprised. The time taken to make a thought is measurable, while the body responses are too instantaneous to measure. It is not like being given even a well-known puzzle and having to 'think' our way through to the answer.

In the 1940s it was discovered that signals move along the nerves as quantum impulses at an extremely high speed. The impulse is a fixed shape, a little like a standing wave, and is not generated until a certain critical mass of information is reached. Then there is a sudden change and the signal moves in a nonlinear way that integrates with everything in its path for rapid delivery. These impulses are called solitons, and some have called them the 'elementary particles of thought.' Together impulse and pathway form a collective operation, a holistic system along which the wave front moves.

In most cases we would now call these nonlinear events. A linear system obeys very specific rules that are sequential, such as addition and multiplication. The laws of electromagnetism, which describe electric and magnetic fields and the behavior of light, are linear to a very high degree. Linear systems cannot be chaotic and unlike, say, the weather, and are not sensitive to small external disturbances.[49] The behavior of these systems is determined entirely by the forces and influences that emerge in its immediate vicinity. There are also nonlinear discontinuous events like explosions, cyclonic winds, and earthquakes. "Calculations indicate [that in nonlinear systems] there is a sort of 'memory' not possessed in any linear counterpart. It shows that the nonlinear world is holistic; it's a world where everything is interconnected, so there must always be a subtle order present."[50] In short, it is in the nonlinear realm that information can move through a system instantaneously.

A new paradigm of energetic communication occurring within the body at the atomic and quantum levels has emerged — one which is compatible with numerous observed phenomena that could not be adequately explained within the framework of the chemical/ molecular model. The concept of fields as principles of organization, and from it the possibilities of holistic causes and action at a distance are transforming our view of the world.

The role of genes:
a willing tool waiting for an instructor

How can the universe be some sort of perpetuum mobile, a self-existing, self-supporting, self-explaining magnitude, wholly complete in itself and thus imprisoned within a pointless circularity of inescapable necessities?

— Thomas Torrance

One of the most fundamental beliefs in biology, taught in textbooks and lectures, is that the characteristics of organisms are controlled by their genes. The concept underlying this is called genetic determinacy. The genes are supposed to control life by being able to 'turn themselves on and off.' From this it was once argued that the complexity of an organism would be proportional to the number of genes it possessed.

Many scientists are now concluding that this Darwinian concept that has held sway over our thinking for the past two centuries should be abandoned. Bruce Lipton wrote, "Single cells are capable of learning through environmental experiences and are able to create cellular memories, which they pass on to their offspring."[51]

When a fetus is evolving in the womb each new cell carries every bit of our genetic code in its chromosomes, and somehow 'knows' what to do next and which part of the body it is to form. Each cell seems to know how many more like it will be needed, and where to go, and needs to know about its neighbors so together they will fit into the overall scheme. This sophisticated communication has to be present in the fetus from the very beginning, and then has to continue for the rest of our lives. Science still has no conception of how this works, how it is possible for the original cells to contain so much information and to pass it on so rapidly with so few errors.

This leads to one of the core issues in our understanding of life on earth: the issue of *how is our creation orchestrated*. The lack of any answer is so embarrassing that biochemists will almost never address the question. Twenty years ago Sheldrake pointed out that genetic theory does not explain how a developing system can self-regulate and still grow normally if some part of the system is removed, nor how we regenerate or repair damage and disease.[52] Today this essential matter still remains unexplained. One wonders whether we have been looking in the wrong direction.

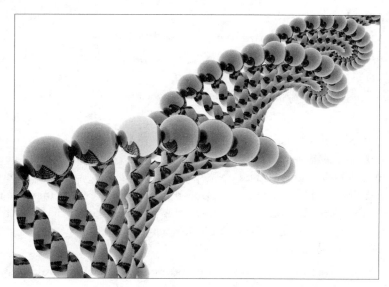

Fig. 2 — Model of the DNA of two helical strands joined
by chains of amino acids.

The Human Genome Project was designed, in part, to answer this question. Before it was completed in 2003, scientists had estimated that humans would need in excess of 120,000 genes to explain all its functions. As genes are primarily codes for creating the chemical structure of proteins, it was thought that there would be one gene for each of the 70,000 to 90,000 proteins that make up our bodies. And in addition to these protein-coding genes, others were needed to determine the complex physical patterns of specific anatomies, to distinguish each cell type (muscle from bone), to determine each organism (a chimp from a human), and that even more were needed to control behavior.

However, these ideas were dust-binned by the results of the Project. This enormously expensive operation revealed that there are only 23,688 genes in the human genome — less than a quarter of the calculated minimum![53] How now to account for the complexity of a genetically controlled human when there are not enough genes to code even half the proteins? This has fostered fresh approaches to the issue and has added considerable complexity to our understanding of how genes function. It is argued that genetic interaction is far more dynamic than was once thought, and that individual genes can have a number of functions, one of which may be to hide the potential function of another, a process called epistasis.

As research continued, this phenomenon became increasingly complex, suggesting there may be multiple reactions from a number of blocking or enhancing genes that can alter the behavior of their fellows. This represents a departure from the concept of genetic independence — the old idea of one gene, one function — to something that appears to be holographic.

The arguments about genes are much more fluid than they used to be, even to such 'heresies' as showing that genes do not wither without the nucleus. Lipton has extracted the DNA genetic code from cells and shown that they continue to function perfectly well without it — perfectly, that is, apart from reproduction. "Cells can live for two or three months without a nucleus," he writes.[54] So, if the DNA in the nucleus does not tell the cell how to operate, what does?

Another conundrum is that the most primitive organisms have huge DNAs compared to their size and complexity. They carry more than half the number of genes required for an enormously intricate higher mammal. As Lipton wrote, "The 50+ trillion-celled human body has a genome with only 15,000 more genes than the lowly, spineless, microscopic roundworm. Obviously, the complexity of organisms is not reflected in the complexity of its genes."[55] David Baltimore, a prominent geneticist and Nobel Prize winner, wrote, "it is clear that we do not gain our undoubted complexity over worms and plants by using more genes."[56]

Compared to chimpanzees, humans have only 450 genes that are uniquely ours, and we share the other 23,238. So what differentiates a man from a monkey? Though scientists are trying to find answers, when one reads between the lines, recent literature is full of phrases like "bound to be…" and "unlikely not to show…" and "could conceivably…," all of which indicate a distinct loss of certainty.[57]

None would deny that inherited genes have an important role. It is apparent, for example, in transplants of fetal eggs in humans and animals in which the baby comes out looking like the parent, not the surrogate mother, and identical twins separated at birth and brought up in very different households, who show major similarities of behavior.

Matt Ridley has suggested that "just thirty-three genes would be enough to make every human being in the world unique, [as there are] more than 10 billion combinations that could come from flipping a coin thirty-three times."[58] What Ridley did not say is that for this combinatory concept to work scientists would have to admit that the underlying organization would need to be holographic.

There is a vast mass of DNA in all creatures that has remained unchanged for 400 million years. It is huge and has been dismissed as 'junk DNA.' Yet these same standardized bits in the helix of all creatures created the enormous variety of worms and dinosaurs and people. Does it provide "the hidden layer of information required to specify the precise placement of cells" in all the living organisms that have ever existed?[59]

It was thought that genes had fixed functions that would never change, but recent work is revealing that the information that actually controls biological reproduction starts with the external environmental signals that trigger regulatory proteins that then influence and even change the gene, which then creates our proteins.[60] This is called the epigenetic mechanism. In other words, the DNA content is not fixed from birth onward, but can be modified during life. This work is little more than a decade old. In one experiment it was found that obesity in mice that came from diet could be passed on to the offspring, even if they were given a lean diet.[61] This is literally food for thought considering our national health problems.

There is also the astounding evidence that organisms can share their individual genes with other species. In this way gene evolution can be speeded up as 'learned' experiences from one species can be acquired by another through gene transfer.[62] As Lipton wrote, there is then "no wall between species,"[63] so one wonders what will now happen to our distinctions between species, or do we have to look on nature as a holographic whole?

Lipton goes on to write, "the sharing of information is not an accident. It is nature's method of enhancing the survival of the biosphere." Equally, through genetic engineering, it is man's method for altering our own biosphere. However, this is happening in ways we cannot foresee, as we have no holographic understanding. It has been found that laboratory genes in crops can, when eaten, alter the bacteria in the human intestine, as well as creating super weeds around trial crops.[64] These are dangerous trends, for through not understanding that everything is a part of everything else, we are threatening our continued existence on this planet.

The possible holographic model for genetic interaction would quite naturally include the proteins, and opens the possibility that the protein that throws the switch to turn on a particular gene may be more important in creating some characteristics than the gene. The differences between species may lie in the process whereby almost identical bundles of genes may be used to create most of the organic world depending purely on holistic interaction. The moment we raise this specter we sideline mechanics in favor of flow. Maybe we should start accepting the growing evidence that there is some other form-creation factor outside the genetic double helix. Maybe the physical sciences can show the way.

3

THE PHYSICAL VIEW

*No theory of physics that deals only with physics
will ever explain physics.*
—John Wheeler

As in biology, the physical sciences have presumed that the universe can be broken into parts and each studied in isolation, that there are straightforward cause and effect relationships in all events, and that there are immutable laws that must apply equally everywhere. Essential as these principles have been in the creation of the modern world, there have by now been enough unsettling exceptions to disturb the serenity of these assumptions.

What the Genome Project has done to undermine the conventional stance in the biological sciences, a combination of paradoxes from the nature of light and subatomic particles has already achieved in the physical sciences. It is in the mathematical modeling of consequences of subatomic research that the first major breakthroughs have come that are only now beginning to percolate into the other physical disciplines.

Though physicists showed that subatomic particles cannot be studied in isolation, but only in relationship to everything else, this property has been applied only to the smallest items and not given leave to influence our thinking too deeply about anything else. Some would like to hold these two realms apart and not apply the agenda from one to the other. For too long it has been assumed that the embarrassing implications of the quantum world resided only in the inert universe of the smallest particles, and that the rest of the world obeyed different laws, those of classical physics in which objects and forces, like cannon balls and gunpowder, *act on* each other, rather than *interacting with* each other.

As a result, and despite believing that the laws of science were *universal,* we have had a century or more in which the science of small particles has been kept isolated in its own discipline. In this way quantum physics has not been allowed to contaminate any other aspect of science.

Were the interconnection of things to be accepted as a possibility for all science and not just particle physics, then it is very hard to see how a lot of modern research would have been undertaken, as we could never be sure we could isolate the primary causes for any effect. In spite of the quantum theory being "the most basic theory of the nature of matter that we have," scientists have not included quantum mechanics in much experimental work.[65]

The real problem lay not in its validity, for in the private views of many scientists there is a belief that the whole must be more important than the parts, but in the inordinate difficulty in carrying out verifiable experiments on such complex interactive issues. There is also the matter of funding, which often depends on being able to independently verify experiments, whereas at the quantum level proof is much harder to come by than demonstration.

Finding answers to the paradox: quantum theory and beyond

In every particle of dust, there are present Buddhas without number.

—Eastern saying

Since the time of the Scottish physicist James Maxwell (1831–1879) the speed of light has been considered a fundamental constant, a measurable speed that could not be exceeded. It was also believed that a field could be a wave, or an object, but not both. By the turn of the century experiments had shown that the inconceivable was true, and that light was both particle and wave, and which we observed depended entirely on the method of observation. The attempts to understand how basic laws could have exceptions have led to the most intensive scientific analyses by some of the best minds on the planet. The outcomes of their work have proved to be the most important factor in directing science toward a more holistic understanding of nature.

In 1900 Max Planck (1858–1947) presented the disturbing concept of 'energy packets' or 'quanta.' In his speech for accepting the Nobel Prize for this discovery he explained, "as the vibrations became faster a gap opened wide. All efforts to bridge the chasm foundered. Either the quantum was a fiction, or it must play a fundamental role. Here was something completely new, never heard before, which seemed to require us to revise all our physical thinking."

Planck introduced the revolutionary notion of "quantum wholeness, which implies that the world cannot be analyzed into independently and separately existent parts; but that quantum wholeness is primary."[66] This is what showed that classical physics, which had assumed that every thing was separate and that each thing could be analyzed and measured on its own, could not be applied to the whole of creation.

The essence of quantum physics is uncertainty. It predicts probabilities, not certainties. The theory implies that all material systems have among their properties two mutually opposite characteristics, called a wave-particle duality.

The second item is that all action occurs in quanta, which are as small as anything can get, and that when many quanta act together there is a collective flow, as with the individual grains of sand in a moving dune. Everything is part of the whole while still being separately itself.

The third item was a new property called no locality in which things can affect each other even though they are not connected. Atomic particles can be both things: they are able to be located in a specific spot in space, and to be without any location when they are occupying all the space there is. The marvel is that it does both at the same instant.

Nonlocality is also known as 'entanglement.' When a quantum system such as an electron is broken into two bits, each part remains entangled with the other so that if one is changed then the other must change as well, no matter how far apart they are. In a way, the particles 'remember' who their partner is.

In experiments it has been shown that whatever happens to one of these bits, exactly the same thing happens to the other. If one of the entangled photons passes through a polarized filter set at angle A, then so does the other. And, if the first of the photons would not pass through a filter set at angle B, then neither would its entangled partner. Or, if you change the spin of one, the other one similarly changes the direction of its spin. How does a photon know what its entangled twin is going to do? Are these little devils psychic or do they have a master plan that tells them what to do in every situation? This has been called the principle of unbroken wholeness, and some propose that it reflects the underlying structure of the universe.

Albert Einstein (1879–1955) wrote a series of papers in 1905 that enlarged on Planck's work. He reconciled space-time with Maxwell's theory of electrodynamics, and concluded that as the speed of light is constant and all natural laws are the same everywhere, then both time and motion are relative and not absolutes. In this way he showed that no event could be defined in all aspects, but depends on the place of the observer. Space and time are not the unchanging backdrop to nature and our observations, but change and adapt to the events that occur within them. The conclusion is emerging that the classical view of the separation between subject and object, useful as it has been, is nevertheless artificial.

In one of these papers Einstein posed the Special Theory of Relativity. The mathematics was confirmed by observations made by the British during the eclipse of 1919. He had proposed that reality consisted of fields, and that particles are regions of intensity in these fields. As more commonly expressed, energy and mass are interchangeable. He revealed that we do not live in a universe of separate discrete objects with dead space in between: the universe is *one indivisible dynamic whole* in which energy and matter are so inextricably entangled it is impossible to consider them as independent elements.[67]

Applying this to the other sciences was just too difficult at that time, and it was theorized that nonlocality applied only to the subatomic level. Then in 1927 Werner Heisenberg (1901–1976) published his uncertainty principle that knocked all of this aside.

He stated that the truth of a subatomic particle — being its location, direction, charge and so on — cannot ever be known exactly as the act of observation actually changes these qualities.[68] Particle and observer participate with each other to such an extent that it is not possible to say whether the outcome came from one or the other.

It transpires that the basis of all matter, being the subatomic particles, electrons and so on, are not precise entities, but are just potentials of possibilities until we observe them, at which moment they 'freeze' into particular states. The moment after an electron appears it dissolves and returns to potentiality. The way the observer interacts with the ensemble determines which aspect unfolds (particle or wave) and which remains hidden. In addition we cannot know both position and direction of movement at the same time. Heisenberg wrote, "The conception of objective reality has evaporated. The mathematics no longer represented the behavior of elementary particles, but only our knowledge of their behavior."[69]

The combination of quantum physics and the uncertainty principle restricted the moment when a particle became a certainty to the instant of observation. Observation 'forced' them into a set state. This meant that the presence of the observer actually *brought each particular reality into being*.[70] From the previous chapter we know that this could include the observer's feelings and desires. Already the concept that mind and body were separate entities was awash with contradictions.

The dilemma prompted Niels Bohr (1885–1962) to offer a convenient way out without resolving the issue. His 'complementarity principle' published in 1928 stated that particle theory and wave theory were equally valid, and that scientists should simply choose whichever theory worked better in solving their problem. While it got physics out of its immediate hole, coming from someone as important as Bohr it gained dominance in future research that appears to have restricted those intuitive insights that might have recast our whole cosmology.

In spite of Bohr's diplomacy, the impact of Heisenberg's uncertainty principle has been shattering on those who have bothered to follow its implications. In a slow-motion drama is destroying the concept of the world 'sitting out there,' and put in its place the *participator.* Every scientist — and every psychologist — is thus a participator. Simply put, the uncertainty principle showed that the prevailing views of "the *absoluteness* of the physical universe are wrong."[71] It showed the opposite, that nothing in the universe existed as a thing in itself independently of our observation of it, though it should be said that some have tried very hard to find a way around the issue. The uncertainty principle implies that the basic structure of the universe and everything in it "is a sea of quantum fields that cannot be eliminated by any known laws of physics."[72]

In 1998 scientists at the Weizmann Institute of Science showed that "the greater the amount of watching, the greater the observer's influence."[73] John Wheeler suggests we not only play a role in the creation of our everyday world, but that we also play the prime role in what he calls a *participatory universe.* The evidence shows that we are not separate onlookers, but are integrally involved with everything that relates to us or impacts on our lives.[74]

The full ramifications of this insight are only now, and especially over the past twenty years, beginning to percolate into general understanding. It lies beyond the boundaries of science, and has not yet altered the common view of our world in any profound manner. Nevertheless, in a process of osmosis the implications have begun to have a seriously deranging impact on other sciences that were based on the presumption of separateness.

This epochal moment should have transformed our deepest attitudes toward life that are based on separateness that assured that the experimenter is a nonintrusive observer without direct influence on the events being observed. There should have been a groundswell in philosophy to incorporate the conclusions into a coherent worldview. But instead the ideas have, in a sense, gone underground to emerge in the Western infatuation with Buddhist thought and New Age holism.

On the scientific side, molecular physics was quarantined so its conclusions would not interfere with the traditional scientific assumption that anything bigger than a molecule would continue to act in the same way whether it was being observed or not.[75] As a result extremely important medical discoveries, such as homeopathy, have been sidelined in favor of direct-contact drugs with the influential drug companies maintaining the dominant conversation. Money has become more important than healing: a recent study showed that death from medical treatment is the *leading cause of death* in the United States.[76]

The implication of Heisenberg's theory is that our notions that the physical universe has any absolute autonomy independent of us are wrong. He showed that the human observer has an intimate influence on the ecology of the material universe. Indeed, the implications are even deeper than this, for the most logical conclusion is that the physical world (as we experience it) exists only in its material state for as long as we are aware of it. In other words, that subjective knowing — or opinions, or beliefs — can change and even create external reality. How we choose to utilize Heisenberg's principle is a philosophical and cognitive science issue that is much discussed. It carries an enormous conclusion that threatens to negate our accepted view of the universe. This book is the outcome of attempting to apply that external understanding to the inner life.

Who said space was empty?

Nothing is permanent in this wicked world, not even our troubles.

—Charlie Chaplin

One completely unexpected discovery was that there is no such thing as empty space. In 1911 Planck showed by experiment that the emptiness of space was a myth, for space was awash with signals and fields.

It was believed that once all the matter had been removed from a space until it became a perfect vacuum and it had been cooled to the lowest temperature possible called absolute zero (being -273° Centigrade), then 'everything' would have been extracted from it. The theory was that at that temperature no more energy could be found. It would be totally empty.

How wrong this has turned out to be. We now know that even in the emptiest space possible there lies an all-pervasive field of energy, a field so enormous that where there should be a total cessation of activity; it still contains more energy than all the matter in the universe put together. The quantity of energy is so staggering that it beggars understanding. It is not just ten or a thousand times greater, but 1040 times. This is enough to create an infinite number of universes like the one we are expending all our efforts to understand and gung-ho-ing ourselves into the stars to visit.[77]

In this empty space emerge elementary particles, bursting forth in pairs that instantly annihilate each other. Electrons and protons and positrons and anti-protons are erupting and as quickly vanishing. This enormous inchoate activity is taking place everywhere throughout the universe. This ground of the universe is "an empty fullness, a fecund nothingness [that] is not a dead, bottom-of-the-barrel thing [but] seethes with creativity, so much so that physicists refer to it as the *space-time foam.*"[78]

This vast cauldron of energy is called the zero-point field. It is the logical consequence of the uncertainty principle, a vast sea of energy that forms the irreducible bedrock of reality.[79] It follows that particles, and all matter that is created from particles, cannot be conceived of independently of the energy fields they come from. Every movement and transformation of a particle gains and loses energy in a constant exchange within the zero-point field. It has been theorized that it is the constant movement out of the field and return to this energetic ocean that ensures the stability of matter.

This vastness is also the medium — if we can call something that encompasses everything a medium — that creates the conditions within which molecules are able to speak to each other nonlocally (i.e., there is no such thing as measurable distance) and instantaneously (i.e., there is no time, and thus without either speed or acceleration). It does not matter how far apart in the universe any entangled photons are, information is instantly communicated between them.

In 2002 Nicolas Gisin and Antoine Suarez performed an experiment in Switzerland in which entangled photons were sent along fiber optic cables to different cities, ten kilometers apart.[80] When the photon reached each city, they passed through devices that allow different paths to be taken. Each time the particles followed the same paths as each other, apparently knowing which choice its entangled twin had made. It was calculated that transmission of this information could not have been less than 10,000 times the speed of light. From this they concluded, "Correlations in the quantum world are insensitive to space and time."

In similar trials by Dirk Bouwmeester,[81] known as the Teleportation experiment, particles were entangled by being passed through a crystal, and were then sent in two different directions, let's call them east and west. The eastern particle became entangled with a third particle that changed one of east's characteristics. The western particle then instantly received the information that the third particle gave to the eastern one. In other words, the concept of "Beam me up, Scotty" may not be too far into the future.

Atoms are more massive than particles. In a recent variation of the Teleportation experiment key properties were transferred between the atoms themselves without using any physical link whatsoever. The gap between protein communication (discussed in the previous chapter) and atomic communication is gradually being bridged.[82]

Instant communication in a timeless world implies that not only does the past determine the future in linear time, but that the future is also determining the past, as proposed and examined by the theoretical physicist, Helmut Schmidt.[83] This has been shown in a number of studies using random sequences of numbers and concealed forecasts that cannot be influenced by any observer.[84] They are called retroactive tests.

In quantum mechanics until an event is observed it does not exist in any particular state, but only as a probability. Once observed, one probability is manifest, and the probability of all other possible states goes to zero. What these retroactive tests have shown is that events that took place in the past have been affected by the present. That is that within the zero-point world of fields where time does not exist, concepts of past and future have no relevance. It demonstrates the mystic view of 'timelessness' in which all is in the eternal now.

William Braud has recently reviewed all the evidence for these retroactive influences on random numbers to study those occasions when some purposeful intention was involved.[85] He wrote that these tests "preclude chance coincidence and mediation by conventional physical processes. The biological target systems that have been influenced successfully have included bacteria, yeast colonies, motile algae, plants, protozoa, [etc.,] as well as cellular preparations (blood cells, neurons, and cancer cells)."[86] In humans many actions and even brain rhythms also, and though the psychokinetic effects are small, they are reliable and consistent and may be reproduced. Braud claims that "these studies provide a sound empirical foundation for considerations of the practical applications of mental or spiritual healing." In short, to think it is to change it.

The zero-point field's presence has usually been omitted from calculations as it is always there — an odd but not uncommon way to quietly dismiss what cannot be understood. This whitewashing procedure was neatly called 'renormalization.' Cancel the inconvenient! "Because zero-point energy was ever-present, the theory went, it didn't change anything. Because it didn't change anything, it didn't count."[87] What was meant was that as long as science concentrated on studying the bits, then in this context these interactive quantum effects taken across the whole system could be ignored.

Leaving out the whole system has left quantum theory standing alone as an aberration that "could predict phenomena accurately, but provides no clear way of conceiving the structure of the world, no deeper reality beyond the subatomic landscape."[88] Though most of the pioneers of quantum physics — Heisenberg, Bohr, and Erwin Schrödinger especially — studied beyond physics to mysticism and Eastern philosophy, they did not formulate a rigorous theoretical alternative that would integrate the particulars of quantum mechanics with the whole. This was left to the next generation.

The four horsemen: Bohm, Bell, Benton, and Aspect

He hath measured the waters in the hollow of his hand, and meted out heaven with the span, and comprehended the dust of the earth in a measure.

—John Milton

Four fundamental approaches, each more audacious than the last, have made considerable headway in resolving much of the dilemma left by the dual nature of light and the only partial, if effective, solution offered by the quantum theory. Just after the last war,

David Bohm (1917–1992), one of the most distinguished theoretical physicists of his generation, conceived the idea of a field below the quantum level that he called *quantum potential.* Like gravity, it pervades all space. However, unlike gravity or magnetic fields, its influence did not diminish with distance. Its effects were equally powerful everywhere.[89]

From this he came to see that the major quality that distinguished the quantum potential from all other states was its wholeness, and that this quality of wholeness was more important than how wholeness 'worked.' Wholeness is by its nature coherent, so that particles are not separate entities, but "through the action of quantum potential, the whole system is undergoing coordinated movement more like a ballet dance than a crowd of unorganized people."[90] The immediate appeal of the quantum potential was that it provided a ground state within which both the world of particles and the world of fields could exist together.

In 1964 John Bell created his inequality theory. The idea was to set the conditions in which the laws of classical physics would be obeyed were quantum possibilities to be ignored. This is a sort of reverse argument, in which one sets out the conditions in which a certain thing must happen, and look for some evidence to disprove what has been done in the hope of proving its opposite.

In his mathematics Bell assumed locality, which means that the position and direction of a proton could be measured. As this was exactly the opposite of quantum theory it meant that the location of one proton could not affect the measurement of another. In his mathematics Bell showed that if classical physics was true for photons a very definite relationship would emerge that could be tested. When laboratory tests were made they showed that the relationship, called Bell's inequality, had been violated.

This was a demonstration that, in contradiction to the accepted belief, the speed of light could be exceeded. Some things could move faster than the speed of light — instantaneously — and could communicate in a way that transcended space and time. This had already been suggested by Einstein and two eminent collaborators thirty years earlier, who showed theoretically that a particle in one place could instantly influence another one far away.[91] But having published the theoretical reasoning Einstein refused to believe it could really happen, and called it "spooky action at a distance."

Bell wrote: "the organization of any biological system is established by a complex electro-dynamic field... This field is electrical...and not only establishes pattern, but maintains pattern in the midst of change. Therefore it regulates and controls living things. It must be the mechanism of wholeness, organization, and continuity."[92] It seems that here we are on the verge of understanding how signals and learning occur in biological systems, with a scientific basis for morphic fields.

The mechanism of Bell's states is coherent. They are conceived as having particular wave functions that remain intact even to the end of the universe. The concept of a signal continuing unchanged into cosmic distances was totally novel to quantum theory, and could not in any way be fitted into classical theory. It postulated a dynamic wholeness across the entire system that ensured that every particle is in touch, no matter how far apart they may be.

A decade later, in the early 1970s, David Bohm reassessed his earlier work and argued that beyond the physical world lay another in which "Parts are in immediate connection, with dynamical relationships that depend in an irreducible way on the state of the whole system. Thus, one is led to a new notion of unbroken wholeness which denies the classical idea that the world can be analyzed in separately and independently existing parts."[93] Bohm was making it clear that the world is more than the sum of its parts, and that by implication science had better include the fields of the whole if it was to reveal more than just the bits. At the level of the smallest particle theoretical science was moving in strange directions that were undermining the assumptions on which most experimental science was based.

Then in 1982 came the first experimental and verifiable evidence to support Bohm's and Bell's theoretical work. Alain Aspect, working in Paris, tested Einstein's prediction that particles should be able to communicate no matter how far apart, and with no lag in time. He and his team established in a very neat and exact fashion that photons did exchange information at virtually infinite distances and that they did so instantaneously, despite there being no exchange of energy.[94] It does not matter whether they are 10 feet or 10 billion miles apart, each particle always seems to know exactly what the other is doing. This implies that everything is connected in the most real and measurable sense and is linked by connections that transcended conventional notions of communication. Traveling faster than the speed of light is tantamount to breaking the time barrier. This daunting prospect has not pleased everybody, and most of those in mainstream science are not very interested in it because they do not know what to do with it.

It was the equivalent of spinning roulette wheels in Paris and in Sydney, and expecting that because the one spun in Sydney produced a seven on black, the one in Paris will be immediately doing the same. This discovery verified the work of Bell and Bohm.

The experiment also showed that signals could be received anywhere without any transfer of energy. Exchange without the need for energy contradicted the Second Law of Thermodynamics that the energy in a system cannot be either lost or gained. It meant that under certain circumstances signaling is possible without any power, unlike our wireless or television. Is this how decisions network out from the brain to activate the most complex responses in the rest of the body?

To bring some shape to this increasingly bizarre situation, and working from the concept of undivided wholeness that is implied in both relativity and quantum physics, Bohm tackled the implications of the Aspect experiment. He defined three states of being that fulfilled all the laws of physics and the new observations.

He demonstrated that correlations between particles are not due to faster-than-light signals, but to their being occupants of a different state of matter, a state that consisted entirely of fields of vibrating energy. Just as the concept of 'field' was becoming a polite word in biology, Bohm reintroduced the concept of fields into fundamental cosmology.

The field he postulated to explain Aspect's findings was what physicists call a 'nonlocality.' A nonlocality breaks one of the most important assumptions of classical physics — that something that happens in one place cannot instantaneously affect an event somewhere else. For example: if a distant star were to suddenly blow up tomorrow, the principle of locality says that there is no way we could know about this event or be affected by it until the light carrying the event has had time to travel from that star to the earth. In nonlocality Gaia is aware the moment it happens, except that we don't know it.

Aspect had proved that photons are able to register each other's presence but, because they have no location, any idea of separateness is an illusion. Location ceases to exist, so it was meaningless to speak of anything being separate from anything else.[95] From this it follows that the basic essence of all matter exists as parts of the one deeper fundamental unity, a unity that includes *everything* that is, including the universe and, beyond that, the boundless promise contained in the zero-point field.

Bohm's solution was to divide fundamental reality into twin states, explicate and implicate, with a third underlying both that was their source or ground.[96] The explicate order is the world of seemingly separate and isolated things and events in space and time that we experience through our senses — tables, hurricanes, and computers, for example. The implicate order is a realm without time or space, in which location cannot be defined. In it all things and events of the explicate realm are enfolded in a total wholeness and unity.

The two realms are so intimately connected that everything in one is simultaneously present in the other. "The implicate order is a realm beyond time, out of which each moment is projected out into the explicate order and back again. As there is no space or time in the implicate order all similar things from all of history and all universes must connect and resonate, so that what happens in one place will interpenetrate what happens in another."[97] We could see the universe being like a stream on which ""one may see an ever-changing pattern of vortices, ripples, waves, splashes, etc., which have no independent existence as such. Rather, they are abstracted from the flowing movement, arising and vanishing in the total process of the flow."[98]

Bohm believed that an electron forms "an inseparable union of a particle and a field"[99] and is neither one thing nor the other, but "an ensemble enfolded throughout the whole of space. When an instrument detects the presence of a single electron it is simply because one aspect of the electron's ensemble has unfolded at that particular location. When an electron appears to be moving it is due to a continuous series of unfoldments and enfoldments."[100]

The sense that there is movement in the enfolding and unfolding of an electron is only apparent, not real. The appearance in our plane stems from the electron's own energy, but through a process in which "the quantum potential acts to put form into its motion, and this form is related to the form of the wave from which the quantum potential is derived."[101] The wave is merely an expression of its energy, and its form is no more than the momentary point of transition from the formless and back again.

Einstein had said all space and time are merged in a space-time continuum. Bohm took this image one huge step further in arguing mathematically that *every thing in the universe* is part of the one fundamental continuum, including space-time.[102] Despite the apparent separateness of everything at the explicate level, every item is a seamless extension of everything else at the implicate level, and that ultimately explicate and implicate orders blend into one another. This is implied in theories of such fundamental concepts as Schwarz's 'super strings' and Penrose's 'twisters,' which are "nonlocal objects concerned with the global structure of space-time."[103]

For Western thinkers, though not for those from the East, such a revolutionary idea "denies the existence of any fundamental constituents of matter — there are thus no fundamental laws, equations or principles," wrote Fritjof Capra. "All natural phenomena are interconnected. Physical theory is an approximate conceptual map of reality, rather than reality itself. They are creations of the human mind."[104] As in the Buddhist phrase of Nagarjuna, "Things derive their being and nature by mutual dependence and are *nothing in themselves.*"

With this deep theoretical understanding Bohm created a framework that many other people (if not mainstream) have since resonated with, and even wished in their hearts to find some experimental way to justify. He created a viewpoint that though the evidence may never be found to a purist's absolute satisfaction, the intuitive in us, along with the spiritual seeker, knows its fundamental correctness.

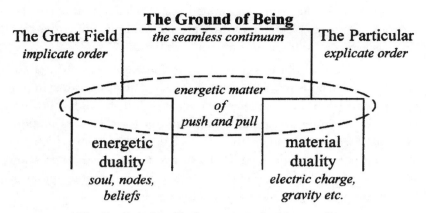

Fig. 3 — Relationship between Bohm's cosmology
and the Great Field.

There are layers and layers of depth at every point in the universe, leading inexorably to even deeper layers each enfolding greater and greater levels of wholeness, so that "every particle will ultimately be found to be the reification of a collective vibration of still finer structures" without end.[105] This structure is reminiscent of a hologram, as used nowadays on most credit cards. Without describing how light from an object is broken up and then reassembled, the principle is that the picture of a real three-dimensional object can be transferred to another place as a virtual image. In a hologram what exists in the whole image also exists in every part and slice of that image (even if to a lesser resolution), reflecting the principle that the part contains the essence of all that exists in the whole.

The concept of the hologram was created by Dennis Gabor in 1947, though it was only thirty years later through the work of Stephen Benton that it moved into the practical world through the rainbow process. More recently this technology has been used for holographic camera focusing, and for optical data capable of delivering information trillions of bits faster than the current generation of computers. Now researchers at MIT's Media Lab have developed a computer-controlled holography system that can actually generate completely animated, full-color, stereoscopic images on the fly at nearly the same speed as video. This mimics the nature of nonlocality in which there appears to be no limits to the amount of information or to the rapidity of movement. The medium, as Marshall McLuhan would say, is the message.[106]

Though the concept is only slowly meeting its potential in our lives, it has been of immense value in stimulating a new view of the universe, the way the brain works and our understanding of fields in general.

Understanding this has added a significant dimension to Bohm's theory. He was able to suggest that the whole universe can be thought of as a kind of gigantic, fluid hologram, in which the explicate order that our senses respond to is just one projection from higher levels of reality. The highest level beyond the implicate and explicate orders Bohm called the superimplicate order that underlies both. However, this does not seem to be necessary as the nature of the implicate is to include all field states from the simplest to the most complex, and the superimplicate is not separate from the Great Field that by its nature encompasses them all.

The theory proposes that life and consciousness are enfolded deep in the generative order and are therefore present in the unfoldment in all matter, including electrons or plasmas. He suggests that there is a 'proto-intelligence' in matter, so that new evolutionary developments do not emerge in a random fashion but are created as integrated products that are already whole from their immersion in the implicate level. The nonphysical connotations of Bohm's ideas are underlined by his remark that the implicate domain "could equally well be called Idealism, Spirit, Consciousness. The separation of the two — matter and spirit — is an abstraction. The ground is always one," or One.[107] He even offered the possibility of an infinite series, even hierarchies, of implicate generative orders, some of which form relatively closed loops and some of which do not.

From here on I will refer to the implicate order and the zero-point field of the physical sciences, and the Ground of Being and God Himself of the metaphysical as The Great Field, or capitalized as the Field.

The Great Field

A holistic tapestry of interdependent influences.

—Paul Davies

In the earlier section on biology we saw that proteins carry memory and signals, and that these exist in fields of vibration. They are influenced by, and in turn influence the whole body-mental system of our lives. In the short term they create behavior, and in the long term the growth of the body itself. They are all-encompassing fields of energy that constantly adjust and direct, rebuild and demolish. Heisenberg's uncertainty principle implies that every particle without exception relies for its existence on a ground field of energy that is interacting with everything everywhere. The concept raised in this book is that these fields are the true directors of the genetic factory, and that through information feedback and exchange all the forms they manifest are reflections of those that already exist in the implicate layer.

In this concept fields are more fundamental than matter. The logic goes like this: as fields cannot be explained in terms of matter, whereas matter can be explained in terms of their energy within fields, then fields must have some prior status before matter. Even the nature of the smallest field, say that of a photon, cannot be explained in terms of anything else except through more fundamental fields, layer upon layer until we come to the original cosmic Field that encompasses all. Thus, material existence is created out of fields, not the other way round.

Observing from the physical constraints of our bodies we cannot tell whether these fields share the qualities of spacelessness and timelessness of the Great Field, though from our understanding of the unity of all things they should. As Bohm says, "The Ground is always One." In the theory of relativity time is a function of space. The Field, on the other hand, does not exist in either space or time. It exists everywhere simultaneously. It has no movement, but only presence.

Jung's theory of synchronicity and Sheldrake's theory of morphic fields sit very comfortably within the nontemporal, nonlinear and nonlocal universe postulated for such a sea of fields.

In this quantum and holographic picture of reality, particles are not separate from one another moving through the void of space, but all are part of one unbroken web, embedded in fields that are as rich and real with process as the matter that moves through it.[108] This description by Jenny Wade is subtle and accurate: "The material manifestation of energy as the explicate order, is enfolded in and emanates from an implicate transcendent order of pure energy, which is infinite and absolute."[109] In short, there is no thing that is not a field. If we move our attention beyond the observation of 'things' or 'states' to the flow and interaction of clusters or nodes of energy within universal fields that are all part of the one Great Field we will get closer to this reality.

Fig. 4—Levels of manifestation from pure energy through increasingly dense fields to organic and then finally, inorganic matter.

Matter is not a fundamental property of the physical world. It is energy. As Einstein proposed, reality consists of fields, and particles are regions of intensity in fields. Matter is energy that stops long enough in one place to give the appearance of solidity. Every bit of matter, from asteroids to toenails, is a collection of electrical charges interacting across a background sea of electromagnetic and other energetic fields.[110] The quantum perspective reveals that the universe is an amalgamation of interdependent energy fields. These fields are mutually entangled in an infinitely complex mesh of interactions. There is no space and no thing that is not inextricably part of this tangle.

As Jung said about the psyche, the Field "is a self-regulating system that maintains itself in equilibrium as the body does," and in a similar way. In the fields that lie within the Great Field "Every process that goes too far inevitably calls forth a compensatory activity."[111] That is, push creates pull, the yes a no, in an endless dance of interdependent duality. But in the realm of the Field itself there can be no duality, for every aspect is evolving in sync, cooperatively.

"This reality is neither one nor many, neither permanent nor dynamic, neither separate nor unified, neither pluralistic nor dynamic nor holistic," says Ken Wilber. "It is entirely and radically above and prior to *any* form of conceptual elaboration. It is strictly unqualifiable... It is true that reality is one, but equally true that it is many; it is transcendent, but also immanent; it is prior to this world, but it is not other to this world."[112] This describes the highest state of unitary oneness achieved by saints and mystics of every religion from Saint Teresa of Avila to Guru Maharishi.

From this highest state we are told that our material selves, what is called manifest form itself, may be compared to a standing cloud over a mountain peak in which the observable phenomenon of the visible cloud has no substance, but is a dynamic process of condensation and evaporation as droplets of water form and unform in the air over the mountain. If we apply this analogy to ourselves we can conceptualize our physical presence as a standing cloud that is 'forming' and 'unforming' in every trillionth of a second from the universal fields of energy that are everywhere and in everything.

This is of the profoundest importance in our understanding of the world and our place in it. We are not just lumps of matter separate from Creation. In this sense we are God in every trillionth of a moment, and human in the next. The glimpses the rest of us get into this ultimate state are so exhilarating that we are moved to spend our lives in a search for more of it.

Some people are naturally more tuned into fields of energy than others. Arthur Rackham, the mystic English illustrator was one of these, as was Dora van Gelder.

Fig. 5—Arthur Rackham, drawing of the
Rhine-Maidens teasing Alberich.

In van Gelder's description of the devas and pixies of the plant world, she noted an enormous range of 'creatures' that share the world with us.[113] Goblins are colorful shimmers with pointed out-pourings of energy just where we would place the ears and toes. Energetically they look just as they are drawn by Arthur Rackham, as little beings with long pointed ears and toes. She describes the energetic forms of great mountains as "clear, clean, uplifted, steady of vision. They are tall and stately and inhabit the principal peaks. They form a company and have a likeness to one another. They have been there for thousands of years, but they convey a feeling of youthful vitality, enthusiasm and a wonderful certainty."

One of her most poignant phrases concerns permanence of the Field: "So many things which matter very much to us do not seem to matter at all to them. Life and death, for instance, are things, which they know all about; to them there is no uncertainty and no tragedy involved…[they] see the flow of life through all things. We live in a world of form without understanding the life force beneath the forms. For us the loss of form means the end of life, but they are never deceived in this way."[114]

The concept of 'permanence' does not sit well with the nature of energy. Fields of energy are, by definition, in continual motion and change. Some fields, such as those of subatomic particles, are created and dispatched within a millionth of a second. Others, like those of the basic laws of physics, remain for huge eons of time. Our daily lives depend on basic laws like gravity and heat transfer remaining constant. Yet it seems they may give only the appearance of constancy.

I have suggested that the mathematical ratios and constants that are embodied in natural laws (whether physical, chemical, or biological) are not absolutely fixed. Recent evidence shows that they adjust in miniscule ways, presumably in tune with the interconnected dance of vibrations throughout the universe. Recent measurement, using the world's most accurate strontium clock, indicate that not all the fundamental constants are absolute — though the jury is still out on that one. It seems that the changes are incredibly small. In each moment of time the tiniest shift has to be reflected throughout the whole vastness of the universe. The energetic 'inertia' that hold the laws in place is enormous, yet being fields every shift and tremor in other fields would cause miniscule changes to the fundamental laws of the universe that we may now be able to measure.

Our laws of physics are immensely powerful means of encapsulating a vast range of natural phenomenon in terms of simple relationships. Without them we would have no framework for understanding our world. But it would appear that they are there, as the old song would say it, because they are there. Once self-molded in the first moments of creation their ability as fields to self-adjust into states of mutual harmony created a semblance of permanence that was not present in their initial formation. And being fields, they continue to adjust and shift in relation to each other.

Our particular set of laws is now so well integrated, and so 'successful' that they have sustained the hugeness and diversity of our universe. Yet, theoretically there are an infinite number of possible universes, each with their own laws and materials. Even within the evolution of our universe the possibilities are endless. If an uncountable number of games of chess can be created with only sixty-four black and white squares with figures given a limited number of available moves, how much greater may be the immense possibilities latent in the Field.

Together the enormous theoretical and experimental work of the past ten or fifteen years has pointed to such a deep change in our understanding of the universe that this book, and many others like it, can be written with some expectation of being seriously received.

Before expanding on the nature of the Great Field, especially in its impact on the human psyche, I need to explore how the Field seems to manifest in the brain and the heart, and on our way through life so that the principles may be applied to therapy. Only then will we return to the Field and investigate its aspects, especially the individual field of each person that we call soul. Soul is, in our experience, the key ingredient in successful therapy that guides us to the inner coherence we need for a deeper communion with the Field.

| 4 |

The Implications of the Field
for Biology

Thoughts affect proteins
and energy fields create form

*The Lord of the mind, the perceiver, is ever aware of the constantly active
mind stuff, the effect-producing cause.*

— Patanjali Sutra

As we have seen, the latest research shows that genes do not on their own create the body, but do so only in conjunction with proteins and thoughts and feelings that tell each part what to do. The double helix of the gene is like a car that goes nowhere without a driver. The proteins that connect with genes are not just switches, but more like thermostats. The gene is activated when a number of the receptors on the surface of the cell have caught sufficient transcribers, or messages from the protein. Small changes in the receptors or in the transcribers can have subtle effects on the expression of the gene. It is the protein-transcribers that tell the gene how to act.

Candace Pert's experiments with receptors showed that their willingness to accept a signal can be influenced by the transmitters. The antennae on proteins respond to a receptor through the vibration it gives off that changes part of the protein so it opens to the receptor. What this apparently circular sentence means is vitally important for the new science. It is that if the *receptor* requires a certain protein it can *create* it, or if the gene *needs* to act in a certain manner, it can *order* the signal from outside itself to start its own program — a sort of bootstrapping, as when a computer pulls itself to life through its own programs.

Bootstrapping may be quite common, for John Cairns demonstrated that changes in DNA show that proteins can choose what sort of mutation they need, which is like saying "if the gene I need is not there, I'll make it."[115] This being so, minor modifications are occurring in the makeup of every species during both the embryonic stage and during the rest of life in an interactive process in which every gene and protein and peptide is permitted to play a part. How much, then, of our makeup is predetermined in the genes of our conception? Maybe all, and maybe a few, depending on circumstances.

Take, for example, the production of vertebrae in a mouse or a human, or a snake for that matter, that is programmed by the same 200-letter gene sequence. The difference between the species would lie in the interaction between promoters and proteins rather than in directions from some command center. These seem more like small alterations of the switching patterns than anything else. In fact, just one change in one promoter will produce a cascade of differences in the organism. Timing is everything — a chimp has a different head from a human being not because it has a different blueprint for the head, but because it grows its jaws for longer and the cranium for less than do humans. This is something D'Arcy Thompson understood sixty years ago.

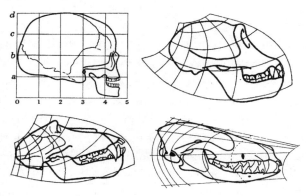

Fig. 6 — Heads of a human and a chimpanzee, and below, a dog and an ape. Four species formed out of the one geometric matrix.

Thompson drew grids over the bones and forms of hundreds of animals and insects to locate the most salient points. This showed that within large groups the points were all located at the same intersections, and that only the bends and twists in the grid determined the final shape. He wrote, "the form of a portion of matter is the resultant of a number of forces, which represent the manifestations of various kinds of energy."[116] The fact that the coordinates that plot the skull of man, chimpanzee, and baboon in the figure form a singular transitional type that can be stretched to fit nearly every mammal shows that they keep their "relative order and position on the grid throughout all distortions and transformations."[117] This illustrates the underlying and relatively simple instructions needed to produce the form of each species, and all that differs are those in-process directions, issued while the object is being assembled, that determine how many and for how long each part will be under construction.

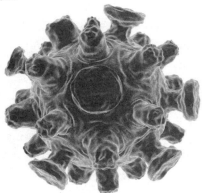

Fig. 7—An influenza virus that is like a sea mine, and just as dangerous.

The 'mutual interdependency' principle is that every protein is created by a gene and every gene is capable of being affected by a protein, while this entire network of genes and proteins is itself influenced by mood and feelings and external factors such as education, food, unrequited love, and fear. This shows that any item in the chain of signals can affect or be affected by any other, so in physical or chemical terms the 'source' could be any or all of them. It means that genes are not immutable creators handed down through the generations, but active participants in the daily changes of our lives. As Matt Ridley wrote, they are "designed to take their cues from everything that happens to us from the moment of our conception [while also being] at the mercy of our behavior."[118]

The material deterministic way of seeing the world denied us power over our lives by giving it to the genes, whereas it also lies in our thoughts. It looks like you can change your life as quickly as you can change your beliefs. All are in the one bath together.

In the 1950s Joseph Hoffman found that feelings could be related to the health of individual cells. He determined the amount of love, hate, and anxiety from the degeneration of the cells, which predated Psycho-Neuro-Immunology research of Borysenko by thirty years.[119] Lots of research has shown that fear and depression weakens the immune system, whereas happiness strengthens it, so it is much easier to resist disease. This is not limited to humans, as Jane Goodall demonstrated when observing how mood affected bodily health among the intricate personalities of chimpanzees.[120]

Over twenty years ago Pert showed how our feelings affect well-being by demonstrating that biological chemicals in the cells, the neuropeptides and their receptors, communicate emotions.[121] They are not limited to carrying signals of function, such as how to digest this or move that, but also signals of thoughts and feelings. Functions are habitual and can remain the same for a lifetime, but ideas and moods change from second to second. Our chemicals therefore form a dynamic ever-changing information network that links our material molecules with nonmaterial energies of thoughts and feelings. Pert concluded, "The fact that memory is stored at the receptor level means that memory processes are emotion-driven and unconscious."

She explained that memories "are stored not only in the brain, but in a *psychosomatic network* extending into the body...from the internal organs to the very surface of our skin."[122] Eric Kendel showed that not only are memories stored in the skin, but they are also stored (through chemical changes) on the surface of the cells that make up the skin.[123] Every part of us, no matter how small, joins in holding our memories. This implies the humbling conclusion that choices about whether a memory or a thought becomes conscious can be made by molecules.

Some memories are held in the cells of the body rather than in the brain. Sometime when people are rebirthed (also called breathwork)[124] the skin lets off a pungent smell of the anesthetic given to the mother in hospital many decades earlier. John Lilly describes a lifelong ache in his left shoulder that he discovered in therapy had come from the time he was a toddler.[125] He was ambling toward a cliff that ran through the garden when his much-loved dog, seeing that he was going to fall over, seized his shoulder in his mouth and pulled him back from the edge. Lilly felt he was being attacked by his closest friend, not being saved. The trauma was locked in the place where the dog grabbed him, and stayed there for the next forty years, gradually adding more and more damage to the tissue.

Thoughts, memories, emotions, and feelings are intangible. They are not visible objects like cells and genes and chemicals. They are part of the 'soft' body of the psyche, the energetic system of moods such as joy and depression. We can be given a meal prepared by a man we dislike and recognize that the bad taste the food leaves in the mouth comes from our feelings about that man. We have introjected into the material (food) an idea (dislike) that has changed our perception (taste) of what we are eating. In real life there is no division between the mental and physical worlds.

As a result, we can now see that "according to energy medicine, we are all living history books...of every event and relationship in our lives. As our lives unfold, our biological health becomes a living, breathing, biographical statement that conveys our strengths, weaknesses, hopes, and fears. Every thought you have had has traveled all through your biological system and activated a physiological response."[126] This is the basis for such terms as 'having a gut feeling' and there being problems we 'can't digest' for they reflect the fact that memories and needs and opinions are stored in our cellular and muscular structure. It is commonplace in therapy to state that "the body remembers everything, and unlike the mind, never tells a lie."[127]

Thus emotions, the signals they give off, and the drives they power occur at every level of the organic chain. Even amoebas, among the simplest of sea creatures, have behavior that corresponds to our concepts of pleasure and pain, of hunger and desire. Wilson

Thorpe in his classic study of animal behavior wrote, "The behavior of a sea anemone is vastly more complicated than supposed. Not only is there a great deal of spontaneous movement but there are elaborate patterns of apparently purposeful activity" that may be observable on speeded-up film.[128] All organic creatures, from the largest whale to the smallest cell, partake in the same complex assortment of feelings and communication systems, and not just individually, but with full cognizance of and, most importantly, adaptation to everything else.

This is new knowledge, but old wisdom. In Proverbs 17:22 it is written "A merry heart doeth good like a medicine: but a broken spirit drieth the bones." This is the basis for all energetic healing. The so-called 'placebo effect' where people in double-blind experiments are given pills with no agent in them, yet still get better because they believe the doctor has done something for them. This is a modern witch doctor or bone-pointing situation. But beyond the placebo effect there are now well-documented trials in which health may be dramatically affected by the thoughts of others.[129] It did not matter what sort of healing was being done, nor did the beliefs of either the patients or the healers affect the outcome. It was just the thought that counted.[130]

It is now understood that the brain changes during life through a gene group called CREB. As members of the group are switched on and off they alter the connections between the neurons in the brain and this can lay down new long-term memory banks. These genes respond to our behavior, not the other way around. They are constantly changing with life. Having created the body in the womb they immediately, under the influence of all around them, start to dismantle and rebuild what they have made. One consequence may prove, under experiment, to be intriguing: To say that some men are gay because they have a certain gene is deterministic. Instead we could examine the possibility that sexual preferences (or any other views, for that matter) may alter proteins, and that this could then adjust the DNA — and does so not in the womb but long after birth. This would provide further evidence that the gene always remains mutable.

The way that proteins are influenced by thoughts and moods can be restated as 'the instructions they give are modified by the mind,' be it conscious or unconscious. From which we may state that our beliefs modify our genetic output, and thus create our bodies, both in health and in disease.

Genes are therefore both the cause and the outcome of our actions and beliefs. "At the very instant that you think 'I am happy,' a chemical messenger translates your emotion, which has no solid existence whatever in the material world, into a bit of matter so perfectly attuned to your desire that literally every cell in your body learns of your happiness and joins in. The fact that you can instantly talk to 50 trillion cells in their own language is just as inexplicable as the moment when nature created the first photon out of empty space."[131] No matter how much we delve into the chemistry of neuropeptides and receptors we will not explain the totality of how beliefs and emotions affect us on the physical plane.

So who conducts the orchestra?

And the demonstration of all these things is so certain that, though experience apparently contradicts them, we will have more faith in our reason than in our senses.

— René Descartes

Once we can accept the proposition that waves of thought from the mind can affect the physical shape and health of the body and the way it operates, we can consider the question: what orchestrates the complexities of growth in the womb, and continues to do so for the next ninety years or so. It is hard to see our bodies being created and sustained by a committee of parts each with their own agendas, and with the slow lines of communication that would occur if information flowed only through direct molecular contact.

Everything points to it being through signals contained in waves of energy through our personal fields of information. The interconnections are neither directed nor random, but more like a dance. Organic systems are so complex one naturally feels there has to be a guiding principle.

Some biologists refer to this guiding principle as morphogenic fields, from which came Sheldrake's concepts discussed earlier. The word comes from the Greek *morphe* or form, and *genesis* or generation. Such fields form the form. They impose patterns on what would otherwise be indeterminate processes. "These fields contain invisible blueprints for the organs and the organism as a whole. In mathematical models the goals are represented as attractors. These attractors lie within 'basins of attraction' that draw the developing organism towards its developmental goals."[132] It is a lovely image of fields that lure the cells into their rightful place and entice them to fulfill their different roles. It is a softer more organic process than an engineer's drawing marked with firm lines and fixed dimensions.

We have no purely biochemical explanation for how our cells are organized into a baby during the first ten days after fertilization. We don't know why the cells that are to form the head end up between the arms and not between the legs. However, there is an electric field around an axis that later becomes the spinal column, and it seems that this axis may form the template around which our cells are organized.[133] The flow of this energy is still felt in the chakras, meridians, and acupuncture points.

The experimental evidence that such action was possible came when it was shown that weak radiation from tissues could stimulate cell growth in neighboring cells.[134] For the first ten days after fertilization the electrical field of frog's eggs determined the yet unformed location of the central nervous system. Harold Burr wrote that the universe "is organized and maintained by an electro-dynamic field capable of determining the position and movement of all charged particles — which is how our bodies 'keep in shape.'"[135]

This is not a new idea. Indeed, the concept that the human body produces and is formed around fields is as ancient as Sanskrit. Dozens of books have been published on this. Over a century ago Leadbeater and Steiner noticed three distinct levels of human energy that differed in each individual,[136] and William Kilner used colored filters to find irregularities in the energy field to diagnose liver infections, epilepsy, tumors, and appendicitis.[137]

For example, my grandmother saw auras. She was a caterer, and knew from 'feel' if her staff were going to become seriously ill.

Over time she could sense coming diseases so often that her pre-scient ability used to frighten her. What struck me as so significant was that she did not have this feeling at the time that the symptoms showed, but at least twelve months before. She knew that her cook was going to get cancer a full year before he knew.

It is often said that breast cancers develop in certain personal-ity types, and that people who have hidden their hearts tend to have heart attacks. It makes sense that if a situation is in the field it is already in preparation on this plane. We all carry cancerous cells in our bodies, along with the viruses of many diseases, but we need to be vulnerable to an attack before we come down with the symptoms. The disposition that creates that vulnerability is the trig-ger, and that may be in place long before the event manifests. The commands do not come from any superficial part, for none of us would consciously want to be diseased. It comes from the deepest energetic layers.

This and hundreds of similar stories suggest that the fields around us become disturbed — or what we might call dis-eased — before illness breaks out in the body. Something alters the tone of the information being sent around the system, which alters pro-teins and receptors, which set destructive processes in motion. This is why Reiki and other energy work on the body, as well as personal development, can have a profound impact on health.

The examples that follow show how people have been investi-gating this relationship. Though this has been going on in an experi-mental manner for more than 100 years, and though results have been positive, the concept still remains outside the conventions of modern biology. They illustrate the diversity of approaches within a common theme.

In the 1920s a number of Russian, German, and American biologists suggested that fields of energy controlled organic devel-opment.[138] Alexander Gurwitsch discovered wave radiation in onion roots and showed that the vibration in the field created by this radiation could have been the morphological field that arranged the cells in the growing onion. Paul Weis wrote "a living system owes its typical organization and its *specific* activities to a *field*…that determines the *character* of the formation to which it gives rise."[139] Playing music to tomatoes is an extension of this idea.

Many similar phenomena have been reported. Dora van Gelder was one of many to observe the lines of frequency in the body that transfer energy from organ to organ, and that health problems arise when these lines are interrupted by surgery.[140] Theodor Schwenk published drawings to show the fibrous lines in bones that look like the flow of energy around the spongy interior.[141] Chinese medicine is based on the study of the body's energy systems.

Burr and Northrup measured the health of plants from the electrical field of the seeds that created them,[142] and used this to select the best seeds for future growth. Burr also found how to measure the fields of all sorts of molds, plants and animals, including humans. The considerable work done since then on how the waxing and waning of the moon alters plant growth originated with Burr's experiment.[143] From these it is being argued that the field is the primary creative principle, rather than the genetic code.[144] The field steers the car, the gene is the engine.

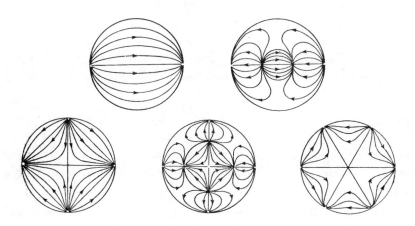

Fig. 8—Variety of regular patterns of movement in a container of water.

Schwenk wrote that the formation of the chicken embryo ""may be initiated by rhythmical shaking," in a procedure that reminds me of homeopathy. The evolution within the egg is accompanied by "countless small movements which interpenetrate one another in the most varied ways" as we would expect of fields.[145] Schwenk was a flawless observer of flowing forms, and was fascinated by the way the movement of water was itself the form that its flow created. In river banks, in the shape of jellyfish and stingrays, in the wind over sand he illustrated how form is not possible without there being some movement in its making.

Fig. 9—Lines of force in the human hip joint showing the flow of energy that created both bones in the early stage of growth, and then the cross lines reflect the moment when the hip was separated from the femur.

It is particularly sad that most of these experiments were completed over fifty years ago, and since then major research in energy work has been sidelined, even sabotaged. The concept that change (and this include healing) can occur without physical contact has become repugnant over the past fifty years. One favorite pejorative phrase is to call energy work 'new age.' The dishonorable treatment meted out to Candace Pert and Jacques Benveniste is only the tip of a very conservative iceberg. So successful has this action been that Benveniste has written that "There is *nothing in any treatise* on molecular interactions in biology that uses the words 'frequency' or 'signal' [in the physical sense of the term], nor 'electromagnetic.'"[146]

There is also a strong financial incentive to keep things as they are. If the power of our energy fields could be harnessed to heal the body, there would be less need for drugs, and the pharmaceutical industry would lose its present dominant position. It is disturbing that in drug trials patients taking placebos will often have the same likelihood of getting better as those who took the chemicals.[147] There are vast profits in antidepressant drugs, yet Irving Kirsch, who has spent thirty years investigating these matters, found that in more than half the clinical trials for the six leading brands the drugs did not outperform placebos.[148] In other words, were our minds to be trained to *believe in their own effectiveness*, and their power over the cellular health of our bodies, then we would be using beliefs rather than drugs to cure many of our ills.

Coherence creates a qualitative difference

When mind control and the controlling factor are equally balanced, then comes the condition of one-pointedness.

— Patanjali Sutra

Herbert Fröhlich has shown that when the vibrations of individual protein molecules reach a certain threshold they begin to pulsate in unison until they bump themselves into another state. At that instant vast numbers of previously disconnected proteins resonate together. What was once separate begins to operate as one. Together they form a single collective vibration with a different purpose to those of each individual molecule. Then all the previously separate parts synchronize to create a new collective.[149] This is coherence.

When molecules are energetically in tune their combined capacity changes and they become more than the sum of their parts, like a crowd or an organization. Together they make a quantum jump to a new level of awareness and operation. Though "coherent states are, as is well known, the quantum-mechanical counterparts of the fields that occur in classical electromagnetic theory,"[150] they represent a very different level of being.

The unexpected transformation that happens in coherence is illustrated in one supremely creative moment among single-celled amoebae called slime mold. When food declines these amoebae huddle together until their numbers reach a critical level, at which moment they reorganize into one single distinct and coherent entity. This is a new form, in no way like the original amoeba, which then moves as one being to a new location where conditions for survival are better. On arrival the collective develops a stalk from which are released millions of spores to create a new colony. It was their aggregation into a mob that created a new field that transformed the individual cells into one self-organizing mobile spore factory. We see something similar in flocks of birds that move as one being, and then disperse to their individual nests.

Humans do this too. The first division into undifferentiated cells in the blastula during the first days of pregnancy comes to a critical juncture when the cells differentiate into the many parts that will become a recognizable embryo. This juncture is the moment of coherence when a mere collection becomes a being. Watching this happening under an electron microscope is a magical experience. You can actually see coherence in action.

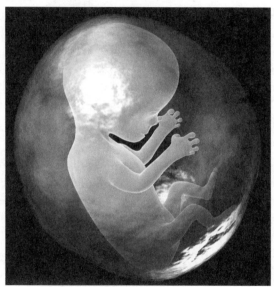

Fig. 10 Fetus growing in the womb.

Another example of coherence is in sport, where success depends on going beyond conscious training or thinking about doing better to that magical zone of transformation where the whole of us operates as one. As Michael Novak wrote about running: "There is a certain point of unity within the self, a certain complicity and magnetic mating, a certain harmony, that the conscious mind and will cannot direct. Command by instinct is swifter, subtler, deeper, and more accurate, more in touch with reality than command by the conscious mind. This discovery takes one's breath away."[151] We know that to obtain such unity more than clear intention is needed.

Communication within the organism of the runner has moved beyond the everyday scale of time and space. The transformation is so huge, and normal rates of order so exceeded, that the organism seems to be moving out of our realm into another. We might say that is it partaking of some of the characteristics found in the virtual landscape of the Field. It can be described as a quantum jump, for in that state long-range molecular forces, no matter how weak, have an impact on others, even across infinite distances.

Emilio del Giudice and Giuliano Preparata have shown mathematically how closely packed atoms act in a manner different to how they would act as individual atoms.[152] They form a collective that behaves in a coherent manner with characteristics that are not found in the individual atoms. As the parts bunch together into more compact groups they form constellations that are qualitatively different. They act together as a whole instead of being random molecules fluffing around in a chaotic soup. It is the same with hungry slime mold and great sportsmen.

We have seen that water shares and carries information. Molecules of H_2O are among the most plentiful materials on the planet. When clustered together as rivers or seas they perform differently than they would as individual particles. Their grouped behavior forms coherent domains.[153] When a molecule of some substance such as lead is placed in water and charged, it transmits the simple signal of that charge. The molecules adjacent to the lead then polarize around it and proceed to do this amazing thing: they amplify the frequency of the lead's signal to such an extent that it may be instantaneously read at a distance without any direct contact.

The information is not just carried within each molecule waiting for a physical connection in order to spread, like when we touch an electric fence, but is augmented so it may be transmitted beyond itself. This capacity inherent in water is important, for it enables signals to be carried throughout every part of an organism with lightning speed. It makes it possible for nerves to move into a coherent mode so signals can travel fast enough for the instant reactions required for survival. At this moment it seems that water can act beyond the time-space constraints of normal life. Water takes a quantum leap into the nonlocal, nontemporal implicate realm. As communicator of signals it becomes imbued with qualities of the Field. It now seems that we have to conclude that the ability to sustain long-range connections is an inherent quality of all matter.

Calculations of the short-range forces that connect one atom with its neighbor are not in themselves enough to hold solid matter together. So, what does? What holds atoms in place so that an object exists, and does not fly apart? For example, how do the atoms in the wings of an airplane stay together when it would be a gross misfortune if the atoms at the tip lost connection with those attached to the fuselage? It was not until the 1990s that this very simple question was being investigated in any depth.

I shall call this maintenance factor the Vishnu Paradox, for reasons that will become clearer as we investigate further.

The Vishnu Paradox

All things can be known in the vivid light of intuition.

—Patanjali Sutra

In ancient Vedic lore created thousands of years ago Brahma is the foundation of all creativity, Shiva the cosmic dancer who creates and dissolves all forms, and most interestingly, and unique to the Hindus, a third force named Vishnu who maintains the system. In a simplistic manner we might rename Brahma as the Great Field, Shiva the endless dance of particles moving in and out of form and time, and Vishnu the coherent mathematician that holds form in place. The importance of referring back to the most ancient religious beliefs that are still practiced is that the truths stated in the Vedas and the Sutras have come from profound mystic experiences by extremely coherent men and women who, in penetrating across the veil into the Field, returned with crystal clear perceptions of the nature of things. Their statements coincide closely with the aspects of modern scientific understanding presented here, and with experiences of today's mystics like Sai Baba, Bernadette Roberts, and Ken Wilber.

Movement without 'purpose' creates random chaos. Without the Vishnu factor the permanence of matter would be jeopardized. Though this is new understanding and the inner strands of connection are not yet clear, one can argue that fields provide direction to the dance of particles while fractal mathematics sets out method and form. The fields would be holographic so that direction and information would be directed to every part at once in the fullest manner. We might consider the possibility that mathematics is just a description of the process by which order is created rather than the cause, and that it is the 'image' in the energetic field that is the ultimate generator.

Fig. 11—Fractal patterns on the surface of a cabbage.

Any collective mode of conduct, according to Giudice and Preparata, can be maintained only by long-range forces that, when spread across a large community of molecules, produce more than what could be expected from the individual behavior of their atoms. A coherent community uses less energy to complete a task. "Packed molecules form coherent domains because such an organization results in lower energy levels. Molecules spontaneously go from a chaotic state to an ordered state if that ordered state happens to contain less energy. The principle involved is that the stable state of a system is the one with the minimal energy" required for its maintenance.[154]

It is a fundamental principle of physics, stated in the second law of thermodynamics, that complex orders tend to evolve into ones using less energy, so that living things die, rocks wear away, and entropy inevitably ensues. Entropy is a little like a crowd of pick-pockets. Sooner or later everyone will have picked everyone else's pockets and the money will be evenly distributed around the crowd. It illustrates how an initially active energetic system eventually runs down. Maintaining coherence is the most important aspect of the Vishnu factor among living systems.

It is also true on the psychological level. When our beliefs and experiences are in conflict with one another, our lives are not as efficient, as energy is being diverted into maintaining coherence rather than toward the tasks of life — and so health may be affected. These conflicts may get to such a pitch that our survival is threatened. Removing or smoothing over these contradictions in order to re-establish coherence is one of the primary roles of meditation and personal therapy by creating inner stillness and through that psychic order.

All energetic healing, including Reiki and Acupressure, reprogram the molecular and cellular fields so they might operate more coherently. Rod Nelson has shown that when we deliberately raise our coherence it creates a cascade of tiny biological processes that can have an enormous impact on health and well-being.[155]

Coherent individuals seem to invariably have great appeal and a stronger influence over others.[156] When we are drawn to certain people, and often deeply influenced by them, those are the people with the most coherent brain wave patterns. This is the same as saying that those with greater access to the Field have a transcendent quality that the rest of us are drawn to and willingly respond to. The feeling of goodness we have when near the Dalai Lama is an inspiring example on the positive side. But coherence need not be only positive. It will depend on the character of the personal energetic fields that we often call charisma. We apply it particularly to political leaders such as John Kennedy, or even Adolf Hitler.

This is clearly demonstrated in distance healing, and has been extensively tested.[157] When someone deliberately synchronizes with another there is a measurable alignment that increases their joint coherence. In the most carefully constructed experiments, completed only in the past decade, it has been shown that healing is most effective when there is surrender to both the belief and the intention. If there is will, especially that forceful will that comes from an egoic feeling that we 'have to do something,' the transfer does not work. When coherence operates between people, as it does in long relationships, they often find they are each having the same thoughts at the same time. It is present in those eight out of every ten adults and children who report they have sensed when they were being stared at from behind.[158]

When we can relax inside ourselves into a state of attunement, a resonating consciousness develops with a higher level of coherence, and then "the ordinary boundary of separateness is crossed. The brain of each member becomes less highly tuned to his own information while becoming more receptive to that of the other. They pick up someone else's information from the Field as if it were their own."[159]

Fig. 12 — In the stillness of meditation attuned coherence is possible.

To achieve this we need to be still within, so that our own vibrations may settle into a coherent state. Without any action being involved, this feels like being pure consciousness. It also acts as the foundation for intentional movement when it generates fields that have been called ch'i, prana, life force and so on. This is the basis for many healing modalities, such as acupuncture, Reiki, and ch'i gong. Practitioners have been shown to produce enormously enhanced transmission of photons and an enlarged electromagnetic field during sessions.[160] In recent double-blind trials a ch'i gong master directed his ch'i at random moments at a man in another room who physically recoiled each time.[161] The ch'i that is transmitted is a field of energy propelled with focused intent, like a Buck Rogers laser gun. It is the intensely focused intent that activates the energy systems of the body to impact on other systems.

Group healing develops an even greater level of attunement, and is more effective than individual healing. If the 'target' is a large social unit, the group needs to be large too. In a fascinating study in Washington it was shown that a group of 4,000 participants could have a dramatic effect on the entire city. The group concentrated on violent crime that had been steadily rising for years. When they meditated on the violence it began to decline steadily. Four months after the group had disbanded, the crime rate returned to its earlier level.[162] During the study they made sure that the decline could not have been due to variables such as weather or anti-crime campaigns. When the project was applied in other cities it was found that if just one percent of the population meditated in unison the crime rate would be lowered — the hundredth monkey effect.[163]

This also applies to huge mass events. The overwhelming feelings that turn a group into a mob in which all individual sense of rightness is swallowed into the crowd's mood is an example of the shadow side of coherence. In the socially constrained cultures of southeast Asia ongoing tension can lead to a total breakdown of conventions and the rules that enable people to live together sensibly, and a whole society will run amok slaughtering whichever group appears as the opposition. This happened in Indonesia during the turmoil that followed the massacre of the generals and the failed attempt by the communists to take over from Sukarno during which over a million people were killed.

We do not even have to be in a mob to imitate a group response, as we realized when we heard of Kennedy's assassination over the radio or the destruction of the Twin Towers. Most people were deeply affected as if they had been together in one place when it happened, whereas they were joined only by devices of communication.

Therapists help to re-establish coherence so that people are no longer pulled apart by the contradictions and shadows and judgments of personality, but may be simple, entire, and whole within themselves. It is from this level of coherence that we may most readily connect with the Field, for we are then in tune and can harmonize, and so resonate with all that is around us. Coherence extends us into another realm of existence that we call samadhi, the timeless union with all that is: to be discussed later.

Replication is both coherent and unpredictable

Evolution is chaos with feedback.

—Joseph Ford

One way to describe coherence is through a mathematical model. In 1975 the French mathematician Benoit Mandelbrot recognized that evolution in nature could be expressed in geometric forms that revealed a similar pattern regardless of scale.[164]

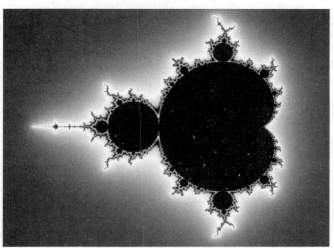

Fig.13—Symmetrical Mandelbrot figure.

He coined the word fractal for these irregular yet repetitive shapes. The mathematics of fractals is amazingly simple. It consists of taking a number, multiplying it by itself and then adding the original number. The result of that operation is then used to start the next operation. There is only one equation that is repeated again and again. The challenge is that even though each operation follows the same formula, the process must be repeated millions of times to create a visual fractal pattern.

These 'self-similar' patterns are nested within one another. The forms that result may be extraordinarily complex, though they are created only by the successive iteration of simple equations. For example, the arrangement of twigs on a branch resembles the pattern of branches coming off a trunk. The pattern of a major river looks like the flow of its tributaries.

Fractals are a description of a tool used in growth. They are not the cause, just as a hammer does not cause a house, but just aids in its erection. Fractals provide a clear way to describe turbulence,

Fig. 14 — The vortices that arise as a pencil is drawn along a straight line through a liquid. It replicates the forms of hip joints, meanders in rivers, hooks in seeds.

as in wind and water, and the apparent chaos of nature as in coast-lines and the branching cells of the lungs. Forty years ago Rudolf Schwenk studied the visual connections between these patterns in the energy flow of nature.[165] Basically, we can say that both turbulence and order are born out of the same underlying processes.

The fractal model predicts that organic growth is based on a reiterated pattern of 'structures' nested within one another. Fractal images of smaller structures are miniatures of larger units. This is why the structure of a human body and how it operates socially is similar to what goes on in our own cells. In reverse, it is said that just as humans are a fractal image of society, so cells are a fractal image of the human. In fact, Lipton would say that cells are a fractal image of society as well.[166]

As D'Arcy Thompson wrote, the manifold forms of nature are dynamically created by *"number* and *relative magnitude,"* and that "the harmony of the world is embodied in mathematical beauty."[167] Number and geometric form are dimensionless, and in these qualities partake of the implicate order.[168] It is through number and regular form that the implicate expresses itself in the explicate, as Bohm might say. Plato and others have been fascinated, if not troubled, by the perfect three-dimensional solids of octahedrons and so on. These forms are so three-dimensionally symmetrical that from whatever direction we contemplate them they provide us with the same patterns. They have been considered sacred shapes that were created, like crystals, to be the fundamental forms of nature.

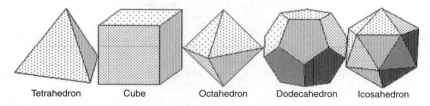

Tetrahedron   Cube   Octahedron   Dodecahedron   Icosahedron

Fig. 15 — Drawing of the five regular Platonic solids.

There may not be perfect symmetry in nature, but equally there cannot be randomness. "In biology randomness is death, chaos is death. Everything is highly structured. When you clone plants, the order in which the branches come out is exactly the same. The

Mandelbrot set obeys an extraordinarily precise scheme leaving nothing to chance whatsoever. The idea of randomness in biology is just reflex."[169] However, the situation is not quite so cut and dried. It leaves out the perplexing problem of irregularities occurring within otherwise symmetrical forms, such as the human face where one half is never exactly a mirror image of the other.

Perfect symmetry is only a probability, and virtually never inevitable. The occasional fractal models that repeat themselves endlessly create monotonous sequences that feel as dull as they look. To create forms that can adapt themselves and integrate with whatever is around them the fractal has to spawn itself so it may "range over many different frequencies without falling into a locked periodic channel" that contains only minimal information.[170]

Quantity of information is the key. Fractal processes are 'information-rich' yet are created from extremely simple mathematical sets. With it comes a higher level of possibilities, which is just another way of describing creativity. Complex multilayered formations offer many opportunities for development and mutation. Where the body has been damaged, tissues may need to re-create themselves with considerable flexibility, creating new bone structure and new ligaments in the right places. It is the many scales possible within fractal systems that provide this creative framework for healing. It seems that the greater the amount of information the greater the potential for creativity and adaptability, and so for the maintenance of a healthy system.[171] It would seem that Vishnu loves complex fractals.

The paradox in stable systems is this fundamental principle that ensures that the universe is as varied as possible. Things arrange themselves so that, while preserving their identity, they produce great variety within that identity. This has been studied in a number of mathematical models that show that without this quality, processes grind to a halt. We only have to examine the infinite range of flows through identical openings, as shown by Theodor Schwenk in his great study on *Sensitive Chaos*, to realize that at one scale all would look alike, and that at another each is rich with diversity without losing any of its apparent wholeness. The fact that we are infinitely attracted to these variable forms and rapidly bored by straight flow shows how deeply *unpredictable sameness* is built into our own system through our way of perceiving nature.

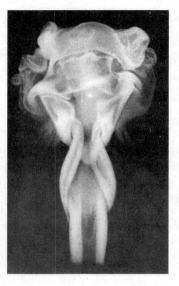

Fig. 16—The flow of a steady stream of liquid into still water creates a shape like the larynx.

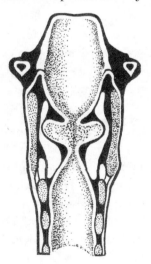

Fig. 17—The larynx in which a stream of air flows between the slit between the vocal chords.

This means that when a gene-protein combination builds the backbone of a snake or centipede there will be those tiny distortions in the system that ensure that each vertebra is very slightly different from its neighbor, without which there would be no possibility of adapting to different situations. Without this unpredictability each unit would automatically be identical to the next. In modern factories we try to duplicate components so that the glass walls of office buildings will be cheaper. But the downside is that identical repetition makes them much less interesting to live with. This is the very boring trap pure rationality has taken us to, and that nature never fell for. To do so would have made it impossible to produce the long-term stability of our environment.

The miracle is that repetition that can self-modify does not become chaotic, but can remain stable. This is true even in complex systems, such as our bodies that contain billions of elements each with its own field. It is the coherence of each field established over eons of time that enables it to retain its uniqueness while adapting and resonating with the 'needs' of other fields. When we cut a finger the different layers of the skin proceed to heal themselves in the right order. The surface skin and the hairs growing out of it do not end up underneath the less robust subcutaneous layers. Each part retains through its own coherence the identity required by the parent system. Yet, were part of the damage irreparable, as is often the case with a tear from jagged metal in which perfect regrowth does not happen automatically, the repair adapts itself to the new conditions even if it leaves a scar as evidence of its adaptability.

It is paradoxical to conceive of growth being both coherent (which is mathematical) and random (which is chaotic). This is why a few clovers have four leaves and the Fibonacci series appears with only approximate truth in the proportion of everyone's bodies. The small differences from the mean in plants, or in hands and faces, express those tiny distortions from perfection that are the guarantee of organic stability. The unpredictable variability in the perfection of the fractals could be called 'consciousness.'[172] Conscious because each replication responds to need and exactly suits its place and the role it is to play in the whole being. If this sea of data were to flow without any guiding principle there really would be chaos.

Instead the Vishnu Paradox applies at every level of existence, even in the outline of the seashore, of the weather, and the design of gothic façades.[173]

Our feelings of beauty reflect the harmony and disorder found in nature, in clouds and trees, and the waves of the sea. Each is a dynamic energetic process that incarnated with its own combinations of order and disorder. When the thirteenth century master Pierre de Celles unconsciously employed fractal principles in the north façade at Notre-Dame in Paris, he created one of the most fascinating and intriguing monuments of gothic. The same principles, and the same elements, are applied at every scale, with a little repetition in each scale of the geometry used in another. This is, in fact, one of the principles of medieval building. The masters developed ways to lay out their churches and to design the templates from which the stones were cut that we can see in retrospect were so aligned with the natural forms around them that they are totally fractal. Notre-Dame may be a supremely appropriate example, but the same principles are found in nearly all the great medieval buildings where variations of similar nonperiodic geometry were applied at every level of the design.[174]

Fig. 18—North façade of Notre-Dame in Paris showing the beauty of repetition through many scales. The photos are increasing concentrated on the decoration within the rose. Notice how the little trefoils behind the cusps of the rose are repeats of trefoils on every level of the façade.

Yet it seems not insignificant that it fronts onto such a cramped street that it can only be appreciated from the back of a narrow lane. The process of design is hidden within the chaos of the town, just as the order in the weather is hidden inside the torrents of wind and rain.

Expansion and contraction

That which is perceived has three qualities, sattva, rajas, and tamas. The use of these produces experience and eventual liberation.

—Patanjali Sutra

At every level of life the organism responds in one of two ways. It can either expand to embrace life or withdraw to defend itself against a hostile environment. It cannot do both at the same time. When a cell, for example, is expansive it supplies whatever is needed for the growth of the organism, and when it is withdrawn it shrinks inward and its functions are impaired.[175] Cells move toward food, away from toxins. Wherever our cells go we go — we become either reflective and intelligent or defensive and combative. This implies that the more protection you believe you need the less you can expect your cells to provide. And this is reflected in the entire system so that we respond to situations with either outgoing energy or withdrawing energy. In threatening situations this is expressed as fight or flight.

The Lyapunov characteristic exponent is a measure of those properties that lead to stability or instability. Devised over a hundred years ago, it has led to some extremely abstruse mathematics that connects chaos theory with dynamic systems. It concerns that fascinating interface between stability and collapse, such as the moment when a stable spinning top begins to wobble.

When a periodic system, such as ABABABAB, or a linear one such as AAAAAA, is repeated again and again the exponent is a negative number. As we might expect such systems may start in a dynamic way, such as the spinning top, but in time tend toward some steady state or entropy. Repetitive sequences contract. However, dynamic and organic systems produce a positive number. These appear as outward-spreading or fluid forms that show the sort of coherence found in fractals. These are inherent in living forms. This means that whatever does not change returns to dust and whatever creatively adapts makes the dance.

We might say that any series that is open to uncertainty is capable of change and expansion (the Vishnu Paradox), and thus adaptability is assured.

Many of the three-dimensional renditions of the Lyapunov exponent produce figures just like those drawn by Chaim Tejman to describe his concept of 'energetic matter.' In 2001 he postulated a fundamental force in all things that simultaneously pushes and pulls. He wrote: "The prevailing consensus points to four fundamental forces — electromagnetism, gravitation, as well as strong and weak nuclear forces — but I aver that there is only one force: energetic matter. Energetic matter creates wave formations that are expressed exclusively by the two principle forces of pushing and pulling."[176] He deals with photons, but the same principle would seem to apply to every level of the universe. He shows that the only way to explain all the interactions between photons and other particles within the laws of quantum theory is to imbue them with two distinct loops. There is an energetic loop that scatters and a magnetic loop that binds. One that disperses, and one that holds. This is the same expansion/contraction response found in all living things.

Fig. 19—Chaim Tejman's drawing of the loops of energetic matter.

He wrote, "a two-loop wave formation...be it swirling, rotating active strings, quarks, rings, loops, or waves, is the primary formation of energetic matter."[177] The different combinations within a wave formation support the many different energetic paths and forces, all created by the one main force-cum-substance — energetic matter. "Two loops in one wave is the building block of nature. Everything works in accordance with this principle."

Today, there is sound evidence of an inseparable bond between these magnetic and electric components of every natural energetic formation. Both components combine to form one entity (the quant) despite the fact that they possess intrinsically different behaviors.

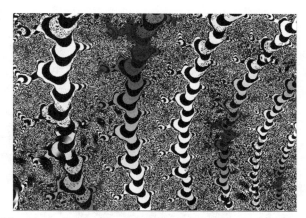

Fig. 20—One of many fractal arrangements that replicate natural formations such as vertebrates, nerves and blood vessels. It shows how complex forms can be derived from a simple formula.[178]

Consequently, wave formation is composed of two perpendicular energetic swirls or loops: one is a largely invisible electric loop that seems to have connections with dark matter, and the other is a magnetic loop that is visible and palpable.

What I like about this unproven theory is that it coincides with observations of larger things, like cells and waves and galaxies, and aligns with what we find in therapy. When a person has an emotional block the client will feel trapped between two opposing yet unequal forces that are acting simultaneously inside him. Exactly as Tejman describes for energetic matter, these forces are like "two loops that are in perpetual competition."

In our scenario energetic matter figuratively represents the conjunction of the implicate world of energy fields and the solid universe of the explicate realm. The loop formation reflects the beliefs of most religions that the manifest world is created around the duality between creation and destruction, night and day, good and evil, birth and death: That Lucifer is simultaneously the devil and the bringer of light, that Shiva both creates and destroys, or that there is a hell to balance the promise of heaven. The paradoxical nature of the universe beyond the Vishnu factor is that all creation is comprised of two contradictory states that co-exist simultaneously, and that the unity of the universe depends on the equilibrium between them.

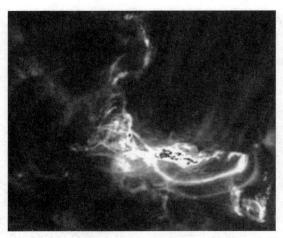

Fig. 21—A NASA double-loop formation in a galactic cluster that
Tejman uses to illustrate energetic matter.

By implication there is a state of rest, a still point between the
loops. This crucial 'neutral' state is often left out in discussion as it is
often such a still point that it seems to be no more than an infinitely
small moment on the cusp between one movement and the next.

The 'yes' and 'no' and 'neither' in the cells is reflected in the
triune nature of godheads in some major religions. In the Vedas
we can read of three fundamental qualities of energy. These are
not states, but movements of the energy within states. Rajas is the
name for Bohm's superimplicate order, the Brahma or the formless
Ground of Being discussed by Ken Wilber.[179] It is pure free-flowing
energy in movement, without any fixed address or appointments.
There are no boundaries, no limits, no time, no fixed density nor
temperature. This is the zone without purpose or limits. It is the
formless and eternal.

Rajas divides into Tamas and Sattva. They are analogies for all
the aspects of division in organic and inorganic things. Tamas is the
enclosing form-making aspect of energy that organizes structure
and holds it in place. Sattva is the opening movement that unties
all restraints. The actions of scattering and binding, of pushing and
pulling, or however this manifests, are the fundamentals of existence, whether they are in photons or cells or planets or the human

psyche. The same forces are present pursuing the same agendas, each in ways that are appropriate to their scale and complexity.

Tamas is like the Yin that draws inward, that holds and nurtures, that encompasses and limits, enfolds, and sucks. It is the inward breath, the closing cycle. It is internal, feminine, cave and the flow of water. In the human condition too much Tamas encourages us to grasp, in attachment and desire, in the closure that generates war and depression. If Tamas were ever to proceed far enough everything would unwind and total entropy would set in. Fortunately the fractal nature of the universe prevents this from happening.

Sattva is the energy of the out-breath and release, the risk-taker that seeks new forms through connection. It is like the Yang, out-thrusting, ambitious, open, desiring, and external. It brings change and new frontiers, it inseminates and manifests with uncertainty and passion. It is the romantic impulse in art and poetry, the open groovy nature in masculine mode, the mountain and the explorer.

Expansion is the scattering and pushing movement that creates the flow in streams and clouds, volcanoes and supernovae, and the excitement of life. Growing organisms and young people have this in abundance. Nature usually provides heaps of it for parents so that life may be renewed. It gradually lessens as we get older, though if we let negative beliefs dominate us, Tamas takes over and we can be quite dead in ourselves while still breathing and talking.

We can summarize the new research in biology over the past twenty-five years as providing the evidence that all organisms connect through signals that are vibrations in implicate fields. If the butterfly in Brazil can trigger a hurricane in Indonesia, then a single peptide in the cell of a finger could spawn a novel or this book.[180] This may be the explanation for such well-acknowledged but poorly understood phenomena as the placebo effect, spontaneous remission in cancer, the health rewards of a strong faith, prayer, homeopathy, and the nonphysical communication that occurs between people and animals.

All in all, we have to conclude that long-range transfer of information is an inherent quality of all matter through invisible fields, and that fields change and transform in response to the matter it has created. Some fields of energy are formed before the organic material is in place, some afterward. So, we are back with the same question geneticists have been asking themselves for a long time: What actually triggers the fields to act in this way?

5

Our Heart Brain and the Cerebral Brain

The three earlier brains

When that which veils the light is done away with, then comes the state of being called discarnate, freed from the modification of the thinking principle.

— Patanjali Sutra

We have a series of brains that have developed over eons, each on top of and created after the other. The first is the cerebellum or reptilian brain sitting over the most ancient part called the brainstem. They form the rapid response team, and are entirely in the here and now. Being concerned almost exclusively with survival, the ability to intuit through access to the Field is a major function.

Around and above this lies the second brain, being the emotional or limbic system that deals with feelings, relationships, and learning. It emerged first in mammals, and deals with past and present. It is the 'gut' of the brain, and affects all the others. If someone is strongly affected by their emotions and connections with other people, this is the part that gets fired up.

The third brain is the cortex, divided into right and left hemispheres. It added the new function of consciousness and awareness of the future, along with curiosity and all its realms of imagination. The earlier parts did not remain unaffected. When "each new brain developed it incorporated into its own functions the more primitive foundations upon which it is built and changed the nature of that foundation into one that would be compatible with the new system."[181]

Between the second brain and the right hemisphere of the cortex there are ample connections, but far less to the left hemisphere. The left and right parts are not always fully connected as the joiner between them; the *corpus callosum* is more developed in women than in men.

The left half of the cortex governs language, creates rigid categories, deals with surfaces and forms, uses logic and reason, while the right is concerned with recognition, the here and now, intensity of feeling, time as process, and artistic enjoyment. You could say that the left is an intellectual scientist, while the right is an ecstatic artist. When you are tired the left brain will often take over. When the right has gone off duty the world lacks insight and value.

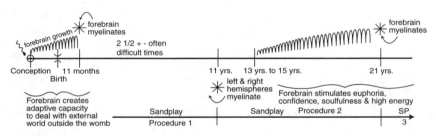

Fig. 22 — Changes in brain growth and myelination at ages eleven months, eleven years and at twenty-one.

Goldberg's recent research shows that the right hemisphere is best at handling novel experiences while the left is best at working with fully developed structures of knowledge.[182] The right, with its rich connections to the lower brains, handles the immediate and unlearned, and only when well established are these signals passed on to the left.

The one on the right is where the architects, designers, and artists are creating new ideas and forms, while the left is occupied by the bean counters, accountants, operations managers, and systems analysts who are responsible for turning the inspiration of the right into a practical reality. In this society and under modern education we mostly 'identify' with the left, as this is where words and concepts live.

However, the left can live in relative isolation, especially in men with their smaller *corpus callosum*. It can enjoy novelty and intellectual adventures without being overwhelmed by the rest, and can easily unbalance the system by rushing off on its own. It can stand outside emotions and events with objectivity, but as it is not directly linked to the heart nor to intuition nor feelings, its brilliant thoughts may lack some of the broader values in thinking we call intelligence — hence the limited intuition among civilized people.

The left is always in a hurry, loves to work out problems, and tends to treat the right with impatience. Where the right immediately *sees* the answer to a problem and passes it on instantaneously, the bureaucrat in the left has to organize its views rather more slowly.

The ideal state is one of close cooperation between the two halves, with the left treating the right as a wise counselor and trusted adviser rather than the village idiot, and the right treating the left as an essential form-maker rather than a boring sentimentalist.

The fourth brain, our neocortex or forebrain, is the most recent acquisition. The important development of these frontal lobes will be discussed in a moment.

Differences between men and women

The properties of matter and the course of cosmic evolution are now seen to be intimately related to the structure of the living being and to its activities. The biologist may now rightly regard the universe in its very essence as biocentric.

—Lawrence Henderson

There are two connective tissues between the hemispheres — the *corpus callosum* and the *anterior commissure*. The former connects conscious material such as words and thoughts between the two hemispheres, while the latter is more primitive and connects unconscious and raw emotions from the reptilian brain underneath. Through here conscious emotional material from the cortex is sent to the limbic for amplification into terror, rage, hunger, or lust, and passed back to the cortex to be processed into the more complex feelings we call envy, anger, or love. Both these bundles of tissue are larger in women than in men.

Women also have more tissue in the *massa intermedia* which connects the two halves of the thalamus. This shunts incoming information to appropriate areas with lightning speed, and is where automatic responses are triggered.[183] This may be why women are usually more in contact with their emotions than men, and why they have an immediacy with words that leaves most men flabbergasted. As the more emotionally sensitive right brain is able to pass more information across to the linguistically talented left, women's emotions are more easily and immediately incorporated into speech and thought.

This is the physical reason that women hold the emotional upper edge over men in verbal battles. Their mates, being less well endowed and slower to respond, get frustrated and naturally move into the one area where they are usually sure to win, their physical strength.

Imaging studies have shown that when women do complex mental tasks they bring both sides of the brain to the problem, while men tend to use only the side that is most suited to it. Women often take a broader view of life, bringing more aspects of any situation into decision making, while men are more focused. Depression is more common among women, for the emotional registers of the brain become overactive through feedback loops that are facilitated by women's enlarged *corpus callosum*, while the action-response sections that help men work their way out of their low feelings remain relatively quiescent.

This physical structure can make huge differences to the way we behave. People with a large corpus and with emotional centers that have been highly stimulated when young tend to be led by their feelings, while those with a smaller corpus and a desensitized emotional body will usually be more mental. The failure to develop the higher mental powers lies most often in a failure to develop its foundations, the older mammalian and reptilian. Such failure leads to an unending cycle of breakdown in which the neocortex cannot integrate the reptilian into its service in order to moderate its behavior. Confusion over which of the three gets to integrate the other two produces most of the problems we find in therapy. The results can be appalling if the reptilian brain dictates behavior without being tempered by the neocortex, for then "trouble brews for that person, his society and the indeed the whole earth."[184]

The deep structure of the brain would be holographic

Union is achieved through the subjugation of the emotional nature, and the restraint of the mind. When this has been accomplished, the Yogi knows himself as he is in reality.

—Patanjali Sutra

It is known that every experience we have ever had can be recalled, in all its details and with all senses involved, if the right stimulation is applied. Were the brain to store all this data in its neural cells on a one-to-one basis, at even the impossibly low rate of one bit of information per second for a lifetime, it would require an incomprehensible $3x10^{10}$ elementary binary nerves — too many impressions for the existing storage capacity. Consider the number of impressions we can take in per second, and you will see how absurdly conservative this is: each second contains thousands of sensory impressions, as well as those from the body, the tug of the moon, the unconscious but current judgments coming from social and familial issues, interpenetration and interdependence of all the available fields, *ad infinitum*.

All our senses are sensitive to the vibrations received by the others. Eyes are sensitive to sound, memory is stimulated by smell, and smell itself is affected by other frequencies. The picture that emerges is that no one sense acts alone, but needs others for the fulfillment of its own role. The brain needs not only to store this unimaginable mass of mixed data, but also needs to be able to shuffle and make sense out of its mixed sources and messages. In addition we need vast areas for the computations, assessments, and judgments without which we could not have survived.

Fig. 23 — The close relationship between the earth and the moon has established the intimate rhythms between them.

Karl Pribram has argued that the brain's deep structure has to be a holographic domain,[185] as only a holographic model of consciousness could explain such an encompassing talent.[186] The argument is that in holograms every part is contained in the whole, so the whole as an entity, not as a set of individual cells or neurons, are responsible for all actions and recalls, even though each one has a unique flavor. As Michael Talbot described it, "if you have a hologram of an apple you can tilt the plate a little to one side and actually see behind the apple…if you cut it in half you will have two complete images — each containing the entire apple. If the cutting is repeated you will get four apples, eight, etc., because each portion of a holographic transparency contains the entire image."[187] Though the image loses detail as the slices get smaller, the principal function is unaffected. In other words, the whole image remains embedded in any arbitrary segment of the original, even if some of the detail is lost as each piece gets smaller.

Roger Penrose and John Eccles have made the bold claim that "some cerebral processes are irreducibly quantum-mechanical in nature" and could be described as holistic, nonlocal, timeless, and nonlinear — indeed all those qualities we would associate with fields of energy.[188] This supports David Bohm's conclusion from his analysis of quantum mechanics that "mental and physical sides participate in each other. Intellect, emotion, and the whole state of the body are in a similar flux of fundamental participation. Thus there is no real distinction between mind and matter, psyche and soma, (and) each human being participates in an inseparable way in society and in the planet as a whole,"[189] all of which is the theme of this book.

The organization of consciousness is, like the hologram, indivisibly whole. There is no sense that some part of you is your consciousness, but you are all together as one in being yourself. This means it has some qualities of the implicate realm, in which sense "every cell of our body enfolds the entire cosmos,"[190] which is where the hologram blends in with the interconnectedness of the Field. The inescapable conclusion is that the holographic principle is found in the behavior of fundamental units of matter, the creation of life, the unfoldment of particles out of the Field, and to the operation of the brain.

This view is not universally popular. It is more usual to compare the brain to a giant computer, with nerve cells that work like transistors or chips, and ganglia of hard-wired electronic circuitry. The brain certainly cannot be hardwired, for Walter Freeman found that the patterns of electrical activity that indicate where this wiring ought to be actually changes location with altered feelings or circumstances. "Patterns are constantly dissolving, reforming, and changing in relation to one another."[191] When there is a new input or meaning there is a new pattern, so that "There are no computers, only meanings...[telling us] that brains are drenched" in endless data flow.

Karl Pribram has shown that "universal events [like telekinesis and telepathy] emerge from frequencies that transcend time and space — they don't have to be transmitted. They are simultaneous and everywhere."[192] This is a statement that fills me with wonder — "they don't have to be transmitted." It is the essence of the most ancient spiritual views of perennial philosophy: that we are all in contact, throughout every domain, but just don't *know* it, as it is across the veil. A couple of well-known examples of new ideas being transmitted without contact are the invention of photography by Louis Daguerre and Joseph Niépce at the same time at opposite ends of France, and of calculus by Newton and Leibniz on either side of the English channel.

It is from this understanding that Jerry Fodor could write, "The brain is a hologram enfolded in a holographic universe."[193] He compared the inability of engineers to create robots capable of the simplest domestic tasks designed to carry out only linear functions with the capacity of the brain to draw complex inferences from the simplest signals by integrating all the senses plus experience plus intuition plus instincts plus any complexes into one instantly-formed conclusion, and to be able to act on it straightaway. The complexity of this sentence is itself an analogy for the holistic qualities of the brain. We can only doubt its holographic implicate nature if we do not wish to face the consequences.

In the field of therapy one consequence is that this holistic approach ends the behaviorist view that all human responses can be examined as outcomes of stimulus and response. If all our thoughts are instantaneously cross-referenced with all other thoughts, then fields of association and symbolical structures are better metaphors for whatever goes on inside. This means that we will be as powerfully directed by an inner constellation of associations and prior energetic fields as by any external event. In the more general sense that includes biology and physics, it means that as we all partake of fields and as our fields are in constant vibration with each other then the subtler fields of nonmaterial reality would have the greater impact than the solid — not only on personality but on all existence.

Our other brain: the heart

See this heart of mine, it weeps for itself and pleads for mercy.

— The Egyptian Book of the Dead

As for the meaning of life, I do not believe it has any — and this is a source of great comfort to me. We make of it what we can, and that is all there is to it.

— Isaiah Berlin

It is becoming apparent that the brain works in concert with the heart to maintain all our human functions. Nevertheless there remains the conventional view that the brain is just a computational device and the heart a pump. Only recently has it become known that there are severe limitations to comparing the brain to a Cray computer or the heart to a Lister diesel.[194] Were the heart just a pump it would need to be the size of a tug to move so much blood along these many kilometers of small piping. In fact, the whole body moves the blood. The vessels themselves join in the rhythmic contractions of the heart, some veins are riffled to smooth the way for the blood, while blood cells themselves get smaller as the vessels reduce in size. In one sense the whole body vibrates and shimmies with each pulsation. The heart is not a separate mechanism, but an integral part of our entire system, continuously communicating with the brain and the other organs of the body.

As with all cells and organs, the heart is part of a signal feed-back system that not only affects physiology, but also our perceptions, our emotions and behaviors, performance, and total health. The heart works with the brain as a dynamic component of the emotional system.[195] Current estimates are that two-thirds of the cells in the heart are neurons in clusters of ganglia with exactly the same axon-dendrites as found in the brain.[196] It is, in short, a management center, that has now acquired its own science called Neurocardiology.

Candace Pert showed that physically the brain *extends through-out the body* via short chains of amino acids called peptides.[197] All the neurotransmitters and peptides found in the brain exist in the heart so that it is able to operate in a similar way. Further, the same molecules in the heart are found in every cell in the body, with particular concentrations in the organs. Now, twenty years later, it has been discovered that there are also direct neural connections between the heart's 'brain' and the limbic brain and all the other major organs.[198] It is through these family-like connections that the balance between the organs is maintained so they are able to work in harmony. It is the heart that ensures that the liver and the pancreas and all the secretions and digestions and so on have the same coordinated aim: our health and our pleasure. And throughout these physical manifestations flow the energetic connections that partner the cellular in what is increasingly being understood as a totality that is as holographic as the brain.

It would seem that the heart has priority over all other organs. In the development of the fetus the heart is formed before the brain. Hence it is the heart that has to deal with signals from the growing organs in the gut — liver, pancreas, stomach, and so on — and to maintain harmony between their differing needs long before there is anything to 'think' with.

Priority also applies energetically, for the magnitude of the fields emanating from the heart outweighs those of the brain by huge amounts. Its electrical field is about sixty times greater than the electrical activity of the brain so that all the cells of the body are continuously bathed in an all-encompassing energy field that binds our whole system together.

Also, the heart produces a powerful rhythmic electromagnetic field that is an incredible 5,000 times stronger than that produced by the brain. Evidence has accumulated that the heart's fields affect water and DNA,[199] as well as having a measurable physiological impact on people at a considerable distance.[200] This is why connections with fields beyond ours is, in the universal sense, the job of the heart. This has produced a growing interest in *emotional intelligence*.[201] As no feeling or desire in us can remain just a local event, but has to have some impact on all of us, the energetic fields of the heart share themselves with everyone and everything, everywhere.

These intimate connections give the heart priority when receiving and responding to key messages from inside or outside. Where priority is given to the heart it means that, in a manner of speaking, the brain is *an instrument of the heart*. In addition, the brain and the body are both fashioned to vibrate from the heart's frequency, "and then respond to the resulting experience and interpret its quality. This qualitative analysis, or emotion, is relayed back to the heart's own neural field...changing those fields."[202] The heart's intelligence is not cerebral, but holistic, relaying data to the brain's emotional system on the bodies' needs and taking feedback intuitively as well as directly.

Though mind is essential to the heart, which has no structure for analysis or logic or contextual details, the brain, and especially the left brain, can streak off on its own if it wishes to, and ignore the subtler messages from the heart. Biologists have confirmed that emotions of love, care, and compassion are linked to physiological changes everywhere in the body, in the heart as well as the brain and the nervous and immune systems. Their positive signals are relayed through particular hormones that specialize in encouraging peaceful emotional states. No wonder we believe intuitively that the heart is the center for love and compassion.

When there is an alignment between the frequencies of the heart and the head there arises a deep sense of inner peace. Chilton Pearce calls the process 'entrainment.'[203] It is a key tool in transpersonal therapy that we call attunement. The term *physiological coherence* has been used to describe this inner peace.[204] It is not dissimilar to the stillness found in certain meditative states and by those who have integrated peak religious insights, or had near-death experiences. From it comes increased efficiency and harmony in all aspects of life, with greater emotional stability and intellectual performance.[205] Such physical coherence seems to underlie the connection between positive emotions, health, and longevity.

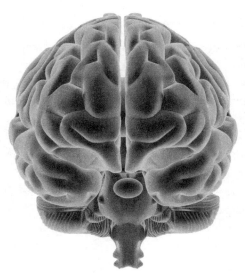

Fig. 24—The brain from above showing both hemispheres.

Limiting the heart-brain

When someone loves you, the way they say your name is different. You just know that your name is safe in their mouth.

—A four-year-old

As the first organ in the fetus, the strength of the energetic system emanating from the heart maintains a strong connection with the Field and with everything round about. The sense of the oneness of all things rests in the very first moments of our lives, so that the newborn baby is totally merged with and open to all the fields around him. Such connectedness and openness tells us that a baby is all love. He smiles and we naturally soften in response. No matter how silly or embarrassing the baby talk of the adult, his smile and outpouring of love remains.

This is a most remarkable time in a newborn's life. Not only is the baby in heartfelt bliss as he smiles on the world, but he is simultaneously aware of the auras and vibrations around him. Whenever people access their earliest memories, especially before the age of four, what scenes do we remember!

I have asked my grandchildren, while still young, what did the fairies look like, and they would tell me with great certitude and detail. One said, "When you see people in love, their eyelashes go up and down and little stars come out of them." I have met youngsters of six who would embarrass their teacher by knowing they were ill when they were trying to hide it, or seeing the gender of the calf while still in the cow's womb. I personally recall the thrill of seeing my godfather's luminous aura surrounding him in incredible colors while he stood at the foot of my cot, and at the same time being aware of a deep inner sadness. In later years I knew him as a very kind man who carried a terrible sense of personal worthlessness.

This capacity to see into the Field is bred out of us, through disdain for what children experience, through schooling, and in the scientific and materialistic assumptions of our society. The Christian churches, particularly the Catholic and Anglican, have minimized the value of the mystic experience and ecstatic inspiration — mainly, I suppose, as it has cut across church authority. One result is that, at a rough guess, fewer than 15 percent of Westerners have regular mystic experiences. On the island of Bali, on the other hand, probably only 15 percent have *never* had a mystic experience.[206] This is expressed in the dancer's self-mutilation by the kris in the Rangda-Barong dance that leaves no scar. The dance expresses their mystical attitudes publicly. It is no accident that Balinese babies are recognized as 'gifts from the gods' and constantly held near their carer's heart until they are old enough to walk.

Karl Pribram has argued that the brain has a mechanism that limits the mass of information coming from the Field.[207] As few of us are advanced enough to integrate the full complexity of information in the Field, we need to be 'slowed down' so we won't be overwhelmed. Yet enlightened people have shown by their example that there is a way the fullness of the Field can be handled without blowing all our circuitry. The realm of matter is, in a sense, the kindergarten level in which lower level information gets processed. The capacity to have peak experiences, and for the left brain to be able to deal with the enormous rush of numinous information, lies in the fourth brain, which has developed to its present size and significance only over the past two or three thousand generations.[208]

The fourth brain of transcendence

Understanding of mind-consciousness comes from one-pointed meditation upon the heart center.

— Patanjali Sutra

The prefrontal lobes of the fourth brain grow in two stages. One comes with birth, and has a governing role not dissimilar to that of the heart. It ensures that the older-style brains form according to the needs of the prefrontals, facilitating the older systems to rise up the evolutionary scale and consolidate themselves into one civilized mind that can be socialized. This is the monastery of the brain, the only part that is free from the constant labor of responding to sense impressions. Its purpose is to be free to ponder. "The prefrontal cortex springs into life and we are jettisoned into full consciousness as though from a tunnel into blazing sunshine."[209]

The process happens during the first twenty months after conception. Thick synaptic connections are made between the pre-frontals and the limbic system and, through it, with the heart. Then around the eleventh month an abundance of links grow between the prefrontals and the foremost part of the emotional brain followed by a rapid growth in the whole brain. But then, most surprisingly, in all the cases studied these links stop growing, and there is a pause.

At eleven years of age all parts of the brain (except the pre-frontal) myelinate.[210] This locks into place all development up to that time and increases speed and efficiency. But it also locks in all habits, both good and bad, and any traumatized responses. This imposes a tremendous shock to the system. Suddenly the feeling that we once had that we could adapt to anything and play rau-cously with the world has slipped away, almost unnoticed. When over the next few years this is combined with the body's sexual transformation, it is no wonder that adolescents often find life difficult and are much harder for the therapist to work with than children or adults.

The second and larger development of the prefrontal occurs around fifteen years of age, in mid-adolescence. It forms dynamic connections to every part of the older brain. Strange as it may seem, this later development was discovered only in the mid-1980s. Its neural structure completes its growth around age twenty-one, and then, as before, the superfluity of these connections is seriously reduced. And for most people that's it.

During these six to eight years the growth in the prefrontals of young people seems to generate that idealism and tremulous expectation that something fantastic is about to happen, that an enormous future lies hidden within them. As long as the prefrontals can overcome the negative input from the limbic system the body is suffused with joy and cohesiveness that stem from the heightened activity in this area. We all know the incredible feeling of invinci-bility and passion, of an unstoppable rush of energy that is usually put down to hormones, especially testosterone. It seems significant that a large number of people with the capacity to cross the veil had major transcendent experiences around their twenties: Satya Sai

Baba, Bhagwan Rajneesh, Robert Johnson, Chilton Pearce and Krishnamurti, to name a few.

Yet the expectations of the late teens nearly always remain unfulfilled, and by twenty-five we find life has imperceptibly dulled. It is a radical change. We have 'settled down' both socially and in our physical brain structure. The enormous excitement of the nineteen-year-old has ameliorated into having a family, paying the mortgage, and starting that repetitive regularity that will last most of us until we die.

Along with Robert Johnson, I have been excited by evidence for the growth in human capacities in recent times. The ability to distinguish the color blue, for example, has developed only over the past few thousand years. "The word *blue* does not appear in the Old Testament nor in Homer nor in any classical writings."[211] This capacity has emerged slowly, and is the most quickly lost in color blindness. In sound too, the pleasure we receive from musical harmony, as opposed to melody, may be even more recent for it appears with Du Pré only in the beginning of the twelfth century. Perhaps sensory consciousness of human energy systems is only now appearing in human evolution, not just for those rare individuals who have guided us in the past, but for all humankind.

So the uncertainty is, what has all this coming and going meant to do for us? Clearly it is meant to be more than growth and decay for its own sake. Our capacities and our potential to experience the whole universe are enormous, perhaps limitless. If everything is, in its foundation, fields of information intersecting within a Great Field of quantum information, and if we with our egoic personalities are granted access facilities that we throw away, what is the Field's next move? Or, is it up to us as co-creators with the Field?

My personal understanding is that the greater fields are remote, with a lack of what we, in our human attitudes, would call *humanity*. Yet here on earth we shower caring and grateful projections on gods and spirits in rituals and prayers and meditations that show how deeply we desire to bathe in their energy. My sense is that the Field may be responding positively to this loving, and is thereby 'instigating' the formation (without intent or design) of just those neurons and synapses that would allow us to manifest those connections in a fuller way.

Our ancestor's god-consciousness may have goaded the Field to make our job easier. The prefrontal lobes of the brain may be the Field's way of installing a higher level transmitter so that our highly developed brain and heart might be known on the implicate level, and exchange the timeless Beingness of 'out there' with the human capacity for conscious love and moral virtues.

Is this new part of us primarily responsible for the extraordinary brilliance of the human species? Is it through the neocortex that we are able to access more memory storage and computing power than is available to any other animal? Building on the work of Pribram and Schepp, Ervin Laszlo has argued that the brain is currently able to read the Field and download vast quantities of memory and other data stored there.[212] The upper echelons of our memories and creativity are just another sense, like sight or smell: a sixth sense designed to gather more information than the other five. Is genius, be it Rembrandt's or Einstein's, just a reflection of a person's capacity to access the Field? As the Field may be likened to a warehouse for all that is or ever was, it has the ability to offer us, as a species, the most awe-inspiring potential. To do this consciously would provide us with the compassion of the Field in which everything is, by its very nature, in right order. What then would happen to greed and fear and hopelessness?

The potential is ours
only when coherence is undamaged

Only in conflict with itself can the human heart or the human soul attain what is best in life.

—Bruno Bettelheim

On both occasions, at eleven months and at twenty-one years, the elimination of most of the cortical connections between the prefrontal brain and the rest seem to happen from the same cause — because in most cases the child has not, during his earliest years, been receiving the extensive and loving nurturing he needed for his fullest development.[213] Full elimination is not always inevitable, and we should not beat ourselves up about this because it is a very complex issue that is not well understood. Mozart and Einstein, who had greater use of their forebrains than the rest of us, did not necessarily have a better childhood than others. The size of the forebrain may be limited by many factors; for example, in the womb by the emotional state of the mother, or by the depth of nurturing between mother and infant in the first eighteen months or so.

The care of the infant not only has an impact on the effectiveness of the first brain spurt, but on the second as well. Allan Schore has found that the way we discipline our children and use our greater power to inject shame are the major causes of "the degeneration...and rewiring of the orbito-frontal columns," and that this minimizes its rich potential in later years.[214] Effective development of the prefrontal lobes that is critical to all higher intelligence as well as transcendence seems to depend on this nurturing, not the genes. Pearce has argued that at midadolescence the prefrontal cortex transforms the limbic system into a potentially transcendent power able to renew its connection to the Field.[215] This may be the most significant evolutionary trait of *homo sapiens sapiens*, yet is still only in potential.

The amount of emotional encouragement determines the degree of development. In our society discipline is usually imposed at the most critical time when the toddler is beginning to explore the world.[216] Schore states that the linkages between both developments of the prefrontals to the rest of the brain depend on the care the toddler receives.[217] It will determine the "lifelong shape and character of the child's worldview, mind-set, sense of self, impulse control, and ability to relate to others."[218] Chilton Pearce comments that "It might be assumed that the genetic blueprints will suffice as the stimuli for neural development. Those genes, however, would need to be stimulated by the child's interaction with the capacities they imply when those capacities are ready for development. That is why one infant cannot model for another. Someone who is fully able to do something in a certain way must perform the role of model if a similar ability is to be awakened in the child."[219] It is why the child with a natural gift for mathematics would not fully develop that gift if he lived in the jungle.

With Anthony Storr, both Chilton Pearce and Schore are concerned with the effect of discipline that blocks a child's natural curiosity.[220] The infant's eager, fearless exploration of the world is filled with joy and humor. This curiosity represents every function the prefrontal lobes are designed for. It is an expression of a child's total coherence.

A newborn baby resonates with the mother, so that all mother's feelings and energies are felt and digested by the baby. The mother's heart energetically mentors her child and "furnishes the model frequencies that the infant's heart must have for its own development in the critical first months after birth."[221] The more in tune they are, the greater the resonance between them and the greater the coherence in the baby's growth and learning, and the more likely the forebrain will develop so that it is able to act as intended.

However, when a child is socialized and educated and subjected to the traumas of other family members the most pervasive loss can be in the child's coherence. Overall wholeness is seriously depleted in childhood as essence and soul and naturalness are undermined. The pressures of adapting to a household seriously affect a child's inner centeredness and belief in herself. As coherence crumbles she feels uncertain and quite accurately senses that something is missing.

Sandplay requires only a tray with a blue-colored bottom filled with sand and hundreds of little figurines, objects of every variety and size, some good and some bad, male and female, gods and mythic creatures, body parts, and soldiers.

Sandplay is the unconscious on view. It specifically directs itself toward the needs of the psyche, and so it sets out problems and will indicate their solution in the most lucid manner. Symbolic meaning is important, but most needed is the energetic field that develops between the client and the facilitator.

Through it we can explore the fullness of the body and the emotions, and more importantly, the soul and the vibrational formations that make us who we are.

Sandplay is a loving and unobtrusive way to work with children. Before the neurons in the brain myelinate at eleven years they can unearth their own meaning and transform them themselves. The play in the sand unravels their uncertainties without having to use words that can be misunderstood.

We use a powerful process called sandplay that is the best diagnostic tool we possess, described in the box. In these four photographs of one sandplay session, we can follow the process of early disciplining and how it was taken by the infant. Some children are not as susceptible to shame and guilt as others, and need not be as deeply affected. Nevertheless the exercise of pressure on the infant can easily create huge distortions in that child's views of life, and through the inner contradictions that arise as coherence disintegrates.

Fig. 25—Sandplay 1, the child in the center background is in grief from the dominant power of mother, on the front right.

Fig. 26—Sandplay 2, she dies inside, or part of her does, and becomes the black skeleton hidden under the tears.

Fig. 27 — Sandplay 3, she decides to limit her potential, shooting herself in the head, under cover of a gigantic scream.

Fig. 28 — Sandplay 4, yet she needs and loves her mother, and attaches herself with the necklace.

The first figure shows the infant on the left, fearsome mother on the right, and my grief-filled client at the back. The large key points at her, the handle is in mother's mouth. Her mother's demands are emphasized by a tiny framed picture of the child as the mother wants her to be (you cannot see the picture in the photo), and to make sure you have got it, a yellow sign saying 'Messages' points at the picture. Mother's demand is that "This is what I want you to be" rather than letting her stay the irascible, noisy urchin she was by nature. It was terrifying for the little girl.

In the next figure we see the first consequence — she has thrust a black skeleton under the mask of grief. Without more ado she shoots herself in the head, then covers all this up with a gigantic scream, in the third figure. This is not a scream at mother, but into the sky, at God for bringing her into such a family. Her loss of herself and her despair is absolute. She is torn between her need for her mother and her passion to be herself. In her growing emptiness need wins, and in the fourth figure she shows her need for her mother, and her love, by linking them with a necklace of beads.

Her coherence had been shattered. She has now accepted she is a prisoner within the family's demands for appropriate behavior and places herself behind bars on the upper right, looking at 'Messages.' There has been no physical abuse here, just the demand that she be 'civilized' to fit in with mother's expectations.

Once coherence disintegrates, for most of us the potential in the forebrain remains dormant for the rest of our lives. It leaves nearly everyone with a sense of unrequited longing. To rectify this and to get the mind-and-heart system to return to the infant's time of wonder and connection a host of meditative and experiential techniques have been developed in all cultures, whether discipline-oriented or ecstatic, along with drugs and mortification — but too often to little avail for the effort expended. Once the connection is lost it may be hard to reform it, though therapy that addresses the energetic body, as I will discuss in Chapter 7, has proved to be as effective as years in an ashram.

When the forebrain connects with the heart we are granted intuition

The intellect has little to do on the road to discovery. There comes a leap in consciousness, call it intuition or what you will, and the solution comes to you, and you don't know how or why.

—Albert Einstein

We find in therapy that intuition comes when there is a palpable energetic connection between the heart and the brain. This can be distinctly felt in the stillness of meditation. Ancient Eastern beliefs are that the 'third eye' in the center of the forehead — right in the middle of the prefrontals — brings down a higher intelligence when, and only when, it is connected to the heart.

In medieval texts we read of the descent of Holy Spirit, drawn as a white dove descending onto the crown of the head. As the *sanctus spiritus* the dove represents holy wisdom descending from the outstretched hands above. The same theme was stated thousands of years ago in the Patanjali Sutra: "understanding comes from one-pointed meditation upon the heart center. As a result, the higher hearing, touch, sight, taste, and smell are developed, whence all things can be known in the vivid light of intuition. This intuitive knowledge is omnipresent and omniscient and includes the past, the present and the future in the Eternal Now."[222]

As an example, when Hilary and I began our search for the valley where we now live and made a home for the Crucible Centre, I went into meditation on what we were seeking, and drew a picture of it. The search took a year, and after we built the house and moved in I compared the two. The picture and the reality were identical, even to the stream, the chickens, the peaked mountain in the background and the open grassy area in front of the house and the dense bush behind. The vision had taken over a year to manifest.

Fig. 29 — Drawing of the vision we had for our land made in April 1996.

Fig. 30 — The setting as it is today.

When building the house and on the day after placing the heavy hot water tank on timber beams in the roof, my ex-partner in architecture turned up unexpectedly. I had not seen him for some years and our new house was a two-hour drive from Sydney where he lived. It was a pleasure to see him and we chatted about this and that. As an aside he suggested a steel joist to strengthen the beams under the hot water tank, something I had not thought of. I realize that but for his fortuitous visit the platform under the tank would have sagged. He has never been back since then, so how did he know this was the day I unconsciously needed him?

Just as the Field manifests images and dreams in us that we bring to consciousness, we manifest our 'images' in the Field that are then projected back as something tangible in our world. In this manner, albeit unconsciously, I 'created' the arrival of my partner so that my unrecognized and professionally incorrect understanding of the weakness in the structure could be shown to me. This reads like double-think, but in the quantum world of fields this sort of occurrence is as real as it gets.[223]

All of us should have highly developed intuition. "It is present in everyone because it is a survival skill, not a spiritual intention."[224] Yet through training, our society denies its validity as unprovable, and we have to rely on mental properties to keep us going. Intuition often looks like synchronicity, which is "the mind operating, for a moment, in its true order, extending throughout society and nature, moving through orders of increasing subtlety."[225] Yet it is immensely more.

At first, intuition arrives as an image, a sense, or a word that is extremely faint. The more we pay attention to these delicate promptings the stronger they become. Then we notice that our sense of time fades, and we can hold our attentiveness and do our work at the same time. We are able to perceive more widely and fully than usual, able to hold many different aspects or processes within the same intuitive band and tire less easily. We are then spanning the two realms, the material and the Field, and partaking of both. With it comes the quality that Gurdjieff called 'youthing' in which the body and mind retain a younger subtlety, no matter what the age. Intuition and increased coherence develop together.

Intuition operates directly and immediately, from a personal space inside. There are neither judgments nor concepts to stand in the way, and there is no thinking nor emotional content. If an emotional impression creeps in then the intuition is likely to be contaminated. Like the Field it comes from, intuition has an impartial dispassionate quality that is unlike intellect, which is invariably slanted to some viewpoint. In the presence of intuition the mind becomes more like a commentator or a foreman ready to act on command.

The way each of us pick up our 'messages' is very personal. The senses involved may be hearing or vision, or just a feeling that transmutes into a phrase or a word from which comes a knowing. Personally, my intuition comes as a 'density' in the body, a sensible impression, a sensed form or image that may be followed by a mental picture and then a phrase. On the other hand, my partner Marg receives clear sentences and, with contact through the hand, a vision in the mind of energy shape and movement that is projected onto the 'real' vision.

As intuition emerges from the Field, we can at times sense occasional aspects of the future as well as the present. We seem to be able, at the subtlest level, to access fields of information that exist in a domain far removed from linear time. Compelling evidence shows that both the brain and the heart process information about the emotionality of a stimulus before this stimulus is presented. There can be a 'knowing' that comes before the event, as if the body is continuously scanning the future.[226]

There is a similar scanning that influences others. We might think that we have the strongest influence on ourselves, yet recent work by William Baude has shown that other people can have almost the same impact on our mind and body as we can when we try to change ourselves. Letting someone else have some intention for you, either good or bad, seems to be as powerful as using meditation techniques on yourself.[227] This may be how bone-pointing and healing by prayer works.

In addition, it has been found that if you believe you can connect at a distance you will outperform those who do not. Here is an excellent test of feedback with the Field, for if we influence the

Field through our awareness of it, the quantum connections that the Field make possible become more accessible. If the analytic left brain is overactive, the Field is less accessible as connections to the frontal cortex are diverted, whereas if the right brain is dominant and the left is relatively quiescent, then connections are much stronger.[228] This just shows the huge influence our thinking apparatus has on our level of intuition. By stilling the left brain a little through meditation the doors of perception open a little wider, and the receptors in the brain become more available to a larger number of wavelengths in the Field.[229]

When we are consciously connected to the Field everything appears much brighter, the colors more intense and everything is more deliciously real. To achieve this we have to dampen all those left-brain thoughts that take up so much of our inner space. Their attachment to survival distracts us from the most intimate aspects of living. The moment the left brain becomes involved, as when input is interpreted, or mental analysis slides into the middle of a process, the connection between the frontal lobes and the heart, running through the right brain into the limbic, becomes disturbed. Activity in the left brain distorts the transmission. Without the left we seem to have potential access to all the information in the universe, every sight and sound and smell. The left brain works primarily outside the quantum fields, and being an analytic filter actually reduces the primary impact from all the senses.

It has been experimentally shown, as with the Russian rabbits mentioned earlier, that every death is registered in the Field, and can be picked up by anything that can resonate with that vibration.[230] There is empathy between all organisms so that a plant will respond to the death of another, even if it is some other species. Humans are the same, if not more so. How many of us have experienced something of a distant event, such as an accident or sudden death of a close friend, even on the other side of the world?

If actualized in enough people, the conjunction of heart and brain could totally alter the consciousness of this planet, and turn an irresponsible species that fouls its own nest and turns a blind eye to its own suffering into a noble and compassionate race. Together the heart and the brain form the roots of compassion. When these are working together all the finest minds have agreed that a natural sense of ethics and personal morality arises. This blessed state comes when we are so connected to the Field that we know, intuitively, where everything ought to be in the world around us. It does not come from thought, but from a heartfelt sense of knowing that within the totality of all vibrations "all is right with the world."

In fact, we exist in a totally interactive and ecological environment in which every level of matter and life lies within a singular ground. There is nothing that is not a part. All is therefore One in the Field. The body, head, and heart "form an intricate web of coherent frequencies organized to translate other frequencies and nestled within a nested hierarchy of universal frequencies, all functioning in coherent resonance, endlessly unfolding moment to moment through the rich dynamics between possibility and actualization."[231]

6

WHAT CONSTITUTES THE GREAT FIELD?

The Tao cannot be known.
—Lao Tsu

Many physicists, meditators, and theorists would agree that there exists a common field referred to in religious texts as the Brahma, the Ground of Being or the Void that encompasses everything from the largest field to the smallest particle. Bohm called it the superimplicate order. I have called it the Great Field. Whatever the name, it is the same. The Field is the superstratum of all creation, the all-pervasive, all-inclusive essence from which all is created and within which all exists. It is as close to the meaning of God as we get.

This Ground of Being gives rise to the two states that we are aware of, the formlessness of fields and the forms of the material world. Mystics experience the Field directly, and for the rest of us we deduct that wherever there is division, as between energy and matter, there has to be a common origin that is one indivisible whole. These states that we call opposites are, in fact, only different faces of the one coin in constant movement from being an individual field to being matter, and returning back again, as two aspects of the one underlying state that "contains the entire spectrum of creation from the most beatific to the most diabolical, but in unmanifest form."[232]

The concept of a Great Field inherent in every single aspect of the universe provides a framework to explain the uncertainties and inconsistencies in our present views of particles and stellar systems, gravitation, and black holes. It could provide a natural explanation for all the forces and interactions of nature, and even of space-time itself. It seems capable of forming a conceptual basis for a unified cosmology that would help to clarify all of creation.

Fig. 31 — Orderly evolution of a conch shell from a single instruction that changes with scale.

For example, the signals that instruct a beech seedling to grow "in the characteristic shape, structure, and habits of a beech is because it inherits its nature from countless beech trees that existed in the past."[233] Sheldrake has called this process *formative causation*, in which "each kind of natural system has its own kind of field [that] shapes all the different kinds of atoms, molecules, crystals, living organisms, societies, customs, and habits of mind." He called them *probability structures* in which the influence of the most common past types combine to ensure that the probability of recurrence of all future types.

Occurrences align through the total accord that fields ensure between each other. Anything else would be inconceivable. Imagine the field of say, strawberries. Small distortions, such as changes in color, size, and number of petals that would not disturb the equilibrium of the field would seem to be allowable. Occasionally some of these may slip off on their own to form separate and coherent fields, and spawn a new variety of strawberry. But imagine what would happen to the field if some berries were produced as beech trees. This is not a small distortion. It changes such enormous chunks of the information resident in the field of the strawberry that the field's natural tendency to return to its original flow would be deformed beyond repair.

It may be ludicrous to imagine a beech tree laden with strawberries. That would be another species corresponding to its own field and would have little in common with either the beech or the strawberry. The continuous integration of flowing fields in the whole would be undone in an instant. Nature has turned out to be neither blind nor mechanistic, but infinitely flexible, intelligent, and resourceful. It works because the Field 'learns' by transferring information back and forth between every vibration and every organism and all collections of energy at every moment and in all time, both past and future. When the fields do not integrate there are failures, in nature and in our experiments with crossbreeding, gene transplants, genetic engineering, and so on.

In a beautiful description David Abram set out the integration very clearly: "Our bodies have formed themselves in delicate reciprocity with the manifold textures, sounds, and shapes of an animate earth — our eyes have evolved in subtle interaction with other eyes, as our ears have attuned by their very structure to the howling of wolves and the honking of geese."[234] The universe is an enormous dynamic matrix of information being continuously shared within a structureless formlessness that contains all potential variations of all potential forms of energy and matter.

In this way we co-create the Field through everything every being on the planet is and thinks and handles. The Field forms a superstructure of hyper-interconnected, information-filled signals that transcend both the material and the energetic realms. Unlike the total sum of matter and energy in the universe which science tells us is fixed, the amount of information contained in the Field is rapidly increasing, perhaps exponentially, a growth that has been suggested contributes to the force that drives the expansion of the universe.

Within the logic of the Field and the point made in this discussion we can attempt to formulate the steps required in the initial acts of creation, as the fields of our universe emerged out of the inchoate soup of the Great Field. This attempt is set out in a concise form in Appendix 1.

Individuality within the constraints of coherence

Things could not have been brought into being by God in any manner or in any order different from that which has in fact been obtained.

— Benedict Spinoza

Variety happens within and through the coherence of all the fields. It is like "a ballet dance, in which all the dancers, guided by a common pool of information in the form of a score, are able to move together in an organized way."[235] Coherence depends on having such a pre-existing score, or form-field, within which each dancer will display their individuality only so far as permitted by the score. This is no different to the beautifully coherent form of a baby that has been evolved by a field that is coherent enough to create a working human body, yet permits the intrusion of individual characteristics that would modify the parts without affecting the essence of the form. We get the impression that the form of the baby has been generated exclusively through other forms, like mums and dads, rather than fields. This consolidates the illusion that only forms can produce and influence other forms. But actually, no form can be understood apart from its ground in the Field. As has been argued, the Field has to be the primary reality.

Bohm suggests that there is a 'protointelligence' in matter, so that new evolutionary developments do not emerge in a random fashion but creatively, as relatively integrated wholes from implicate levels of reality. The mystical connotations of Bohm's ideas are underlined by his remark that the implicate domain "could equally well be called Idealism, Spirit, Consciousness. The separation of the two — matter and spirit — is an abstraction. The ground is always one."[236]

The Field is primarily information, as it is communicable data encapsulated in vibration. It transcends the physical world. It underlies all fractal and biological processes. This sea of signals that flood the Field has to contain eons of information, many trillions times more than there is matter. Benveniste showed that signals of information need not have material substance in order to affect, for they impinge from field to field with equal potency at any distance. The enormity of both the size of the Field and quantity of data could operate only in a nonlinear implicate setting.

Fig. 32 — Fractal pattern in which the smallest parts can be seen to replicate the largest.

This setting, at least in our universe, is molded by the purity of mathematics that is expressed in fractals. The deep and pervasive creativity that we notice is everywhere, from the unbelievable variety in the stars, and even in the types of planets in our system, to the inventiveness in human cultures and beliefs. The key material is water, and if this substance did not exist anywhere in our universe entropy would set in and all structures would become more and more crystalline. In a perverse way the manner in which probability determines many outcomes rather than linear cause-and-effect ensures that the universe is as varied as possible. The Vishnu Factor makes sure that *unpredictable sameness* saves our universe from ossifying. It is significant when we are involved in stressful situation we tend to close down and become more conservative.

In an almost deliberate move to counter this, the Field would seem to have 'decided' to be both unpredictable and coherent. The possibilities for choice and selection being offered by particles and

135

cells and mental ideas are extremely varied, if not infinite on the micro scale. Yet most simply pass away as soon as they have arrived without finding a sympathetic receptor. We know how many sperm it takes to fertilize one ovum, how many books full of fresh ideas make it only as far as the dustier stacks of the public library. Being unrecognized is the most common event in the universe.

But to be recognized means finding a home, a resonance in some pre-existing system that, in a sense, takes you in. A new idea meets other ideas or group-needs and is taken up because it satisfies those needs. It fits in, just as any signal from a protein fits in with the 'needs' of a cell's receptors. Order then appears spontaneous, when in fact it is very precisely determined by the fact there is a space 'waiting' for it. Did the new idea satisfy a need, or was the need a response to the creation of the idea in the first place? Or were all of these a part of the mixture of fields common to all?

We may call this free will, opening a vexed question for which there are few answers. The potential asymmetry in the flow of all nonlinear fields ensures that things do not get stuck in dull repetition. It inputs creativity and flexibility, for were every plant to grow identically there would be neither evolution nor adaptation. The limits to choice are determined within each field's range of coherence. In our personal lives we have choices, but as in Luke Rhinehart's novel *The Dice Man*, the hero — who has decided to let the throw of dice make every decision for him — is in fact limited by the range of choices he selects in each throw. As an American he chooses only those alternatives that fit his social mores, which would have been entirely different were he from India or Madagascar.

Freedom is, as Karl Marx said, the "recognition of necessity" — a very limited operation that is never entirely free, but has to be constrained by set and setting. We may have many parallel futures stretching all around us, but I would doubt there are an infinite number, as we operate within the limits of our form-fields. We cannot fly like birds, for example, nor can a rich person imagine how he would be were he impoverished.

There is a possibility that within the infinite connectivity there is infinite 'choice', maybe not conscious, but certainly present in every moment, and that the future stretches not in front of us, but all around us. In this world of parallel universes there is one in which Hitler won the war, leaving us with a present so unlike the one we know that only our grandparents would recognize it.[237] The possibility that the thousand-year Reich might be actively present in the Field along with a billion other historical alternatives raises the amount of stored information to astronomical levels.

An ever-expanding warehouse of information

If we do discover a complete theory, then we shall all be able to take part in the discussion of why it is that the universe exists. If we find the answer to that, it would be the ultimate triumph of human reason — for then we would truly know the mind of God.

—Stephen Hawking

Anyone who has had a glimpse beyond the veil, or a near-death experience, knows that the Field is jam-packed with collations of every event and experience and thought that has been part of their lives.[238] It looks like all our experiences are stored holographically in the Field, and that nothing is lost, unless there is some mechanism for outdated obsolete fields, like those of extinct animals, to gradually decay taking their genetic memories with them.

Many people have had near-death experiences in which they were given a review of their entire life, all in the blink of an eye. People repeatedly describe it as "an incredibly vivid, wrap-around, three-dimensional replay [in which] every moment from every year of your life is played back in complete sensory detail. Total recall. And it all happens in an instant."[239] The replay includes knowing how others felt in each experience, as well as their own feelings. It is a total evocation in precisely the way Bohm describes the implicate zone where everything happens in one moment, timelessly, spatially and totally inclusive of everything related to it everywhere.[240]

Such a moment of total retrieval implies an enormous storage capacity. When the entity having the experience is 'dead' or in a coma we have to face the question, who or what and where would this storage be? Where else but in the fields of the Great Field? It is the nature of the Field to be the universe's memory bank, an information storehouse that maintains the uniformity of nature through its totality.

We think that much of our memory is stored in the brain. Maybe. But maybe those brains that have a more direct contact with the Field don't have to bother holding all that data themselves, but simply have a better connection to where it is kept off-site.

It has been suggested that many memories are stored in the cells of the body. For example, Graham Farrant discovered in a series of rebirths that his mother had attempted to abort him. He telephoned her to see if this was true, and she denied it. When he described how she had taken a handful of pills and then a very hot bath without success, she broke into tears and said, "You couldn't know this, I never told anybody."[241] He argued that physical experiences, and especially those of the birth, are retained in the cellular structure of the body. The body remembers,[242] as with the woman who was almost choked on her own umbilical cord at birth, who always had difficulty breathing and whose neck produced a ring of scarlet when she recalled the event. It was the cells of the neck that held the reaction and restricted her breath.[243]

However, could this be because all our cells get replaced every seven years, leaving nowhere for the memories to reside? Therefore such memories have to be contained in something common to every generation of cells and passed on each time a cell is replaced. I am arguing that this would be in the fields that direct the replacement of the cell. They could be retained in the energy of the soul, but as the memory is usually specific to a location, such as the neck, it is much more likely to be in the forming-fields of the cells, contained not in a free flowing way, but as nodes. This is a reminder that the fields of energy and vibration that form us in the first place continue in each and every replacement. They are the ground of our bodies that ensure our rejuvenation as recognizable humans, but as they ingest the events and traumas of life their ability to replace age with youth is increasingly diminished. This will relate to our later discussion on karma.

Definable aspects within the Great Field

This invisible source of all that exists is not an empty void but the womb of creation itself [that] turns the chaos of quantum soup into stars, galaxies, rain forests, human beings, and our own thoughts, emotions, memories, and desires.

—Deepak Chopra

Can we unscrew the inscrutable?

—The Weavers

From the nature of our universe every matter and event and thought has its own field with different levels of complexity. The field of sand may be simpler than cats, metals more homogeneous than humans. Each field reflects and emanates a particular essence — be it as protein or a belief. And each cohabits the whole. For us, the energy we find most available, and the most personal, is the human soul. As this is such an important matter I shall leave discussion of the soul until Chapter 8. Soul appears as our personal aspect in the Field, a sort of connector like the air we breathe that rests within us.

Beyond the field of soul there are larger fields, larger not necessarily in size, which would not be a characteristic of fields anyway, but larger in being coherent conglomerates of many individual fields. Some fields are conglomerates of many others, some small, others vast beyond any imagining. Like fields interact with their familiars through the common vibrations in each 'knowing' and communicating with others of their kind. Each molecular group associates with similar molecular groups, and souls with souls.

A person, a crowd, or a nation each reflect their collective fields, yet contain a host of smaller definable fields. There is the field of our blood type, and of our propensity to be afraid and, say, the urine in our bladder. Each is a distinct field in its own right and will maintain itself as blood, fear, or urine whether in the body or not. When all are operating on each other within us they form the auric field of the individual, a field of enormous complexity that co-exists with all the others without being of any of them.

As with the parts of us, the Great Field itself is therefore made up of many gradations all entwined. We might call them hierarchies, though in a field of holographic wholeness no such concept could exist. Some, such as electrons, may have less complex vibrational systems than coconuts, but since they each co-exist equally throughout the Field how could nuts lord it over electrons? We might call them different levels or conglomerates of consciousness, but purely on the basis that some are more complex than others. Certainly none are 'superior' in that egoic sense in which a field would contain an 'opinion' about another on which any human sense of hierarchy could be established. It is just that some have a greater zone of influence or a greater range of information than others. Numbers may be as important as complexity.

For example, molecules of H_2O mingle and create a field in lakes or tanks or streams of what we call 'water.' The common vibrations in all of these conjoin to create unimaginably enormous fields of the essence of wateriness. Some water is pure, some salty, some polluted. The salt water in the ocean would partake of a different field to the sparkling freshness of a mountain brook. Each of these states produces different vibrations and, as Emoto showed, different crystalline structures. Every connection forms conglomerates of larger interactions, many of which share in a multitude of conglomerates simultaneously. This continues up more complex levels of the Field until, at the ultimate pinnacle of wholeness, every vibration shares in every other in an immense holographic dance — a miracle of universal consciousness.

Together they form blueprints for the major dynamic components of existence, including the human societies and individual personalities. They are constellations of energy so huge they can trigger and sustain a renaissance or a holocaust. Being conglomerates they have structures that are autonomous. They have recognizable outcomes that would usually have a greater influence on individual fields than any individual has on them. I would prefer the word 'outcome' to 'goal,' which suggests a conscious intent that is not possible within the Field, where every moment of past and future is a cooperative alignment in a timeless now. They are impersonal collective forces that influence everything that is created and, in the human psyche, form the deep structures that Jung defined as ordering principles.

Such collective forces have been called many things. Plato called them 'Ideas,' or ideal forms or patterns already existing in the divine mind that determine what will manifest in the material world. John of Salisbury, the medieval bishop of Chartres, referred to "exemplary forms which are the original plans for all things permanent and perceptual, such that even if the whole world were to come to an end they could not perish."[244] Two of the more cogent definitions have been Jung's terms of archetype and the collective unconscious.[245] The word 'archetype' comes from *arche* that means 'the first' and *type* meaning 'imprint' or 'pattern.'

There are as many archetypes as there are character traits among human groups, from which Jung concluded "that single archetypes are not isolated...but are in a state of the most complete, mutual interpenetration and interfusion" with one another and with the human psyche that both sustains them and is affected by them.[246] At this level most of the archetypes we know are involved with human thought.

Their huge energetic fields form a large part of the personal unconscious that is an immense collation of human beliefs and experiences and gives rise to both the fantasy lives of children and to the mythologies of whole cultures. Jung called these fields the *collective unconscious*, because they form the unquestioned foundation for the behavior and beliefs of different races and cultures. Being incredibly more effective than any individual field these conglomerates determine patterns of behavior for those that lie within the group.

Every individual of a species, such as the Koshima monkey, will have been influenced by their group field. A collective of similar fields connects or 'holds together' as a band or tribe. And on a wider plane all the tribal fields of the one species will resonate together as a collective. Some species are more implicate than explicate, in that their personal fields are less powerful then the field of their group, the individual members being less independent. Birds and ants and many species of fish that act as a group are closer to their collective field than, say, lions or dolphins. Germans thus become 'typically' Germanic just by living within communities of other Germans, all resonating together in the same linguistic and religious cultural field.

Concerning the spiritual journey, Ken Wilber refers to collective and archetypic fields as the highest beacons on our return to the formless, the final barriers to be deconstructed on the edge of radiant infinity.[247] The enormous power these collective forms possess, due to being such huge conglomerates, means they certainly are one of the hurdles on the journey. But we should not con ourselves into believing they are the last ones. The veil may be deeply embedded in our world-view, but this is all we have to get through. The journey is *within ourselves*, not against any outside force or through any external barrier. Indeed the very thought that this is something we have to jump through is itself a barrier. There is nothing outside us that keeps us separate.

Projections onto the Field

What do I have to do to get you to admit who is speaking?

Admit who is speaking, admit it and change everything!

This is your own voice echoing off the walls of God.

—Jalal-ud-Din Rumi

So what do we make of the multitude of visions we humans have of gods, cherubim, wrathful devas, entities and other spiritual forms without number? Do they exist in their own right, or are they the creations of our imagination, or a bit of both? The Field is neither uniform nor undifferentiated. It is just full of fields, and that's that. It is full of energies and flows that reflect-and-create all the other manifestations of the universe. Just as material reality is infinitely varied in qualities and substance, so the vibrations in the Field are equally varied. Every field vibrates to its own tune, where one is peaceful and another wrathful, or one tune is creative and the other destructive.

From our point of view we would prefer to have the creative and peaceful in our lives rather than the wrathful and destructive. This is our assessment, our choice, and our projection, not the Field's. The Field can have no purpose, no aim for our lives. In a nondual world there can be no power of *direction*, none at all. It just is, without opinion nor intent nor meaning.

Yet we humans seek the solace of feeling that we are not alone, and that there is some Being out there who can look after us and make sense of our often chaotic lives. We create this Being by projection. A projection is, like transference in therapy, the relocation of something in us, a feeling or a need or a pain, onto someone else. Someone who lost their father when young goes on to dream of how perfect he could have been, and then later transfers that dream of male perfection onto another and expects him to have all those qualities this father should have had.

Though it is the nature of humans to project, when that is extended onto the vast canvas of the Field we project on a huge scale. Whatever desires we project onto the Field, the Field will supply as required, and in any language. If we believe in hell, then that concept is transferred across and provides exactly what the saints have found when their meditations have taken them through the veil. If we come from a warrior culture we will find Götterdämmerung, and if from a matriarchy, our prayers are illuminated by goddesses. Since a thousand generations have helped to project their vision of heaven, by the time it is our turn we should not be surprised to find in our meditations that heaven is exactly as the books describe it. As has been said, "if God did not exist, we would have to invent Him," and this is exactly what we have done.

In doing this humans have peopled the Field with the most enormous collection of beings. Most religions infer a spiritual zone that is occupied by many varieties, all numinous and all with particular characteristics, both beneficent and fiendish from the most divine archangels to the most malevolent demons. Christians refer to hierarchies of angels, cherubim and so on, as do Moslems, Jews, and Tibetan Buddhists. Unconsciously over tens of thousands of years the urgency of our cultural and psychic needs have prompted us to vision them into existence. The more humans have thought or talked about them, prayed or meditated to them and brought these visions into daily life the stronger their presences have become in the Field. And being in the Field their influence over us, especially at the unconscious and subliminal level, has grown stronger with use.

This does not mean that there is no god. There are hundreds, if not thousands, all created in the Field by all who have believed and worshipped over the millennia. Every type of god to suit every human condition has its vibratory presence in the everlasting wholeness of the Field. In logic it is not possible to be an atheist or an agnostic, because gods exist — we have made them. They are not made "in our image," but in the form needed to invest them with all the attributes we most needed.

Even ancient gods, such as the Norse Woden and Thor, will retain some presence in the Field after a thousand years of neglect. As our creations over millennia, the gods themselves participate in our creation in the eternal interplay that ceaselessly saturates all realms. Those humans who participated within the ambience of any particular god-field are affected, very deeply, by what their ancestors have projected, and to this extent each god remains a creative force.

But no god is the universal creator, the first principle. It is not possible for us — a very small part of the universe — to have created the ultimate creator. As long as gods are projections we can rely on them to affect our lives, why should we not worship and praise our own creations, as we do to some extent with our culture and our scientific achievements. At the simplest level singing our love to our god imprints our feelings into the god-field that will return that love to us, we hope in the most compassionate and nurturing way.

Once we release our god-field from responsibility for having to be universal, we can take a great sigh of relief — for more people have been killed by religious conflict than in any other way, with every crusade and jihad being spawned by our belief that one god was more 'universal' or 'true' than another. The power to destroy in the name of a projection is strong enough to fund repeated onslaughts to annihilate any opposition. Normally religious beliefs include clauses that inhibit wholesale slaughter of false believers, but the horrible tragedies of religious wars and modern fundamentalist terror show that these clauses are failing in the attempt to hold these powerful psychic forces at bay. If it is ever released, for whatever reason, the door will be opened on the most terrifying holocaust that modern ingenuity can devise.

Arguments for an entity that is a separate and autonomous being cannot be proven. Philosophic and religious arguments of god's existence have been offered by the cleverest and most subtle minds for over 5,000 years, and equally often amended or disproved.[248] They are founded on the presumption that there has to be something out there, some sort of first cause to match the big bang, some watchmaker, even if reduced to eternal physical laws. But when we alter our perception to consider that all gods are our projections, then most of the complexity of religious argument disappears — as would persecution and bigotry.

It is natural to understand how this may have happened, for when we connect with the Field it feels so full and present, and our experience is so rich and enthralling that it is natural for us to invest it with god-like qualities. We then make the unwarranted assumption that the 'out-there' god is able and willing to exercise control over the unfolding of its own domain. Humans are, on the whole, insecure, especially about the future. It is important for us to have somewhere something that might promise some certainty, and the bigger and more comprehensive it is the more secure we are likely to feel.

Being stuck behind the veil we pray to our own image in the Field to do this or that for us, on the childlike assumption that we cannot do it for ourselves. For all of these reasons I have some hesitation in using the word 'god' or 'spirit. In my understanding of the Field we cannot ask god or spirit to do anything for us because the place where we are looking is a nonspatial, timeless void that goes on reflecting our reflections and illusions back and forth like a stack of gigantic mirrors. The fact that these feedback loops suit each culture so well is confirmation that we are getting from the cosmos exactly what we put into it. Put another way, we are feeding the cosmos with the images that will most readily fit in with our needs and longings.

So, if we project our needs on the Field, what of the reverse?

We may be projections from the Field

The thing that most interests me is whether God had any choice in creating the world as it is.

—Albert Einstein

If our projections create the gods, what are the Field's projections on us? The physical and biological evidence shows that fields affect and create thoughts and matter, just as ideas and matter create and influence fields. It feels like a kaleidoscope of two-way mirrors, each bouncing reflections back and forth in an endless continuum of cross-referenced information in a universe in which everything is seamlessly indivisible. Can this explain, as one example among hundreds, the influence of astrology on us and the apparent role of the planets and the sun?

In every religion people pray, dance, sing, and meditate on goodness and ask for grace. Everywhere rituals are created to remind the faithful of the particular gods in their creation. This all ends up in the Field. We receive back well-being, security, and hope. But not all reflections from the Field are equally blessed.

In August 1914, for example, an overwhelming feeling of belligerent righteousness swept through nearly the entire population of Europe. For a few short weeks a communal madness drove the leaders of these countries to rush into war.[249] A mass jingoism swept Germans, French, and British as strongly as Russians and Austrians. Monarchs who knew each other intimately and who had married into each other's families drew their swords and rushed to the attack. And once started it could not be stopped until the terrible convulsion of that war destroyed the social order that had permitted it. Not one community survived intact. The so-called cause in Serbia was only the trigger to an inevitability. Once the war began the mood passed as quickly as it had come, but by then it was too late. The way so many were blindly influenced by something outside of themselves, so that intelligence and compassion were exorcised, seems like it was a projection from the Field.

The Field may be wielding an influence in minor ways too. At times we are affected by changes of mood that seem to come out of nowhere, and there are days when we and all our friends seem beset with problems or stress, or days when every motor in the house breaks down.

Fig. 33 — Sandplay of a projection onto the Field.

Fig. 34 — Taken from the opposite side of the tray showing the Field's projection back.

In this study of projections in a sand tray the client was asked to depict how he saw his world and how he felt the world saw him. Away from him were his own fears and dreams that he projected onto life, and which summed up his experiences. What he projected is what life gave him in return — the childhood fantasy, the brutality, and the insurmountable. In the other direction (in the next photo) are the archetypic figures that ruled his life that were often in conflict with each other. On the far left is the King and his dreams of rulership, and on the right Prince Charming and the

the servant. Though they seemed to him to be the qualities of his personality they were also associated with elements in the field that were projected back on to him.

However, there is no need to imbue the Field with powers of planning and foresight. It is enough that the forces resident in the Field came together in a certain way, gathered and interlaced with Europe's political and racial dynamics, into a potent mix that affected all. No need to postulate anything intentional. The energies had been gathering in Europe over the previous fifteen years.

My school history was stuffed full of cogent reasons for the war, so many that none seemed really potent enough to have started such a catastrophe. But looked at purely from the aspect of fields of desire, greed, nationalism, and disappointment, launched and fostered on national scales, shared through newspapers so that few were unaware of the great imperial issues, is it any wonder that the fields this created coagulated into a gigantic reverse projection and 'produced' just that which was most feared? The minds and feelings of so many became bent upon such purpose that everywhere people were affected and the sum of them manifested the whirlwind. It is a terrifying thought that humans could so transmit their own vibrations that they could be returned to us as annihilation. Are we doing the same today with fossil fuels?[250]

Whatever your imbibed beliefs, whether you are Buddhist, Catholic, or Fundamentalist, you get a feedback loop of your own stuff. The feeling that this stuff exists outside of ourselves is an illusion: the origin of all spiritual beings is the ground of energy onto which men and women, individually and in tribes and cultures over millennia, have projected in a manner that is totally holographic.[251]

On the personal level, our projections influence the archetypes. These are not permanent and indestructible, but are vast dynamic energy systems formed over millennia that will naturally continue to adapt to changes in the human psyche out of which they have been formed. Having created these energetic forms, the forms have in return manifested themselves back onto earth to power our deepest drives. Jung, and many after him, has presumed that archetypes are the primary forms on which all others will rest. They have been called the highest forms of our potential.[252] For the reasons just discussed, I believe this is incorrect.

They were not there from the beginning, for how could the archetype of the human Hero be present when the dinosaurs roamed? There are also newly minted archetypes, such as the gay warrior and the masked terrorist that are surprisingly powerful in spite of their newness. Some archetypes are naturally more available than others, such as the Great Mother (the Goddess movement) and the Spirit Father (Mahatma Gandhi, Luther King), the Patriarch (Bob Menzies, Adenauer) and the Wise Old Woman (Eleanor Roosevelt, Elisabeth Kübler-Ross). Some are fearsome and from recent memory, such as the holocaust and its companion, today's fascination with an armageddon of terror.

In the midst of this we have disengaged from the suffering of our planet and the real possibility that the earth will not provide us in future with the abundance it has offered in the past. Our heartlessness for the only home we will ever have is now being projected onto the Field, and one wonders how — rather than when — it will be sent back to us in some awesome manner. Since whatever feeds into the Field is returned in some way, be it large or small, there is an opportunity for responsibility on our part. In this holographic universe what we put out in life, from the deeper levels of ourselves, is precisely what we get back. We are the future of our planetary fields, so it is up to us to initiate such a deep relationship that were we to connect with Gaia in love and harmony we would receive the same back in equal measure.[253]

When the Field gives us all we need: isn't this Love?

A four-year-old saw his neighbor in tears, and climbed onto his lap and just sat there. He later said, "I just wanted to help him cry."

—Found on the web

As we are all in the Field and as every state and movement beyond the veil is meshed with every other, then everything that occurs or flows or is an event must be in conformity with every attitude and agenda and belief within the Field. It follows that every birth, as much as every joy and every war, is codependent. It is not possible for anything to be out of step with the whole. Whatever happens to us in life has to be in resonance with the Field, so whatever we put out as our deepest needs gets dished back to us.

Being coherent means that life becomes simpler. We need less energy to hold our lives together, and therefore there are fewer incompatible fields woven into its fabric. This changes our level of vibration, for with less energy and fewer self-contradictory fields the resonance is greater. Fully coherent systems have higher and lighter energy systems than those that are struggling within themselves to maintain completeness, and more coherent people have a greater influence over others.[254]

If a person is happy and contented, look how the rest of the world agrees with him, and how joyfulness seems to accompany him all the days of his life. Those who are distrustful seem to be constantly faced with untrustworthy people. People who love dramas seem to accumulate more of them than the rest of us. Here is the universe providing us with situations that match the energy we are putting out.

It is not the surface energy of daily needs and cares that the Field responds to, but those deeper levels where we are most coherent. It does not give us what we think we want, but those core requirements that are so deeply embedded that we are often unaware of what they are.

One person I knew would expect everything to end in disaster, but he continuously found that others went out of their way to help him, and make his way smoother so that calamities almost never happened. His belief in imminent disaster was just on the surface of his life, encouraged by political and national issues that were outside his control, whereas his core was that of a hopeful child who knew that he was loved and cherished. This deeper level of himself was coherent from the experiences of his earliest days. It emitted a vibration of harmony and positivity that others readily responded to. It was not the surface opinions and hopes or the desires that came from the mind that affected others, but the much deeper, more coherent aura that emanated from the heart.

Coherence does not necessarily emit only positive vibrations. Abused people tend to attract abusers into their lives, and even though the relationship may be unhappy, the interplay suits both. It is common for the victim of violence to run for help, and then afterward to return to the abuser. Below the anger and hatred many ill-treated children have contradictory feelings about their molester, and cannot do without him. One who literally became her father's 'wife' found there was some small comfort to be found in having his attention, and this felt a little better than being totally ignored. When she left that embrace the injured child in her attracted manipulative figures into her life who were like her father. In a sense she was asking for repeat performances. This story is a far from uncommon.

Fig. 35 — The skeletal structure of a fish reflects its movement through the water.

In this way the universe provides companions and situations that are perfect responses to the deeper 'needs' in each. These needs are unconscious, and as long as they remain so no amount of thinking or talking will alter them. In each case there is such a perfection of interweaving, such an appropriate melding and adapting that we can only call it *love* in the sense that the universe is being totally compassionate. We might call it essential love, or even divine compassion. By 'asking' to be treated in a certain way we are being actually given exactly what we have sought. Is this not what Christ called the 'infinite love of the universe,' the total capacity for life to give everyone exactly what is most deeply 'needed'?

People who have traveled through a near-death experience have found again and again that after a short ride through the tunnel they were utterly swamped by the overwhelming power of love and compassion that met them. This seems to be the true nature of the Field. Most who have had this experience are changed for life.[255] It is awe-inspiring to become aware that in the Field every energy and vibration tunes in with ours and returns to us whatever we need in such a way that there is no opposition and no conflict. All is in order.

This is love acting to a greater purpose than asking for something. "Love is the fundamental attractive process. It is the process through which you receive information...it exists in all systems at all levels... Love is the unified field theory."[256]

To live within a perfect setting that supplies all our needs is paradise. Eve's 'sin' had nothing to do with apples, but everything to do with self-awareness. She ceased to be like the animals that lived for the moment, but became conscious, and this consciousness brought with it beliefs, morality, and so on. It looks like we were tossed out of the garden for coming to know ourselves and then believing in the illusion that the self was not part of the whole.

How can we be a victim?

Why do you weep? The source is within you, and this whole world is springing up from it.

—Jalal-ud-Din Rumi

Being created in, descended from, and evolving within the compassionate embrace of fields, we totally participate in our formation and our lives.[257] At every point we are influencing the scene we are in. At the deepest and most terrible way we have placed ourselves in this life, with all its experiences and outcomes, exactly as we have energetically co-created it. So we are not and cannot be the victim of events, for being part of the whole we helped, albeit only unconsciously, create every event we have ever lived through.

The Sufis state that we are only a pipe through which the wind of God may play its tune. If our pipe be true — that is, really coherent — then we won't need unconscious stuff to be thrown at us, but may allow the quantum energy of the Field to be marshaled in our favor.[258]

Maharishi once said that while young he had wished to move mountains and cure the ills of the world, but after he was enlightened and could do now these things he no longer wanted to "because he had put the mountains there in the first place."

In *Seth Speaks* Jane Roberts reported how this applies to every event, even when someone is the accidental victim of a mudslide, or a child caught up in a war, or the baby born with disfigurements.[259] The cause-and-effect relationship may not be obvious, but in the total oneness that exists between us and the Field, it cannot be otherwise. Yet one would say, "what of rape, of abuse of an innocent baby, or someone caught in an avalanche — how could they have created what happened?" Emotionally I would agree, yet from the evidence of universality and from the logic of what we understand of the Field, each event must already be in the Field and waiting to become manifest. In the light of this it is hard to recognize anyone as a victim.

Some therapies define their clients as victims and abusers. In this, as in everything else, the Field is manifested in extremely precise ways. If we need a dominating woman to replicate our being overwhelmed by our mothers, then the system provides it. If we need a violent man to replicate earlier beatings or bullying we will find him, and if the man tends to be mild our needs may still turn him into an abuser.

Once in place this pairing nearly always develops into a triangle. The third role is played by a healer who wishes to make it better, whether that is a friend or a therapist. Most therapists are healers in this sense, for they loathe injustice and truly want to help their clients out of the impasse they find themselves in. Does this mean we do nothing? I believe not, for we are creators of the Field, and the compassion of the universe is ours to share in. So how should we act? The one requirement for action, Ram Dass explained, is to do what we do with the utmost attention and passion, but to remain unattached — not unattached to the person's pain but to the outcome.[260]

Many therapists have chosen their profession, consciously or unconsciously, to resolve unfinished issues in themselves — certainly I did, and so did most of those I have worked with. When questioned about their role in the triangular game, there is often anger and disbelief, because their life's purpose has been assembled around solving their own problems in the shape of another. The unfortunate outcome, at least until the therapist has dealt with her own issues, is that the involved healer helps to perpetuate the problem by maintaining their client's belief that they are in a victim game. There is the additional attraction that if there were no problem there would be no need for the healer, and no job for the therapist.

Each person in the triangle — abuser, victim, and healer — has manifested exactly what was most needed to satisfy their own deepest yearnings. Each is dependent on the other for the creative unfoldment of their manifestation within their game of life.

A basic experiential understanding of Aikido practitioners — and it also applies to the other martial arts — is that no person can successfully attack another without there being a deep, unconscious agreement between aggressor and victim.[261] Whenever we put out at the deepest level — that Chilton Pearce calls the nonordinary or unconflicted level — is what we get back.[262] The victim energy acts with the perpetrator to create a mutual dance between Tamas and Sattva, mixed with the complex feelings that follow of self-blame and anger, and so on.

Betty's parents lived separate lives, because dad smoked so much that mum banished him to the shed. Betty longed for them both to be together in the house with her, but was compelled to choose. She loved her companionship with her dad, but he was too easy going to oppose her mum. On the other hand her mum was a sad and critical woman, who Betty wished to make happy. She found it hard to know where to be, contented with dad or anxious with mum. Her need was to have her parents together, not mum alone and angry and dad banished to smoke in the shed.

In adulthood she tried to reconcile the irreconcilable, hoping unconsciously to resolve the childhood struggle that remained locked within her. So she chose partners who were easy going like her dad, but who needed healing like her mum. Unconsciously she knew it was an unattainable and impossible struggle. In every partner Betty found just the right person to fit into this game, and expecting defeat, unconsciously made sure that the relationship failed each time. Here is the compassion of the universe providing the right people to act out preconceived dramas to give us exactly what our deepest nature expected.

There is no plan, so what of good and evil?

Truth, goodness, and beauty are not always found where we look for them; often they are hidden in the dirt or are in the keeping of the dragon.

—Carl Jung

The quite unbidden yet uncomfortable conclusion of a universe of fields is this: As all is in tune there can be no plan, there never was and never could be. To have a plan demands a definable purpose. But who or what defines in the world of sympathetic fields? Were there to be a vibration called 'the planner' it would have coordinating powers over other fields. The free flow of information would be hampered by the mere presence of a plan, let alone the attempt to enforce it, and then we would no longer have the Field. The logic of this appears unassailable.

There is a rightness to it all to the extent that everything is intimately connected to everything else. Everything fits perfectly because that is the nature of the coherent information that is the Field. As each moment is created solely by the sum total of all moments there is a natural inevitability and unforced order to it all. Everything flows together harmoniously so that every marvel in nature, no matter how numinous or how ordinary it may appear to us, is essentially a reflection of the inevitable coherence of the Field. But none of this signifies a plan, let alone an ultimate purpose. The concept would have no meaning in a timeless non-localized environment as everything that ever was and ever will be is already present.

Everything is relative, nothing is absolute. This was reflected in Geoffrey Chew's 'bootstrap' theory about subatomic particles in which he argued that no particle is more fundamental than any other.[263] If there are no fundamental objects of any kind, whether they are particles, laws or equations, then the universe is a dynamic web of interrelated events. Only overall consistency determines the structure of the whole or a part. This includes consciousness.

Where Chew writes of a self-promoting bootstrap, Buddha speaks of 'codependence arising,' a phrase that is extremely profound. Arising refers to the emerging of particles of fields from the Ground of Being to be manifested as matter, and its continuous falling back into vibration. None of this is happening independently, but bring fields together in concert with every other pertinent field in a way that can only be called codependent. Over time this arising and falling create morphic patterns. Those that we call laws seem permanent only because they have been around for a very long time.

I had earlier described Sheldrake's concept that the laws of the universe, that appear to be eternal and immutable, may have been just those rules of vibrationary behavior that, in evolving and becoming comfortable with each other, became the foundation of our universe over billions of years of repetitions. I had also described the zero-point field that showed that at absolute zero temperature there a window opens into a trillion other universes, each possibly operating under quite different 'universal' laws. Together they indicate that without central planning any number of universes with different yet coherently workable sets of rules could exist on the other side of the window — and we will never know.

Just as it has no plan, the Field itself can have no opinion nor judgment of right and wrong since ethics arise only from within the attachments of our material world. Opinions do not have any absolute existence of their own outside our material needs. If there is to be moral consciousness in the universe it must be introduced and nurtured by those with such a conscience, though we might consider whether our moral values have any absolute significance outside our human landscape. This is the danger lurking in the dragon of morality.

Whenever humans identify with any great field of power the influence on us can be profoundly negative, as it was with the Nazis.[264] Were we to take on the role of the superior race, the great mother, the wise guru, king, hero or savior there is a "serious danger to personality, for when it is awakened a man may easily come to believe that he really possesses the mana, the seemingly magical power and wisdom that it holds."[265] If we become possessed by a greater authority, we feel that we have tapped into a huge reservoir of suprahuman power — and we become inflated. We feel it as a charge of energy, something outside us, something so huge the conscious mind may no longer have control. This is "the expansion of the personality beyond its proper limits by identification with an archetype. It produces an exaggerated sense of one's self-importance."

Being merged with the greater we readily become impersonal and lose some measure of our humanity. It imbues us with lots of energy and zeal in daily life so we may be called 'spirited,' but we are to some degree possessed in such a manner that we become isolated from the Field by trying to wield power over it.

The unpalatable truth is that the crucial quality of higher levels of the Field is that they are essentially not interested in humanity's needs or moral values. This is why Jung called these higher levels "forms devoid of context," and after his own peak experience admitted that he felt "a strange cessation of human warmth."[266] Like animals in the wild, fields have little concern with human ideas of fairness, justice, or morality. They serve a realm that is fundamentally instinctual with no plan or thought for human needs or evolution.

I would conclude that there is nothing in the nature of the Field that can have purpose or attitude. The Field has neither plan nor morality. Humanity is not uppermost in its mind, as it should be were it our concept of a loving god. Instead, there is only responsiveness within the interdependent flow of signals that arranges itself in codependent ways that enables the next moment to arise. This may sound accidental, but not really, for no response is made that is not within the enfoldment of the surrounding signals. It is just that there is no ultimate, or even short-term, purpose in it all. It is just the enfolding and unfolding of codependent evolution.

Is human consciousness of benefit to the universe?

The therapist is not just working for a particular patient, but for himself and his own soul, and in doing so he is perhaps laying an infinitesimal grain in the scales of humanity's soul. Small and invisible as this contribution may be, it is yet an opus magnum, *for it is accomplished where the whole weight of mankind's problems has settled. This is a supreme responsibility.*

—Carl Jung[267]

The fuller parts of the Great Field seem to have no intrinsic interest in anyone or anything, not even itself. If planets fade or whole galaxies disappear into a black hole with everyone aboard, the Field would not care. Caring is a human quality. It involves allied feelings of relationship, and love, and wanting to make things better. There is no evidence that any of these qualities exist 'up there.'

Most animals and all plants live and die without consciousness of what they are or of their place. They are born and live through instinct, eating across the prairies, mating and rearing their young, carrying on in their allotted roles without change over eons. Like the mountains and the rocks, theirs is a timeless and unreflective world.

Consider the salamander that changes color with the branch, becoming a perfect match so it is invisible to prey and predator. Does the salamander *know* it is changing color? Is it able to alter colors so it becomes brightest gold on a blue flower, playing symphonies at will? Can it produce an individual art form on the branch? And what of the branch and its azure flower, are they aware? Dolphins and elephants, and perhaps some other species, seem to have some level of consciousness, perhaps equal to or higher than ours, though we have no way of knowing — yet. Compared to the rest of the planet humans have a quality of consciousness that operates beyond the information we get from our five senses.

This is not transferable on this plane, for our being conscious of the salamander will not enable it to become conscious of itself, or of the Field. However, it is transferable in the other direction, for unconsciously human values must be altering the Field by the input of our vibrations of care and responsibility. There is an historic moment, noted in the Biblical story of Job. Job is God's most faithful servant, seeking to be totally at one with Him. Yet God plays loose with his sincerity because he is so stung by a retort from Satan that he decided to give Lucifer power over all that Job possessed. It was a wager. God accepted Satan's taunt that he could test Job to such a depth of misery that Job "would curse Thee to Thy face."

God gave the opposition permission to destroy Job's life, kill his wife and children, bankrupt him and drive him from his tribe just to prove that his servant was incorruptible. Under contemporary law God could be sued for professional irresponsibility. At the end of all his suffering Job turns to God and criticizes him for not having the same faithfulness toward Job who is his servant as Job has to him as his god. "Is it good that Thou shouldst despise the work of thine hands, and shine upon the counsel of the wicked?"

In spite of the wrangles in the later chapters, Job has shown God up. He has brought a higher consciousness to their relationship, and a very high order of integrity and honesty to his own life through this encounter. He, as a human being, affected God's level of awareness by taking responsibility for no less than upgrading cosmic consciousness. In a way this led some centuries later to the new covenant introduced by Jesus of mutual responsibility.[268] There is of course a prior rapport here, for this God contains the projection of later generations of Job's people who wished for some mutuality between them.

At least since the time of Job, if not before, a few people have been trying to alter the spirit in the Field. These are almost invariably those who have had some experience of the Field. They are sensitives who have developed the intuition of their hearts, like Buddha, Confucius, Lao-Tzu, and the authors of the Hindu Vedas. These rare beings have for centuries attempted to 'teach god' and to imbue higher human values into the amorality of the Field.

I do wonder at times whether this impulse to change the spiritual realm, no matter how subtle, has not created its opposite in a shadow-field that has counter-projected onto us the very inverse of what we desire. The enormous forces pulling our planet apart, from loss of species and destruction of the rain forests, to the bombing of women and children, and hideous racial and religious divisions are possibly being stirred by this shadow.

This would not be the first time such negative forces have been in evidence, though the scale today is beyond the level any culture could have enforced in earlier times. Whenever there have been powerful religious movements a similar cosmic shadow has invaded cultures. Remember the purity of the early Christians at the same time as the excesses of Rome, and the deep mystical movement of the Sufis and Cistercians at the same time as the terrors of the inquisition and the crusades.

Are we wrong to share our values for compassion and gratitude and the well-being of the heart with spirit, or should we just leave it as it is? Certainly, we do face an enormous inertia. Our numbers and short time in the Field offers only a minimal input. It is our nature to keep trying as we do while it is the nature of the universe to move into duality and give us our own back, both in light and in shadow. It is certainly an interesting situation.

Many peoples have found their place in the universe by becoming the servants of the cosmos. Jung tells that when he visited the Pueblo Indians they told him, "We are the people who live on the roof of the world. We are the sons of our Father the Sun. From our beliefs we daily help our father to cross the sky. We do this not only for ourselves, but also for the whole world. If we were to cease our practice, in ten years the sun would no longer rise. Then it would be night forever."[269]

In the early morning in Kenya people spit on their hands when they rise and hold them up to the sun. Their moisture is offered as a reminder to both themselves and to the sun to remember. By bestowing consciousness on the sun, they ensure it won't forget to rise again. In Columbia an isolated and deeply religious people, the Kogi have built their rituals around a similar belief. They call themselves the Elder Brothers, and we the Younger Brothers. In the older mountain villages of Bali the Tenganum people respect a similar cosmic cosmology. Their role is to heal the planet and to bringing the world's consciousness to a new level.

Nature never introduces a new component, especially one in a species that is successful, without good purpose. It is as if the Field is 'in need' of what our heart energy could do when partnered with our previous acquisition, the large forebrain with its huge unused powers. Chilton Pearce suggested that "nature's evolutionary aim" is to make such a direct connection between the discipline of the brain and the radiant fields of the heart that would turn us into an antenna to connect us directly and permanently with the wisdom of the Field.[270] Our desire for enlightenment may be partnering with the Field to remake us so we can connect, and thereby be able to help transform the implicate realm. I will discuss this further a little later, but the thought that we may be the means for the Field to know itself may lie behind that wonderful Sufi phrase "that God longs to be known."

The transfer of consciousness from a lower vehicle into a higher is part of a natural creative and evolutionary process. Since the universe is the evolving outcome of mutual creativity, and we evoke the universe just by being within it, we should consider how higher conscious could best evolve. My personal feeling is that the way lies in our highest virtues, those of compassion and gratitude. These too may become humanity's greatest contribution to the evolution of Cosmic Consciousness.

The way mankind has quite naturally decided to improve the spiritual realm (even if unconsciously) has been expressed in these awesome words from Jung's autobiography: "Man is indispensable for the completion of creation; he is himself, in fact, the second creator of the world, who alone has given to the world its objective existence — without which, unheard, unseen, silently eating, giving birth, dying, generations nodding though hundreds of millions of years, the world would have continued in the profoundest night of nonbeing down to its unknown end. Human consciousness has created objective existence and meaning. Man has found his indispensable place in the great process of being."[271]

Other universes with different laws

The existence of living organisms seems to depend on a number of fortuitous coincidences that some scientists and philosophers have hailed as nothing short of astonishing.

— Paul Davies

The Great Field is the outcome of billions of years of evolution. It could have evolved in almost any direction, co-creating any combination of laws and outcomes, manifesting almost any type of environment and filled with whatever style of organism would replicate and flourish. This idea has been explored as 'multiverses' by Hugh Everett in the 1950s and Bryce DeWitt and Neill Graham more cogently twenty years later.[272]

Sheldrake suggested that our immutable laws of nature are merely what have emerged out of the average sum-total of all the uncountable interactions between fields and particles over the whole of time. In the beginning any change to the rules governing any of the particles of the gas cloud emerging from our big bang would affect every other particle, until some consensus emerged. These became the laws of our particular universe.

I mentioned earlier that the amount of energy-plus-matter in our universe has now been calculated as representing much less than one percent of all the measurable material. This being so, we need to consider the possibility of many incommunicable systems within the Field, all with different laws and different agendas. The world of negative matter may well be one of these, not waiting to destroy us in an instant fireball, but simply an invisible neighbor existing within its own set of 'universal' laws.

There is an assumption that our world of classical linear physics arose naturally from the quantum chaos of the big bang. It does seem odd that an orderly world with well-defined physical laws within measurable concepts of time and space would arise out of the nonlinear nonlocal explosion of the initial state of our universe. Ten years ago James Hartle calculated mathematically that "for the majority of initial states, a classical world would *not* emerge. In that case the separation of the world into distinct objects occupying definite positions in a well-defined background space-time would not be possible."[273] There would be no locality. "It seems likely that in such a smeared-out world one could know nothing without knowing everything. Indeed the very notion of traditional laws of physics should be regarded not as truly fundamental aspects of reality, but as relics of the big bang, and as consequences of the special quantum state in which the universe originated."[274]

Fig. 36 — The radiation of the big bang.

Recently Victor Stenger has postulated that all the laws of physics are human interpretations that are theoretically consistent and experimentally valid because they are nothing more than a means of correlating observations "so that they appear independent of viewpoint."[275] In attempting to answer one of the perennial questions in science — how did the things of this world come from the nothingness of the void — Stenger argues that something came from nothing because something is more stable than nothing.

This prompts the vital question of what is time and space, and when did they originate? Are they both creations of the process of incarnation, or are they *a priori*? Does our life cycle create time so that infants can change into adults, and adults may themselves wither away and die? Does the reality of organic things that start as seeds and grow and die need time to justify their transformations? Or, more conventionally, does growth and death itself originate from being in time? And is time what a million species over a trillion years has evolved with enormous thoroughness that now we too are trapped in the same historic delusion? Is time essential to all creation, or does it exist only in our universe and not in others?

Were we to be open to greater levels of the Great Field itself and observe everything in all its wonder are we sure we would not see all of creation generating itself without beginning and without end? Scientists see the big bang as a single event, but considering what a small part of the Field the mass of our explicate world takes up our act of creation may be only one of an infinite number of created universes endlessly and simultaneously presenting themselves through gigantic fractal fields. The Indians believed that Brahma is continuously creating new universes by breathing out, and discreating others by breathing in across vast epochs of unconnectable time called yugas.

Stephen Hawking, working on the presumption that the universe is completely self-contained, and therefore having neither boundaries nor beginning nor end, concluded that "it would simply be. What place then for a creator?"[276] As the Field is capable of changing, albeit slowly, as our events modify its fields, creation is the natural unfolding of events and states, each connected within to such an extent that they profoundly influence the other. The single act of creation out of nothing, the *ex nihilo* theory, does not apply to the Great Field, which is everywhere without time, and therefore just is, whether it includes this universe or any others.

Sidney Coleman's theoretical concept of 'wormholes' — massive protrusions of space-time within our universe that connects two distantly separated regions — has the potential to stretch beyond our universe to connect us with many different universes. Were we able to make this connection, we would be propelled beyond the world of mathematical certainty that colors ours. In spite of there being a general agreement that wormholes are possible — as between the black hole at one end and the quasar at the other — the essential disparities between universes with different basic laws means that, as Gerard Hawkins said in a recent talk, such phenomenon would be fundamentally incalculable: To which Gerard 't Hooft exclaimed, "Goodbye Law and Order!"[277]

It does not necessarily imply that other universes consist of anti-matter or shadow matter, but simply that their physical laws are consistently their own yet different to ours. This probably means that nothing and nobody formed within our laws would be able to communicate with other universes formed through other laws. Then the earth and our universe would be just one possible configuration in the Field, our earth-world just one sample in which all possible systems are present and are self-sustaining and self-validating.

Can the future determine the past?

Can machines think?

—Alan Turing

There is an integrated wholeness to everything in which all things that arise do so through a codependence on everything else. As this occurs first within the Field, which is a timeless zone, all that will be and all that was is a current factor in creating that codependence. Being timeless there is no forward or backward, and no sense of past and future. Being mired in 'timefullness' we cannot see the future, but for the Field our personal future would already exist within the 'timelessness' of its present.[278]

Brandon Carter wrote that the laws and forms of our universe must have been so organized from the beginning "as to admit the creation of observers within it" and according to what is sometimes called the 'strong principle' "claims that the universe is tailor-made for habitation [and has been from the first moment], and that both the laws of physics and the initial conditions have obligingly arranged themselves in such a way that living organisms are subsequently assured of existence — akin to the traditional religious expression that 'the Lord made the world for mankind to inhabit.'"[279]

This is part of what Carter called the Anthropic Principle to explain the observed fact that the fundamental constants of physics and chemistry are just right to allow the universe and life as we know it to exist. They are so fine-tuned that what one might call the seemingly arbitrary constants in physics have one startling thing in common — they are precisely the values you need if you want to have a universe capable of producing life. These include the relationship between fundamental forces of gravity and electromagnetism that, if only slightly different, would have already turned the universe into a fireball, and had the weak force been any weaker hydrogen would have become helium and water itself, the foundation of life, would have been as rare as gold. We have already met this already in Lovelock's concept of Gaia.[280]

In other words, as has been repeated again and again in this book, no law or event or field is possible *without the agreement of*

every other field and law and event. Creation is replaced by evolution in the only way it could happen when all is one, without
conflict, nor disagreement nor disturbance. It is in this sense that
Wheeler's argument for a *participatory universe* should be true. He
concludes with great logical force that "the existence of an observer
at some stage in history is actually responsible for the creation of
that particular type of universe."[281] He points out that even the size
of our universe is perfect, for he calculated that were it to be less
than 10^9 light years across it would have collapsed so rapidly that
life on Earth would not have had the time to develop.

These deliciously anti-time ideas strike at the heart of our perception of things. For humans, indeed for all explicate creation,
time moves in one direction with the possibility of infinite choices
and accidents at every point. From this perspective for an uncertain
universe to produce the subtle integrations of the Gaia concept can
only be seen as pure magic. But what if it were not? What if our
creation was, in a sense, foreseen in the impenetrable silence of the
solar energy fields before even the earth was born? If so, then each
future inevitability is implicit in wholeness.[282] Bradbury's dead butterfly could not then be responsible for the next choice of president
in the elections that followed, for that was already 'foreseen.'[283] In
which case free will is a terrible illusion. This is the ultimate causal
world in which, like Gaia, all the individual parts work together
in a communist-like harmony for the benefit the whole, and where
willful eccentricity has only a minor place.

7

THERAPY AND THE FIELD

When religion lost the cosmos in the West,
society became neurotic and we had to invent psychology
to deal with the ensuing neurosis.

—Otto Rank

Everything presented in the earlier sections of this book, from biology to subatomic physics, and from astronomy to neurocardiology, affirms that the psyche consists of and within fields of energy. Just as it has been shown that water responds to energies, and that the messages are passed from one token to another via water, we, being 70 percent water, are necessarily integral with the same fields. The point of view that we have been discussing has not yet been integrated into mainstream therapy. That remains, for the most part, reliant on behavior modification and medical solutions. This chapter is about the egoic issues that arise from an energetic source, and is followed by an analysis of the vital role of soul in our lives.

The word 'therapy' usually refers to mainly verbal counseling, the sharing of tales and wisdom, and evolving strategies to deal with everyday life situations. Psychology includes behaviorism, cognitive and neuropsychological issues, child and family therapies, and many related schools, in which there is very little consideration of anything beyond the five senses. It is not surprising that soul is absent, as the psyche develops in a Western world that believes in the split between mind and matter, between body and soul.

I will use therapy here in the broader and more powerful sense of the in-depth psychology required for deep personal transformation. I use the word 'transformation' because it has a more profound meaning than healing, and is the correct word for those on a spiritual path or who wish to continue Job's work on the Field through raising their consciousness. The rest of this book explores how an ever-present intimacy with the Field can affect our attitudes and our personal work on ourselves.

Transformation means seeking below behavior and childhood dramas and beliefs into the decisions that underlie them, and then going below that to the very core energies of personality, and then even deeper into the fields of vibration out of which we were formed. If we deal with the root issues of our initial creation, which underlie all the early decisions we took in creating ourselves, then all other issues and contradictions on the surface will adjust of their own accord. We should not have to work on the surface to get into the depths, but on the foundations if we want the house to move.

Therapy deals with the psyche. It could be described as being like a crossword puzzle in which, at first, there is nothing but an unknown jumble of spaces and blank holes, but that the solutions to independent clues link together in a consistent and supportive way to form a coherent completeness, so that the more clues we solve the easier we find it to access the missing features. The dictionary tells us that the word *psyche* means "soul or spirit, as distinct from body and mind." However, it may surprise you that the original meaning in Greek comes from the word for 'breath' or 'to breathe,' with the same root as Prana in Sanskrit. Somewhat like the breath, the psyche has no material presence; it is seen only from its product.

The process presumes that the Field is primary, and that all those elements that are part of the Field — soul, energetic nodes, entities, spiritual forms, and so on — offer us tools that are broader than those of more traditional methods. Behavioral psychology that implants new techniques for living certainly helps, but leaves the deeper impulses with all their original powers intact. Since these have not been accessed, components that derive from the Field remain at war with the newly learned behavior. This is why all modes of counseling based on mental and verbal procedures would benefit from being widened to include fields of energy.

Conventional psychology is extremely wary of the word 'energy,' let alone the concept. Energy work smacks of the unprovable, the mystical, and the ungrounded. They are correct in that the outcome of energetic healing is seldom amenable to proof. The deeper we enter the Field the less we can know about it through our instruments because the instruments themselves belong to the explicate zone of matter, space, and time while energy belongs to the vibratory implicate zone that possesses neither. Tools developed to measure space and time have no significance in a timeless and spaceless environment. Since we have to let go of any attempt to 'prove' our experiences, we have to rely on the intensity of the actual event, the feedback from intuition, and in the end the effectiveness on this plane of what we do when we use its gifts.

The experiences and events described here occurred in sessions and workshops held at the Crucible Centre. The Centre lies in the western foothills of the Blue Mountains outside Sydney. The theoretical structure described in this book has evolved from these experiences, and reflects what we have learned in the clinical work we have done since 1989. The outcome of this work is the ultimate test. If a concept works, no matter how bizarre it may at first seem, that is the final check for the effectiveness of the theoretical structure. Indeed, in all therapy it is only the described outcome that confirms the method, and no matter how carefully organized the testing procedures, we come back to people's opinions and reflections in order to judge our results. Consequently, what we and our clients experience, and the format of their descriptions are the basis for this investigation, not any preconceived notions.

The trigger for writing this, and sharing our work is that there is now sufficient scientific evidence from biology and physics to provide a coherent context for these experiences. Together they support the basic tenets of the theoretical structure that we are building at the Centre.

We have found that deep self-investigation reveals the patterns behind the decisions we made on how to deal with life. There are not a lot of patterns. They come down, in their essence, to energies that open and energies that close. It has been fascinating to discover that each human pattern reflects similar patterns in other levels of the universe, for the *modus operandi* of molecules and galaxies are also ours. This universal consistency convinces us that our theories on the human psyche are not too far from the truth.

Our particular discipline has been called Transpersonal Psychology, a term created in the late 1960s at the Esalen Institute in Big Sur by Abraham Maslow and Stanislav Grof. Transpersonal refers to all those levels of reality that are not directly discernable by the five senses. Unlike modernist psychology, the transpersonal paradigm is based on these 'insensible' human qualities and works with them to heal. These include all the unseen forces of the Field, from archetypes and souls to the energetic formations within each of us that direct our behavior. Jung, Huxley, Laszlo, Rowan, and Wilber, to mention only a few, have discussed these issues in great detail.

It seems humans have always had some knowledge of the body's energy systems

The stuff of mind is constantly active and constantly manifesting.

—Patanjali Sutra

Human beings have, it would seem, always been interested in the energy systems that run through our bodies. The oldest mention of an energy field is in the Patanjali Sutra of 3,000 B.C. The Chinese called it *ch'i*. John White refers to ninety-seven different cultures that recognized the human aura.[284] In 500 B.C. Pythagoras wrote that auras could be used in healing. Barbara Brennan mentions the twelfth century French monks Boirac and Liebault who described an energy that impinges on individuals at a distance, in which one person can affect another just by their very presence.[285] This particular phenomenon of knowing when we are being stared at has recently been described by Sheldrake,[286] and successfully tested experimentally by William Braud.[287]

A mass of photographic evidence has accumulated over the past century that shows that all living creatures generate and emit radiation. Photons of light, electromagnetic frequencies, heat, sound, and scent are all emitted from our bodies in direct response to our internal states. In the mid-1920s George de la Warr and Ruth Brown took the first photographs of the human field. Semyon and Valentina Kirlian in 1939 applied this technique to natural objects as well as people. As in Emoto's work on water, photography can be very persuasive.

Shafica Karagulla discovered that energy fields interpenetrate, Leonard Ravitz[288] that the human field fluctuates with mental and emotional changes, and Vladimir Popov of Russia that healthy individuals have stronger fields than the ill.[289] In 1979 Becker mapped electrical fields that follow the shape of the body and the central nervous system, and found that electron-sized particles moved through them.

Bohm and Aharonov found that electrons can 'feel' the presence of a magnetic field even where the situation has been created in which there is zero probability of finding the electron. Bohm concluded that the "tangible reality of everyday life is really a kind of illusion, like a holographic image. Underlying is a deeper level of existence, a vast and more primary level of reality that gives birth to all the objects and appearances of our physical world in much the same way as a piece of holographic film gives birth to a hologram."[290] As *everything in the universe* is part of a continuum, the apparent separateness of things at the explicate level is an illusion. At the implicate level of the Field everything is a seamless extension of everything else, and this may well be the basis for the fields in our body's energy systems.

Electrical-magnetic fields affect a person's biological makeup. Lipton states, "pulsed electromagnetic fields have been shown to regulate virtually every cell function, including DNA synthesis, protein synthesis, cell division, cell differentiation, morphogenesis, and neuroendocrine regulation."[291] He says that these findings acknowledge that biological behavior can be controlled by "invisible" energy forces, and this includes thought.

In the 1990s Hiroshi Motoyama found that the levels of light emanated from Yoga practitioners could be measured. Zheng Ronglian in China that shown that ch'i gong masters produced a pulse-like energy, while some emit a low frequency sound that appeared both as a wave and as particles. The presence of these fields shows that the medical view of the body having separate systems for the digestion, blood circulation and the lymphatic, and so on does not include the energies that join them all together. Ronglian argues that the body should be "viewed from a quantum concept of energy stemming from the atomic cellular nature of the body, which cuts across all tissues and systems...The hologram concept emerging in physics and brain research provides a unifying cosmic view of reality which demands reinterpretation of all biological findings on another plane."[292]

All views of energy and the presence of the Field are based on each observer's own personal level of truth and clarity: including those in this book. This sandplay provides a very clear picture of one person's 'vision' of the other side.

Fig. 37 — Sandplay of desire that prevented further entry into the Field.

She hears music-like vibrations within the shell, symbolic of her openness. She remains aware of the duality that exists in all realms, shown by the pair of cymbals joined by a leather strap, and a pair of bells farther back. Beyond the cymbals lies an open book held out to her by her 'guide.' Yet she feels a sense of childish loss at being open to the Field yet not being given it all, for behind him, hidden by his body, are all the other records in the Akashic library, unavailable to her. The possibility of obtaining everything she sought is disguised by her emotional desire for the one book she did have sight of. This attachment closed off the rest of the Field from her. In an exquisite paradox, the duality caused by her attachment to wanting more from the library actually stood in the way of her being open to further insight.

The fields of the human body

Recognize yourself as you are and you will see yourself everywhere. All you have to do is clean up your house.

— Gangaji

The creation of the egoic personality follows the same process as the creation of any other part of the material world, except that its reality is purely energetic. The psyche consists of a collection of fields that inhabit one person. It does not stray or wander. It is a slice of the Great Field, yet it remains uniquely ours while being influenced by all that is around it. We do not enter the Field, rather it enters us. There is neither possession nor occupation. The union is as a mist appears in the air, soft, effortless.

Mae-Wan Ho, an English biologist, expressed it in the loveliest way: "The visible body just happens to be where the wave function of the organism is most dense. Invisible quantum waves are spreading out from each of us and permeating into all other organisms. At the same time each of us has the waves of every other organism entangled within our own makeup. We are participants in the creation drama that is constantly unfolding. We are constantly co-creating and re-creating ourselves and other organisms in the universe, shaping our common futures, making our dreams come true."[293]

There is an enormous literature on the visible fields of the body. For those who can see them, they are beautiful to look at and reflect our inner selves in unique ways. Some people have found in them ways to heal, or to read the qualities of personality, and even with a lot of fun, to draw and photograph. Mostly, they hint at levels of ourselves that lie beyond the usual limits of the body and the boundaries of the skin. Nearly all of us saw them when we were young, and gradually lost the ability the more we were told that the fairies and devas in the garden simply can't be true.

Personally, I find that observing the fields that shine out of people is distracting. It is my bent to feel these fields sensuously in my body, though this way does not work for everyone. Intuition, for me, is a whole-body feeling that rapidly translates into either a spatial sense or into words. It is an inner awareness that comes through focused attunement with my client. Robert Heinlein in *Strangers in a Strange Land* called it "grocking," a word I particularly like because it onomatopoetically combines the deepening feeling of a "growl" with a hard consonant of an immediate experience. Brian Josephson has proposed that focusing with intent changes the level of quantum probability in any interaction, which supports the therapeutic technique of attunement that we use and the development of the unseen 'space' of consciousness that forms between therapist and client, that some call the *Metvelt*.[294]

Attunement is like the ch'i gong master's use of ch'i, which is expressed in the saying that "the direction directs the ch'i, the ch'i directs the body." Attunement is a subtle, delicate attentiveness that is sensitive and flexible and feels like a soft sensuousness that explores the terrain without any agenda but the exploration itself. The client responds in kind, with a willingness to allow their own curiosity to guide them in their self-investigation.

We find that to work therapeutically within the Field allows the psyche to integrate in a trice. Many therapists have experienced the rapidity of these movements and the instantaneous release of old traumas throughout the whole structure the moment the old energetic forms have been unpinned. Though the cellular structure in the body may need a little time to adjust when deep and ancient traumas are loosed, yet in the psyche such moments are over in a second. There is some preliminary work needed to 'loosen' the system and to soften the hardness of the ego, but once we can work at the level of the Field transformation can be extremely quick as the information is networked throughout the system.

Among the thousands of ways to use energy to heal, and the many books written on it, one by Barbara Brennan describes the procedure as "rebalancing the energy field...that is intimately associated with a person's health and well-being. To deal with the source usually requires a life change that ultimately leads to...that deeper part of ourselves that is sometimes called the high self."[295]

We are socialized to turn reality into illusion

When that which veils the light is done away with, then we become discarnate and are freed from thought. This is the state of illumination.

—Patanjali Sutra

Karl Pribram's work on the brain has shown that when we use our senses we don't see an object reflected at the back of the eyeball, as suggested in all high school diagrams, but as a virtual image sitting somewhere outside us.[296] What our eyeball responds to is not the object as it is supposed to look, but only particles and waves. The mind has to learn not to struggle with all this data. The explicate world is, in his view, a holographic blur of frequencies, and the brain that makes sense of it through a matching hologram that selects only those frequencies that can be transformed into acceptable sensory perceptions. In reality, concrete reality ceases to exist. As the religions of the East have long upheld, the material world is Maya, an illusion, and although we may think we are physical beings moving through a physical world, this too is an illusion.

The brain has to interpret the data to suit what *we are conditioned to see*, and projects that outward as the object itself. Through experience we learn to place this image of our own making in the same place as the original so that all our perceptions coincide with it.[297] When we reach out to pick up a thing, we are in fact reaching for the image of that thing as 'formed' in the brain. Experience and feedback gradually make enough of the qualities of the outer projection coincide with the original vibrational reality to feel 'true,' but the process still alters and diminishes the outer reality in many important ways. We see neither the original particle-plus-energy reality, nor a pure interpretation of it, but a censored and narrowed picture that we deign to call the 'real world.'[298]

The holographic potential within the brain enable images, signals, and memories to be stored multidimensionally in their totality. Our brains are able to read this information, and from it create our image of the world. As Pribram concluded, the brain functions like a quantum in holding in itself all the past and all emotions while redesigning the present and including impressions from all the senses. It integrates all these in every moment as a complete projection of itself within its own holograph. Pribram argues that the brain does not do this in a logical or orderly manner, not in images or in words or in chemical impulses (though these are what we can measure), but in the language of wave interference, of phase, amplitude, and frequency. This indicates that the resonant awareness in the brain is also the language of the Field.

The theoretical understanding of how the brain reads information to create a personal image of the world has been confirmed by Walter Schempp, the creator of brain imaging technology, and

English physicist Peter Marcer. They discovered that "perception occurred at a much more fundamental level of matter — the netherworld of the quantum. We don't see objects *per se*, but only their quantum information and out of that construct our image of the world."[299] Perception is not a direct process of light and sound impacting on the eyes and ears as receptors, but an indirect system that operates as if it was the Field itself. In Schempp's phrase, the brain conducts itself as a quantum holograph.[300] It is like a gigantic internal internet in which every neuron is able to log on and exchange information with every other neuron at the same time via the quantum processor that it sits in.

The uttermost cleverness of the illusion! Our brain is so adept we are able to turn the reality of the Field into any illusion our society would accept, and operate on it as if it were truly what is out there.

More importantly for our purposes, Pribram demonstrated that the mass of information available to us in every second does not have to clog up the system.[301] We store enough as it is. There is a mechanism in the brain that limits what gets accepted. A 'filter' censors what we perceive so that the vastness of the Field does not flood us. However useful this mechanism is in ordinary life, for the spiritual man it is one of the factors that creates the veil we struggle to get through. We use this mechanism to agree with ourselves that a certain view of the information our senses bring us is enough, and that there is no need to sense more. This may be useful in the jungle, but when we wish to reconnect with our higher vibrations and to link with soul and the glory of the Field it stands in the way. Our struggle on the spiritual path is to redirect one of our most deep-seated and well-consolidated survival mechanisms so we can move through the illusion to embrace a wider reality.

The process of change begun by Heisenberg eighty years ago has come home to roost. He had shown that the consciousness of the observer brought the observed object into being, and that no thing was independent of the person who observed it.[302] The fact that the act of observation 'made' the object could now be further refined, and rephrased as "the act of observation 'makes' the object *as we sense it.*"

"As with a hologram, the lens of the eye picks up certain inter-ference patterns and then converts them into three-dimensional images."[303] It requires this type of virtual projection for you to reach out to the images where they really are, and not try to touch them inside your head. As we are continuously projecting images into space, our sense of the world is actually a virtual world. We are creating our world. The trouble lies not in doing this, but in then believing that this is the only reality.

To use our senses is to transform what is being sensed. We are censoring the timeless, spaceless world of vibrations and pat-terns and standing waves into the concrete and separated world of space-time. The word 'censoring' means in this context that we have trained our senses to restrict information. We have limited the universe to space and time, and by so doing have "eaten of the tree of knowledge."

As Pribram's work has hinted, our eyes actually perceive beyond the objects themselves to the most fundamental level of mat-ter — the uncertain and insubstantial world of the quantum parti-cle. "We don't see objects *per se*, but only their quantum information, and out of that construct our image of the world."[304] Perceiving the world only comes after we have tuned into the Field, for in medita-tion and in certain similar states the eye sees fields of energy, sees that all things are in movement and surrounded by intensely colored radiance. In deep meditation, or samadhi, or occasionally on drugs we go beyond the constructs of our minds to respond to the fuller reality of the outer world in a way that is closer to what it really is. In these moments objects are shorn of their civilized constructions and appear instantaneously as both matter and field.

The only difference between the vibrational world and the physical/biological lies in the images we make from the vast amount of data we receive. In reality there is no distinction. As Bohm argued late in life, "mind involves participation rather than interac-tion" and cannot be divided from matter.[305] The belief that the two are separate is only a concept. The mind is doing its level best to cope with the tornado of information driving at it from all direc-tions, and understandably creates a workable exclusion device, cutting out all that is not useful in its immediate context. We have to agree with Robert Jahn and Brenda Dunne that there are not two unconnectable worlds or realms, but only one.[306] It is our minds that create restrictive exclusion zones, mainly because we need to identify with an image for the security it gives us. Censoring is a simple tool for survival.[307]

The Vedas state that this illusion is of our own making. Over 2,000 years before Christ people knew that all is one and that by believing in the external validity of our own projections we are caught in a fantasy of suffering. This reminds me of the famous argument at the time of King Charles on whether a particular table existed when no one was in the room to observe it, for Bishop Berkeley remarked, "It is always there, even when you walk out of the room, because it is in the mind of God." That is, it is pregnant in the Field.

Duality in the human field: Tarzan v. Jane

If you identify with your body, emotions or thoughts, you have not discovered yourself. You have been lying to yourself. Just stop lying. Do it now!

—Gangaji

The Field being a reflection of the way things are on earth, there must be duality in fields just as there is down here. It would seem that the more complex the field system of a material or a species the more likely it is to induct its opposite. The most commonly experienced are the archetypes for the masculine and feminine. "Jung called the feminine figure the *anima* and the masculine the *animus*. These two words mean 'soul' and 'spirit' in Latin."[308] Their differences among all organic things provide one of the most wondrous fundamentals of life on earth.

Making form is one major aspect of the male archetype, resting in formlessness is an essential aspect of the female. The male archetype is upward striving and ambitious, while the feminine is downward, accepting, and empathetic. The male is open, and works best in open spaces, with mechanisms and cars and in action and competition. The feminine closes in and is best in homes, in the garden, with patience and talk. One is akin to Sattva, the other to Tamas.

The differences seem to be present even in the act of conception itself. A single egg waits passively for a maelstrom of hyperactive sperm during intercourse. The hundreds of millions of sperm seem frantic to get there, but once they touch the egg they go into an extended 'hug' around the ovum until one of them is drawn in, when all the others are excluded.

In the Gospel of Thomas it is written, "They said to him, 'Shall we then, as children, enter the kingdom?' Jesus said to them, 'When you make the two one, and when you make the inside like the outside and the outside like the inside, and the above like the below, and when you make the male and the female one and the same, so that the male not be male nor the female female, then you will enter the kingdom.'"[309]

How do men match the regular way women bleed? Only ritualistically, by bloodying one another and themselves. Women are self-sufficient in their product. Men have to go out to make it. Women are naturally part of the moon's cycle; men have to be solar warriors. But warriors have no natural rhythm, so the tension builds to a point of catharsis, like an ejaculation. The posturing side of the animus leads to most power play in politics, much of which lies in the shadow.

Combine these differences of behavior with the physical differences in the *corpus callosum* and other structures of the brain that have been discussed earlier, and we can see that remaining ruthlessly self-aware in a relationship may provide the most important road to consciousness. By the male and female following the play of their differences they can see themselves each day with clarity.

There is one very important reason for this. It is commonplace to say that we are attracted to people like our parents. But in fact this matter is much more complex. Our ego has been created to make us safe in the face of our parents (which is why they remain in our lives forever). But we choose our partner not because they are like the parent, but because they have the ability to trigger those defenses we first developed in the household of those who reared us. The role the partner plays in this aspect of the game is to be able to get in under our best-prepared defenses and to stimulate the ego to be stronger. Our partners are a daily reminder of how we protect ourselves. They know exactly how to best prod the most vulnerable wounds, and our response hones the strength of our personal citadel,[310] at least until we develop consciousness.

Fig. 38—Sandplay of couple around fixed and conflicting desires.

Vulnerability is illustrated in this first sandplay done by a couple. She put in the dog and the house, he the spiky shell under the money and the picture of the mountain. House and hill are elementary symbolic archetypes for female and male qualities, though other issues became apparent in the sand. As a child she longed to be patted by her dad, but had to fight her sister to get it, while in his childhood he had resisted all attempts to be touched, working hard and taking comfort in money. Their marriage had broken up after only six months, and she brought him along as she still longed for them to be together. By seeing, right from the beginning of therapy that their vulnerability came from childhood there was an opportunity to rekindle their relationship.

There was a second issue: that she would not share the house she owned with him, and he needed to keep all his money for himself for comfort. At this stage in their young relationship this had not yet become a major difference between them (though one suspects it would in time), everything was dominated by her longing to be held and patted, and his to be left untouched.

Disguising our contradictions creates shadows

He who is drawing his shadow off others is doing the most significant political work. The problem is not the hydrogen bomb but the psyche of man that manifested it

—Laurens van der Post

Human beings are walking contradictions. We call the outcome the games people play. There is only one purpose to a game, and that is to win, through acceptance, recognition and so on. We say, "How are you this morning?" without ever expecting the other to tell us how they really are at that moment. It is a pretence phrase that covers the truth of what we want and we would normally be aghast to receive a truthful answer in return. And, as we know, there are a million other games we play, seldom as pleasant as this one.[311]

Then what happens to the truth behind the question? "How are you?" may have hidden the appeal "Please notice me and tell me I'm alright" or some variation on that. But we seldom want to know the real answer, because it may not be to our liking. So we disguise, and this is how we usually win — "How are you?" is a game in which both parties win. Disguising is a subtle form of resistance that allows us to hold a bundle of contradictory states and beliefs within us without breaking up and having to face our vulnerabilities. The fields in us remain together, though coherence may be considerably strained.

As an example, a child who was abused sexually decided that only by beating all odds could she protect herself and control her life. Her anger came from knowing that she had already failed to adequately protect herself. She used that to drive her determination to succeed. In adulthood she made prodigious progress and appeared able to manage everything, but frantic panic lay just below the surface. When investigated, she found that there was within her an energetic node that had the shape of a fist thrusting outward, but the wrist was disguised. She realized that the wrist had been covered to hide the knowledge that there was no arm behind it. The lack of real strength in the muscles of the arm had to be disguised.

The node included the contradictory qualities of determination and weakness. When she designed buildings, spoke at meetings, or went to buy clothes, this contradictory quality would appear. Designs were forceful, even a little outrageous, but never too extravagantly personal. At site meetings she related well with the men and wore clothes that were strong in color, yet they were formal enough to be unthreatening. Under every action, no matter how small, lay this common combination of aggression and submission. The duality limited her choices. She felt trapped, and not wanting to relive the trauma that was the cause, disguised the game as best she could.

One far from uncommon outcome is to align with one aspect of this inner struggle and to condemn the other. In this example she found it more protective to be determined and strong, and so pushed down the accompanying feelings of weakness and submission.

These repressed parts do not go away, but continue to live in the unconscious where they grow sour. Like a pressure cooker, the more we repress the more explosive these parts become. We call it the 'shadow' because it walks behind us through life, whether we like it or not.[312] The energy in it does not disappear because it is not used. It vibrates inside us, and like a magnet attracts to us those people and events that tune in. They have a matching vibrational energy. It is not surprising that those with lots of suppressed anger continuously find themselves in the presence of aggressive people, and so it is with every variety of shadow. The process is often called projection, for we are sourcing our needs from outside and then dealing with them not as mirrors to our problems, but as external reflections.[313]

Indeed, the less we like it the stronger it gets, and becomes a major force behind out judgments and opinions. The most powerful have been disguised so deeply they are completely unconscious. Judging others is a favorite pastime of the shadow energy, but it is readily extended to include spiritual and cultural judgments of other beliefs, races, colors, and ethics. This is why Laurens van der Post could write, "He who is drawing his shadow off others is doing the most significant political work. The problem is not the hydrogen bomb but the psyche of man that manifested it."[314]

Here is a typical scenario: After years of untidiness Bill decides to clean up his shed. Finally his *drive* to clean has become greater than his *desire* not to. But the old desire will come out of the shadow and reassert itself, and instead of cleaning Bill will fiddle, read old magazines, and generally play about rather than carry on with his decision. In doing so he alienates the inner drive and begins to project it. Now the drive is seen as outside him, that *someone else* wants him to do it. He does not know who, that someone has at first no name. At this moment, enter wife Jill. In innocence she asks if he has finished cleaning up. Now he is relieved, because he now *knows* who is pushing him, and Bill tells Jill to get off his back! The projection is complete, for it is now Jill who appears to hold his drive, and willy-nilly has to take on the role of pushing Bill to clean up. Bill feels, and will no doubt restate it in innumerable arguments in the future, that his wife is *pressuring* him.

As in this story, the shadow exists only in those parts of the explicate realm where there is a capacity for self-deception, at which we humans are expert. We disguise large parts of ourselves in a way that is detrimental to our coherence. The shadow cannot exist in the Field, which is whole and undivided and therefore unable to 'hide' any part of itself from itself. This is why becoming conscious of our shadow and taking our projections off other people is the most significant work we can do.

The shadow seems to be increasingly supplied these days, particularly as the virtues taught though religion are less and less important, and are reduced to a private issue. The grand and numinous aspects of soul may be pushed there, as may spirit and our karmic heritage. Even the archetypes, and even God Himself may play a shadow role. Here their authority is so great they have the power in the shadow to wreak great damage that, in the collective, could have cataclysmic consequences.

As God and Job both realized, ultimate power over our place and role in the cosmos resides in the collective unconscious. Man has already received so much knowledge that he can and is in the process of destroying his own home, this planet. Where the ordinary shadow expresses itself in negative outside judgments, the cosmic shadow expresses itself in the infinitely more terrifying dimensions of Armageddon, annihilation by pollution and global warming, and the omnipresent insecurity of suicidal terrorism. This is Hal Stone's personal Killer Critic gone cosmic.[315]

The solution lies in recognizing through our energetic reality that we are all one in the Field. The most direct way to access this oneness is through soul. Whether this is in meditation or therapy or sacred practices, it is through soul that we connect. Where all is interconnected there can be no shadow.

Fig. 39—The dark side of the moon.

8

Soul is Our Personal Aspect in the Field

In the day of my trouble I was not deceived.
My soul remembered God, and was delighted, and was exercised,
and my spirit swooned away.
—Psalm 76

There is no clear consensus on the nature of soul. There are as many views of soul as there are religions. In our therapy we have had to separate ourselves from all opinions no matter how ancient or venerable, and rely purely on the experiences of our clients from their investigations into their own souls. This has shown us that souls are the creative principle behind humanity, perhaps behind all living creatures. This would not surprise most of you. However, it may be surprising that soul has neither ethics nor desires. Souls just are, existing in the Field as the prototypes of humanity, but without our judgmental or emotional baggage.

Soul with a million definitions

Man has no body distinct from his Soul; for what we call Body is that portion of Soul discerned by the five senses.

—William Blake

"In all cultures and religions since the beginning of history" wrote Robert Johnson, "the idea of the soul has sprung up spontaneously. Humankind has always intuited the existence of an entity within that was invisible yet active."[316] Soul has been defined in so many ways it is hard to be convinced by any. The variety shows how everybody and every group interpret what they intuit in their own way. There is little harm in this unless opinions become fixed beliefs that are then used to restrict our own and other's experiences.

Established religions are obliged to produce a consensus for their members, and will naturally adjust their opinions to suit theological and political agendas. That is natural, but it inevitably distorts personal experiences from within the Field.

There are two basic approaches to soul, the Middle Eastern that includes Christian, Jewish, and Muslim, and the Asian that includes Buddhism, Zen, and Taoism. The first group believes that soul is an intrinsic part of each of us, and is gathered to God on death, and has just this one opportunity to get it right. This approach has a finality that is time-driven, eschatological, and remorseless.

The second approach is timeless and reiterative. It refers to the soul field of Brahma as the Atman that incarnates and then becomes clouded by identification with the form it inhabits, which is us, and thereby forgets its real nature. This identification creates the illusion of separation. Without transformation the soul keeps on returning again and again.

Within these two lies many variations that would be tedious to describe. Some place soul in the mind and feel it operates though the brain,[317] some limit it to the muscular system,[318] while others refer to multiple levels of souls.[319]

When human psychic systems are considered there are just as many differences. Sigmund Freud denied a spiritual soul, though used it as a metaphor for "that which is most valuable in man."[320] James Hillman, and his populist Thomas Moore, bring to soul the combined qualities of the magical child plus some inscrutable archetypes and the anima.[321] This suggests a *potpourri* of mysteries and uncertainties that makes sure we never get stuck in any set of beliefs, yet does not permit us to work with the qualities of any, which is in any case one of Hillman's aims.

Michael Murphy stated that soul intermingles with all consciousness, interacts with other entities in a way that "does not always depend upon sensory processes."[322] John Rowan defined soul as that which is multiple and symbolic, and that "We discover the soul level when we fully go into and accept our own imaginative qualities."[323] Hameed Ali wrote, "Soul is the locus of our own individual awareness."[324]

Carl Jung aligned soul with the anima and animus, and from this decided that men feel their soul is feminine, and that women may sense theirs as masculine — though in our experience we do not find this alignment particularly accurate. "Since the complex represented by the anima and animus best corresponds to what has been described as soul at all times and by all peoples, it is hardly surprising that they bring an uncommonly mystical atmosphere along with them as soon as one tries to examine their contents more closely."[325] Our clinical evidence indicates that Jung is correct in this, though not for the reasons he gives.

Mellen-Thomas Benedict described the actual experience of soul with that numinous excitement that is common to most direct insights. During his near-death experience he saw that "all the Higher Selves are connected as one being, all humans are connected as one being, we are actually different aspects of the same being. I saw this mandala of human souls. It was the most beautiful thing I have ever seen. I just went into it and it was overwhelming. It was like all the love you've ever wanted, and it was the kind of love that cures, heals, regenerates."[326]

The notion that is common to any direct experience of soul is of a beautiful and fulfilling presence. It is sensed as an energy that is separate to the egoic personality yet is in some way personalized, and that acts as a medium or gateway to more rarefied energetic states and fields. It is from here that Jung could write, "soul is the transcendent energy in man."[327]

Experiencing soul

The man who can discriminate between soul and spirit achieves supremacy over all conditions and becomes omniscient.

—Patanjali Sutra

At the Crucible Centre we have worked with many hundreds of clients since the late 1980s, been part of a small ongoing group of seekers for more than a decade, read widely, and talked both privately and publicly. We recognize that we too are explorers in this uncertain realm, so when a process works in therapy, in the sense that a client is cleared of a major trauma through soul-work, we have adopted the concepts that have come out of that process to refine our understanding of soul. Through feedback and by testing our understandings against the inner reality described by our clients, we have come to certain conclusions. These we will now share with you.

The 'we' in this story refers to my partner in life, Hilary James, and our partner in our therapeutic work, Marg Garvan. We each bring very different qualities to bear, and though each of us has our own strengths and limitations, we have found that in combination we are more than we are on our own. Though there is no simple way to adequately describe the intuition we bring to therapy, Hilary works primarily through her heart, Marg through her clairvoyance and I through understanding form.

This is not the place to describe how we facilitate clients to access soul, though four aspects could be discussed. Firstly, we as facilitators need to be in touch with our own souls and with as much of the Field as we can during the session, for this makes it easier for clients to be open to the same levels within themselves. Secondly, most clients need to have already cleared some of the more pressing personal material out of the way, and have had a glimpse into the spaciousness of the Field to be awake to their inner states and to be as self-aware as possible. Thirdly, we 'hold the space' energetically so that the clients feel secure and safe, while we tune into their process. Forming a field between us is common in therapy: the Jungians refer it is as the *Metvelt*. Lastly, we avoid in any way directing our client's process, so we may trust the truth of what is presented.

In process clients recall memories that are felt as real experiences in present time rather than thoughts. The recall is in the body, not in the mind. In this setting people can effortlessly regress to infancy and experience what it was like to be born. With support they can go further and feel what it was like in the womb and beyond that to the moment of conception. It is from regression into this space that much of our understanding of soul has come. It is a privilege to experience what other professionals tell us should have been forgotten. The experiences feel real, as real as any other intensely moving moment in life: and accepting such depths as true is the basis of psychotherapy.

We have concluded that the experiences are held holistically, not only in the brain, but also as 'memories' in the cells of the body and in the soul. The deeper the process goes the more the client is feeling the soul's own experience. It is through energetic regression that we have brought together the information in these chapters. Other researchers have come to similar conclusions over the past twenty-five years, mainly through hypnotherapy, like David Chamberlain, Michael Newton, and Jenny Wade, whose work we will discuss shortly.

I will refer to the soul-field as 'it' rather than she or he, just as we do with the body or the mind. Many writers prefer to personalize the soul as a reflection of its very *gemutlicht* nature. Using the impersonal pronoun is more appropriate for an element of pure energy, no matter how closely it sits within us. This in no way moderates our knowing that it is a part of us nor, as our connection with soul gets deeper, does this limit our coming to know that soul is such an intrinsic locus of consciousness that no distinction will be felt between us.

The following descriptions of soul stem from these direct experiences, not from any prior religious theory or dogma. But it was not until I grew to understand the nature of the Great Field that we were able to dovetail these experiences into a more general theory. Jung was, I believe, incorrect in merging the concept of the soul of religious language with that of the anima and animus, and in claiming that these archetypes "act like the soul."[328] We find that the therapeutic methods used to work effectively with archetypes such as the anima are completely different to the methods required by the soul. When the therapy requires a different approach we feel confident in concluding that the nature of each energy would be significantly different.

Our conclusion is that *Soul is a personalized aspect of the Field, an individual unit of consciousness with a more permanent existence than our bodies.* Soul lies further into the implicate order than the ego. It connects Field and matter more readily. It is free-flowing, open to influence and induction, yet coherently itself. It does not fade away nor come and go like a cloud, nor vicariously alter its nature. Like ego, each soul is an autonomous entity, uniquely different, yet without any substance in the material sense.

Soul is that transpersonal energetic form that can be sensed within, that has a voice that can clearly articulate and has qualities that feel quite different from those of the ego. It influences matter, records experiences, and responds to our ideas and will, yet it cannot drive a bus nor give birth. Thomas Moore writes that, "Fulfilling work, rewarding relationships, personal power, and relief from symptoms are all gifts of the soul. They are particularly elusive in our time because we don't believe in the soul and therefore give it no place in our hierarchy of values."[329] Without connection to soul we are dry and jaded, and we find ourselves pursuing material possessions and excitement to fill the emptiness.

Soul is not the same as spirit.[330] This is a very important distinction that should be clear from the beginning. I use the word 'spirit' for certain higher levels of the Field with less feeling for humans and less consciousness of what makes us human. Though I am aware of the inadequacy of a language based on things and actions to describe something that possesses neither, this description in the box (with some help from Hillman[331] and Moore[332]) may describe the difference.

"You will know your soul by a special taste or flavor, like a sweetness, a delicacy, or fullness. The soul will saturate you with an uplifting Beingness. Soul removes a certain dryness in people, and a thinness. It is like having an inner companion that is nothing like the child. It has a certain presence and density, as if all the inner crevices have been filled. We have no senses with which to sense soul, yet we know — and humans have always known — that soul is as real as anything we can put a sense to. Any feeling that we are being guided by deep inner truths probably involves soul. When we can adore our partner while leaving him totally independent, we may have reconnected with soul."[333]

A poetic discourse on soul and spirit.

Soul is not all light and fancy goodness. Soul is a powerful force, an archetypic presence that, when fully aroused, is far more willful and powerful than us. She carries the mystic darkness and the unmentionable as well as the bountiful and the warmth. She is not always what we would like, but offers us the richest and sweetest life if we will take the risk with both hands and all toes.

Soul draws us uncannily inward to the dark of the uncut forest and the deeps below the waves. She is the soul of the water without which we are dry, the green of trees and shrubs without which we are blighted, the black of the night without which we become lazy and smug. An intimate relationship with soul will transform both of you, for soul is also open to change, and a higher purpose in life comes when we dedicate our whole being and total energy to supporting that transformation.

She is the lady of the beasts riding our passions, she is our father's daughter, and our sister and our lovers. She is the worrisome succubus drawing off life's juices and the Sophia of Wisdom, she is the cold wraith in the mist and the hallowed nurse, the Cinderella nymphet and the harpy temptress, the bearer of fate, the Persephone of destruction and the Maria of Compassion. She is the darkness of our dreams, the intimacy of love and death and the black night.

By comparison the world of spirit is different indeed. Its images blaze with light, there is fire, wind, and generation. Spirit is fast, it quickens all that it touches. Its direction is vertical and ascending. It is arrow-straight, knife-sharp, powder-dry, and masculine, the active principle in making form, order, and clear distinctions. It exemplifies the higher and more abstract disciplines, the intellectual mind, refinement, and purification. It is purpose incarnate, pure, and implacable. Spirit does not desire relationship, does not long for contact, is not intrinsically sensitive to our humanity. Hence, merging with spirit carries the present danger of inflation and being carried remorselessly beyond our genetic condition.

But soul moves in circular ways where retreats are as important as advances. She prefers labyrinths and dark corners. Soul involves us in the flow. She is vulnerable and suffers, passive and remembers.

She is water to the spirit's fire, like a mermaid who beckons the hero into the depths of her passions to extinguish certainty. Soul is imagination, a cavernous treasury, a sepulcher of manna. Whereas spirit chooses the higher path and seeks to make all One, soul prefers uncertainty and curiosity. She is love and the intimacy of sharing. She is a slate waiting to be inscribed.

Where spirit says "this and not that," soul whispers "this too has a place, may have significance, and may have its own myth." We can be taken over by spirit, and if soul is not present, as the lubricant, spirit may be impelled to limit and discipline soul, to empty her imagination and dry her intimacy. On its own, spirit will feel that soul is mere fantasy. We need both to receive the fullest fragrance within — for soul is liquid like the fish while spirit is as focused as fire of the sun.

But in fact, it is only through the connection of soul that we may be with spirit and remain human — otherwise we too are taken over. Soul is our guarantee of ordinariness and humility amidst the temptation of inflation and certitude. It is through soul that we may actively participate in the daily creative unfolding of our universe — because this is the realm where we cannot know, where certainty is impossible and the future sublimely mysterious.

We, in our society, are on a precipice right now. We are in the process of losing the place of soul in our lives. Our material society has reduced the trinity of body, soul, and spirit that has lived in our culture for tens of thousands of years, into a duality — the duality of matter and, often as an afterthought, spirit. Our materialism recognizes only that which we can sense.

This prospect is more disastrous than many think. What we lose with soul is a world of imagination and passion, of fantasy and inner reflection, that is not physical or material, nor is it abstractly spiritual — yet is bonded to both. To sustain hope, no matter how hard the times nor how painful our circumstances, we need to know that soul holds a winning card of crucial importance: Soul guarantees to lie in wait, dormant yet expectant, until our longing emerges, and then our ache for its fullness and sweetness, its companionship and strangeness will inevitably draw soul to us. With soul we are never on our own. Without her we are lost in our own emptiness.

The intense sense of beauty that we feel empathetically when in immediate connection with a soul, as we do in therapy, was described by Benedict: "I saw how beautiful we all are in our essence. We are the most beautiful creations. The human soul, the matrix we all make together is absolutely fantastic, elegant, exotic, everything. I just cannot say enough about how it changed my opinion of human beings in that instant. At any level, high or low, in whatever shape you are in, you are the most beautiful creation."[334]

The world of souls is described in many ways. The most common feeling we have when we touch that realm is numinous, a term loved by Carl Jung to describe that ineffable feeling of grace and gratitude that accompanies any peak experience, any profound meeting with the divine. Michael Newton concluded from his many subjects that: "The more distant concentrations [of souls] have been pictured as 'islands of misty veils'…[with] a continuous feeling of powerful mental force directing everything in uncanny harmony, a place of pure thought."[335] He described these veils as "loosely wound arms of a mighty galactic cloud" that, from their home in the "unified celestial field," peel off as individual souls to enter our sphere.

Some have argued that only humans can have an individual soul, while others have wanted our closest animal friends like dogs and cats to also have souls, though at a different level to ours. Some believe that animals that operate in groups could not have individual souls, but just one group soul. Yet whenever one member of a species that shares a strong common field is separated from its flock, as in a cage, a fish tank or a zoo, they do not fade away, as they would if they relied on only one common field that was diminished or even broken by separation. Every living thing has its own field of energy that creates and sustains its form.

Flocks of birds are not unlike gangs of humans. As we have discussed before, when a large number of fields collect in one place the coherence of the group raises the individuals to another level. Flocks of geese can fly much farther than will one goose on its own, and a mass of people will act with less individual conscience than would its members. The obvious example is a rampaging mob, but it applies equally to ecstatic religious practices.

For some animals, such as dogs, their personal fields are extremely adaptable and merge with those of humans in a way that creates real partnerships. Domesticated animals such as cows and cockatoos will resonate with us in a different way to cattle roaming on the prairie or flocks of birds screeching in a tree, and the field of rocks and pebbles may be even simpler.[336] All aspects of creation have fields, and all are to their own degree connected to the Field.

Though this is reaching into realms beyond anything we have studied in therapy, I think it would follow from the principle that every 'thing' in the explicate realm emerges out of its own field, that the difference between the fields of a pebble and that of a person lies not in whether they have a field, but in their level of consciousness. I would not argue that the pebble has no level of consciousness at all, that is yet to be established. But I would argue that the fields of organisms are more complex than rocks, or even crystals, and that the quality of consciousness that would produce self-awareness would seem to be available only to higher organisms. Grand collections of pebbles, like the earth itself, have a level of consciousness that is self-sustaining and adaptable, which James Lovelock called Gaia.[337]

Soul in our energy system

It is through the realm of the soul that we find the heavens that govern the skies of the world.

—Jalal-ud-Din Rumi in the *Mathnawi*[338]

I would liken the nature of soul to that of a dolphin that has a well-developed cortical structure and enormous empathy and compassion, but no hands. The key difference between man and the dolphin is that it cannot physically alter its environment nor change its appearance. A dolphin is consciousness without the potential to manipulate. Lacking that potential, the dolphin can only play within its medium, the ocean. When we meet they appear to smile at us, and we feel their love and joy. Here are intelligent beings that don't have *to do anything*, and consequently when we approach them with the innocence of a child, they join with us and we play.

All the great company of souls would seem to be, on the etheric plane, like shoals of dolphin mingling and mixing and honking and touching in the timeless landscape of the Field in which all is in compassionate empathy. Dolphins do not act like a swarm with a purely common mode of being and acting. Even in large pods moving in one direction they are no less individuals than a crowd of humans on a bus. Like dolphins, souls have individual consciousness. It is through the consciousness we share that relationship between us and dolphins, we and our souls is possible.

We can get a sense soul within us when we recharacterize our own feelings as vibrating fields rather than emotions. One of my first learnings about this was when I was given three sheets of paper with outlines of the human body, and asked to use color to show how the body felt on one sheet, how my emotions felt on another and then my energy system on a third. The colors in the first two drawings were scattered and confused. My body was full of aches and pains and my emotions were all over the place. Yet in the third drawing the colors and shapes showing my vibrational system were clear and straightforward. Though I was feeling neither happy nor confident at that time, my deeper energetic nature was completely in tune. After that I began to pay more attention to the sensations under the emotional turmoil on the surface.

In our emotion-based language we may describe an emotion as 'aggressiveness,' 'abandonment,' 'jealousy,' etc. These are all energetic states that derive their particular coloring from our beliefs about how things ought to be. When we separate from the beliefs and view ourselves energetically, aggression may appear as an up-and-out explosion, abandonment as a compressed inturning or turning away, and jealousy may be a combination of both. By observing them as vibrations we take the traumatic edge off the emotion.

The first time we do this, it is a remarkable experience to observe how the complexities that the mind and emotions bring to a situation lessen. The discriminating mind moves back, or even disappears, and we may realize that at our deepest level our state is pure attentiveness, or what meditators call mindfulness.

Below thoughts and emotions lie subtle flows of energies that are constantly changing. I would sense, for example, that when I was drawn positively toward someone there was an opening sensation within me that seemed to peel me apart as if I were singing, accompanied by a soft radiance. At the same time there was a grounding feeling, a descent of energy that was my wariness establishing a footing. These two systems were quite separate within but present to each other.

I might experience caution taking over at times, sometimes quite brutally when I perceive a threat, and as it did the radiance would close, but more slowly. One was instantaneous, the other gradual. In human terminology I would call this joy and love mixed with reluctance and uncertainty. But sensed exclusively through movements of energy, the two systems represented a tendency in me, a particular and unique combination that was one of the essential components of who I am.

This is the level at which I relate to soul. The sensation of soul is purely energetic. When we are in contact with one another there does not seem to be any distinction between my personal energetic body and that of my soul. It is like smoke meeting smoke without any limiting conditions. Both feel like pure consciousness.

It is through soul that we can rekindle our connection to the divine. Soul is the part of us that loves beauty, music and nature and, as Hillman suggested, the soul is the source of our creativity.[339] Our hearts sing at the joy of knowing that we are sacred beings. This gives us a sense of pure love, confirming Frances Vaughan's comment that love is the awakener of the soul.[340] It would then be true to say that each of us can, with consciousness, recognize our origin in the 'source.' This is the profoundly moving and transforming experience that Buddhists call 'seeing our original face.'[341]

When the soul is awakened people see their inner core. It is the moment every transpersonal therapist waits for. It is the moment when clients suddenly recognize their divinity. My partner Marg Garvan wrote: "Soul energy is contagious, it fills the whole room and because we are all one the therapist can't help but be part of the transformation."[342]

However, it will become apparent as we proceed that the incarnate soul need not follow our system of virtues, though the beauty it inducts suggests it could. We feel exhilarated and (this is the only word for it) blessed in the presence of soul, but it seems that we sense this from being immersed in a higher level of the Field rather than the particular energetic constellation in each soul.

9

THE SOUL INCARNATES

The ultimate state is soundless, touchless, formless, imperishable; also tasteless, constant, odorless, without beginning, without end, stable — by discerning That, one is liberated from the mouth of Death.
— Katha Upanishad

This ancient quotation refers unambiguously to the Great Field. In much of the literature it has been called the Void because we experience it as being incredibly spacious while being empty of thoughts or things.[343] We sense there is nothing anywhere, yet at the same time we also sense there is no thing missing. This haunting paradox is the essence of our experience of the Void that is utterly still yet includes all existence. As the word Void does describe our sense perceptions of what it is like to connect to the Field, I will use the term interchangeably with Field when discussing the sensation that mystics call *spacious emptiness*.

When we meet this state of nothingness we actually cease to think or to experience in any emotive way. There is an ineffable sense of no-thing. No-thingness is the ground of everything, the cradle of all being, the ultimate source of existence. It is the ground within which fields are present, rather than being the fields themselves. It is a still space without movement or information. It is matter-less. In the East this state may be called 'the nature of mind.'

From here we recognize that the ultimate nature of reality is the Void. Nothing 'happens' in this space because there is only flow. Personal will cannot create any disturbance in the Field, as there is nothing that is not in alignment with the flow. The Void transcends the usual categories of time and space. As David Bohm noted, within it there are no "dichotomies and polarities, such as light and dark, good and evil, stability and motion, microcosm and macrocosm, agony and ecstasy, form and emptiness" because no thing (no condensation into form) remains present for more than a micro-second, even existence itself.[344]

When during therapy clients re-experience their time in the womb, the sensation has the same timelessness and spacelessness that we find in deep meditation and many religious practices. These are the qualities of the Field that are present in our creation. From the moment of conception we take shape within the Void. There is no sense of separation as the fetus is one with the Field, and therefore with mother and with soul. Grof has described this time as one of cosmic engulfment.[345]

The whole of our evolutionary past from sea creature to human being flows through us as we are being created in the womb. This includes our basic drives, our animal needs and survival instincts. In addition the fetus grows within the behavioral fields of the parents, and their parents before them. To a lesser extent we include the fields of all related families back to our simian ancestors and all tribal and group consciousnesses. Our essential nature is formed there, with its elemental balance of will and joy, of mind and curiosity and, most powerfully of all, the form of the soul, its particular collation of qualities and characteristics.

The interaction of all these fields turns the womb into a furnace of transformation. The old expression of a pregnant woman having 'something in the oven' is very true. The holographic simultaneity of the Field presents our entire human potential to the growing consciousness of the infant in such an integrated way that every characteristic that lodges there plays in a symphony of incredible diversity in which nothing need be discordant.

We are created in the whisper of the soul

The soul is our personal inner field of experience, the matrix where all inner events and processes happen.

—Hameed Ali

The nature of our lives reflects that of our soul. As we manifest the changes in our lives we are the vehicles for manifesting soul's nature on this plane. As soul existed before us and was present while we were being formed from the moment of conception, soul's qualities become ours. The vibrations of each person's soul help create the pattern of that person's life. John Nelson wrote, "As a human sperm penetrates an ovum a soft whisper gently permeates the background hum that fills the universe. A new being is forming within its essence…acting as a vortex of spirit, imparting the unique attributes that comprise the human personality."[346]

Soul is one of the primary manifesting agents in our creation along with genes and our parents' own energies and emotions. In the womb, soul's energy system is folding around us transferring its personal mix of characteristics and capacities to the fetus.[347] That is when our evolving cells are most sensitive and delicate and malleable. The larger part of our personality comes from the individuality of our particular soul.

Our soul work has shown that we are not only connected with all fields all the time, but that through the vibrations of our fields we are co-creators of our birth and our lives. However we wish to understand the nature of our existence, and the 'reasons' for our dramas and suffering, there is only one salient and overwhelming fact: soul with a little help from parents and caregivers set up the dance of this life, the way we reacted created personality, and after that it is up to us. At no point are humans victims, and we can change our present and our karmic future the moment we accept that, soul will change with us.

Our clients have experienced their souls participating in the moment of conception. During lovemaking the soul may be just outside looking in, or more intimately traveling with the sperm. The act of conception is a very sensuous moment, accompanied by vibrations of both softness and firmness, of fluidity and excitement. George reported, "I was my soul watching out for the moment of conception. There were no emotions in this space. I was just deeply interested. And on later reflection I realized that I knew I was part of the Whole, though with energetically a slight sense of direction, with the bulk of the Whole being somewhat behind my center of attention."

Another client wrote, "I was very aware that feelings came in as the cells became more complex. I saw that feelings were created within the brain stem and spinal cord and morphed in gradually around the end of the first trimester. I knew them as my animal inheritance when life was driven by hunger and fear. They added great richness to the energetic tendencies that I live with." Another reported that the most prominent energy in their soul was like a thrusting forward, with "no sense of being in the midst of the Whole. This is affecting the entire emotional side of my life, for I have felt separated from other people. It has created the trail of abandonments that have dogged my life with a bottomless longing for something outside of me: But also drive, purpose... and wariness."

The recurring feeling of abandonment would seem to have originated in the energetic form of the soul. There is no emotion in the energy, just a movement. Yet we instill that movement with feeling content, and thus turn it into an issue or a trauma. One client reported, "I traveled back into the womb. It felt very still and enfolded. Then there was a flip, and I was just outside, very aware of the bigness of the penis moving within the softness of the vagina. I was my soul watching out for the moment of conception. There were no emotions in this space. I did not experience the conception, but only a very clear movement out of the Field into the cell. It felt like being squeezed through a narrow opening into a new state of being, like a jelly of toothpaste. My total attention was on the way forward. This has affected my entire life attitude — I am not with the Field, in its completeness, but separated. I have therefore had a life of separation that is full of longing to be in the midst of Spirit that I suspect exists but do not experience, save in tiny flashes."

In this way soul continues throughout life to reinforce the personality it has helped to create. As long as we remain unconscious of our connection with soul, and make no effort to alter any of its vibrations, this influence remains in our basic makeup, but unrecognized. However, energy is no one-way street. Our actions and decisions mingle with those of soul and alter it.

A woman had over the years terminated six pregnancies. Her soul and her aura were cluttered with the impressions of every fetus she had conceived. Her ability to nourish herself was diminished by the energy of those other souls she had been unable to nurture to birth. It was not that she was actually carrying these six other souls, but that her soul had taken on her anguish at what she had done plus the unfinished grief. This is an immeasurably greater issue than most of us think. Any termination, no matter how justified, leaves a residue of sorrow that is carried in the soul. Healing lies in the recognition of both the grief and our need for forgiveness. Without it, soul serves these conflicting energies back to us, and so maintains the situation.

We reflect what soul becomes to the same extent that soul becomes what we are — we continue to mutually modify each other. In time, this mixture of vibrations moves into the next incarnation, and thus is the nature of our lives that is carried into the Field and returned, again and again.

Is the reverse possible, that we create our own souls? Is the soul as an energetic form created out of our genes and parental energies while in the womb, so that our soul-form-in-the-Field is man-made and naturally adopts its energetic system from ours? This is like applying Carter's anthropic principle to soul (see page 160, "Can the future determine the past?"). From the level of consciousness that soul displays during the inter-uterine stage of life, I would say unambiguously that the radiant community of soul-fields is primary. It is right order to place soul first. There is no natural truth in placing the less conscious that partakes less completely in the Field in front of or 'above' soul that is already one with the Field.

The soul is present in the womb

Everything you see has its roots in the unseen world.

The forms may change, yet the essence remains the same.

Every wonderful sight will vanish, every sweet word will fade,

But do not be disheartened,

The source they come from is eternal.

—Jalal-ud-Din Rumi

The soul is nearly always present with the fetus in the womb. Soul may or may not be inside the womb itself, though it tends to remain fairly close to the mother. About one-fifth move into the womb at conception, about the same hover nearby until the birth, and the remainder at times in between. It would follow that the legal arguments that use the presence of soul to determine when a fetus should be aborted are meaningless. The soul is always present.

In one example, a young woman in her twenties remembered under hypnosis seeing her mother sitting on the lounge wearing a dress. She described it in great detail. There was a print on the wall and a woven rug. The radio was playing. Her mother confirmed every detail of the memory. Under hypnosis the mother pointed out this could only have happened when the daughter was six months in the womb. At that time of gestation the fetus can neither see nor distinguish colors, she could not hear nor in any way make sense of what was going on, yet the memory was there, clear for both of them, and verified by third parties.[348]

The observer may be outside the person, as in many near-death experiences. John Lilly wrote that during a particularly hard birth he "split off [and] moved out briefly and watched from the outside for several hours until the head broke through, the baby came out, and he moved back into the baby's body."[349] Chamberlain reports a very young child commenting, "I keep looking through the nursery window. It's weird. I can't be on both sides of the window, can I? But I'm looking at the baby; it's me."[350] The fact that the observer is away from the body is shown from the information they remember, for it could not have been sensed by the body because it happened somewhere else, in another room or even another country.[351] This very clearly shows that memory is resident not only in the body, but has other locations. It may even be that memory is just where our personal energetic key fits into the information larder that is the Field.

A young child remembered an event that had been kept a secret from the parents. Cathy was an assistant midwife, and when she was left with the newborn baby she stilled its crying by offering her own breast until she slept, but told nobody as she felt guilty about being the first to nurse the child. Four years later Cathy asked the child if she remembered being born. "The girl not only proceeded to give an accurate account of who was present and their roles during labor and delivery but, apparently sensitive to Cathy's unspoken guilt, leaned up close and whispered in a confidential tone, 'You

held me and gave me titty when I cried and Mommy wasn't there.'"
At less than an hour old she was aware and remembered, and in
addition picked up Cathy's feelings.[352] Who could the rememberer
be but soul?

Jenny Wade describes how children were regressed to recall
their time either *in utero* or experiences at the time of their birth,
using acupressure, hypnosis, and breathwork. Clients were able to
recall such details as the moment of conception, what their mothers
were wearing, what was said and what their birth was like. "Often
accounts contain accurate reports of complex impressions, such
as abstruse medical conditions of procedures few laypeople would
know about."[353] Wade then interviewed or regressed the mothers,
contacted relatives and obstetricians, and obtained medical records
to test the validity of the information.

She has tried to relate these events to possible real memories
from the fetus, and recognized this is improbable. "Aural memories
are not possible until mid-term…yet subjects can repeat conversa-
tions."[354] She went on to ask whether sounds that would be meaningless to the fetus could be retained in memory and later decoded
into language by a more mature subject under hypnosis? That idea
is untenable as the neurons in the brain that hold memory are not
formed early enough to fill this role. Her explanation was for the
existence of a "materially transcendent awareness," another name
for what we would call soul.[355]

Wade included research by Helen Wambach who regressed
more than 750 people and had them describe their experiences of
fetal life. This showed "two intermittent streams of awareness, one
assuming a vantage point within the uterus, the other one located
outside the baby's body, and apparently outside the mother's body
as well."[356]

Some memories come from long before there was any significant brain development, and in the following case even before the
actual conception. "Ingrid remembered her mother and father making love on a couch before they were married. The doorbell rang to
announce that grandmother and aunt had come back from shopping
when they weren't supposed to. Ingrid says, 'Mother was beside

herself. She knew she got pregnant. She was ashamed. She didn't want to do it in the first place.'"[357]

The connection of soul to the Field is apparent when David Chamberlain's subjects report a sense of a timeless present. Even where the situation is stressful their reports are devoid of emotion when observing from outside the body, but sometimes a little emotional when observing from inside. Add to this that the observer is aware of other's thoughts and feelings without having to hear anything and we know we are dealing with an observing medium that can connect with the vibrations of others.[358]

Though many people will tell you that their soul does not want to be here, and though Wade reports an occasional feeling that life is a rather unpleasant thing to go through, we find in therapy that there was no obligation to incarnate. Even in extreme cases, we have never found souls being happy at attempts to abort them. Being threatened with termination nearly always leaves a negative impression in the field. If souls had an opinion about liking or disliking incarnation, we surely would have sensed that when clearing these cases.

One of Chamberlain's clients remembered being a very tiny fetus, "just a little blob," when she was attacked by a chemical. She described it as having "a strong harsh smell, almost a disinfectant smell, like ammonia, strong, vile." She wanted passionately to live and reacted to the invasion with, "I was determined, I was a fighter even then."[359]

I have my own experience of a conversation between my mother and my granny, who was appalled that my mom had jumped headlong into marriage with an artist, and a broke artist at that, rather than arranging a more 'suitable' match to a rich stockbroker. Granny urged my mother to abort me. I must have been three months at the most. The memory of their voices is absolutely clear. The impact was so shocking that when I remembered it I cried and shivered and curled up on somebody's lap and wanted to stay there for half the day.

Twins are often studied for the clarity they shed on issues. Identical twins have so many behavioral similarities that researchers are fascinated by the questions raised, particularly compared to nonidentical twins who have no more ways in common than the rest of us. One pair who had been separated at birth and met only in later adulthood showed that without any intervening contact they shared the same preferences for stock car racing, carpentry, and vacationing on the same beach in Florida. The both disliked baseball, named their dogs Troy, and not only had wives named Betty but each had earlier divorced women named Linda. Their firstborns had been given the same name.[360]

Genetic determination cannot provide a sufficient explanation for such bizarre 'coincidences.' Morphic fields and extrasensory perception are not enough either. Our research shows that it is the soul that provides the essential personal characteristics that are integrated into the fetus from the moment of conception.[361] The presence of different souls during parturition may explain why children from the same womb are so different.

Very close connections are made between the souls of twins. There is a widely disseminated photo called the "Rescuing Hug."[362] The Massachusetts hospital staff felt that one twin would die. Nurse Gayle Kasparian flouted orders and placed both babies into the same incubator. Instantly, the two nestled together, the stronger one placing her arm across the shoulder of the other, who calmed down and changed her breathing to her sister's pace and so survived.

Fig. 40—The Rescuing Hug.

Simply experiencing touch and sharing energies made her stronger. "It was so instantaneous," Kasparian said. "What happened to that baby was miraculous. Nothing else had worked."

This closeness is even deeper among identical twins. They come from the implantation of one sperm into one ovum. The division into two blastocysts from the one source creates cells that are very different to two cells coming from separate impregnations. They create two people that have many shared characteristics that cannot come from nurture that we surmise there would have been a single soul at conception that divided in two as the cells themselves split to form two people. It suggests that the instant of insemination is when the soul attaches to the embryo, and that among identical twins the personal soul-qualities destined for one fetus were shared between two.[363]

Sometimes identical twins develop opposite qualities, even to the point of deeply disliking one another. We have not had the opportunity of working with such a pair, but have met them. Logic persuades me that the split in the soul may create a variety of vibrations. Some of these would be coherent so that the two would remain synchronized and their lives would be in tune with each other. But some would react against each other, perhaps from the shock of splitting, and this would set up a pattern of vibrations that would, over time, develop antagonistically. However, though this is only a guess at this stage, the possibility emphasizes that the soul energy is not a fixed form, but is changeable and malleable.

Soul is affected by death in the womb

When the soul comes to the nameless place, she takes her rest. There, where all things have been God, in God she rest.

—Meister Eckhart

One example of the changeability of soul lies in what has come to be called the Vanishing Twin Syndrome.[364] This is when a twin dies in the womb. The outcome can affect the whole of life without giving any clue to the cause of the feelings that come from the loss. The client in this sandplay has given up on life as pretty worthless. She works steadily yet without much sense of achievement, as if there was an incommunicable abandonment. She combines this with a constant and eager search for a man, but cannot form intimate or lasting bonds. After repeated attempts she drifted into deeper lassitude.

Fig. 41 — Vanishing twin sandplay.

At times the four corners of the tray have specific meanings. The top left may occasionally refer to a spiritual issue while the bottom right may refer to the material present.[365] She created an axis between these two with an almond-shaped mandorla marked in the sand — an ancient spiritual symbol for higher unity. She drew a circle in the center.

The pieces, in order of placement, are a glass ball enclosing a skull on the axis of the mandorla closest to the spiritual quadrant; a fossil near-right, and between them clasped hands. A little goanna was placed on the fossil, which she described as "soft and uncertain, longing." The cross points to the skull and outside the mandorla a magic carpet and didgeridoo player.

In the session she gradually regressed into being very young, and the discoveries that were stimulated by the sandplay surprised her. She remembered that when she was about three she had been told she had been a twin, but that the other had died well before her birth. She knew this had been a boy.

She then became very emotional as she identified with the goanna and the fossil, helplessly holding on to the departed brother and feeling as dead as the fossil without him. Her inner 'center' lay in the white hands, clasping onto the male who had abandoned her. It was perceived as a frightening emptiness, not as the 'fertile void.'[366]

This was a fetal memory of a broken connection between two souls while in the womb.

Over the past fifteen years we have found that the impact of the 'disappearance' of a prenatal twin is profound, and can affect all of life. The syndrome can create some of the most powerful forces within a psyche, and has an ongoing impact on later life.[367] Besides the psychological trauma, there are often physical consequences from the toxins and poisoning of the mother's body that affects both the mother and the fetus. There is also the profound question of where do the memories of someone's inter-uterine relationship with their twin reside?[368]

A client lived her life with the feeling that she was outside herself, experiencing events as if she was not inside her body, but outside. She had little connection with feelings, and her greatest joy was in collecting and assembling things, like picking up shells to string them into beads. Her twin had died early and she felt she was chasing him here, there, and everywhere. It felt like life was a broken string of beads, and that she was endlessly on the hunt to pick up the lost parts of herself.

Sibling death in the womb has been variously estimated as affecting between 15 and 35 percent of all conceptions.[369] We have now worked with many dozens of clients who have presented such a history, and consider the proportion closer to one-in-three. It is nearly always the boy twin that dies and the female who survives, reflecting lots of evidence that males are the weaker sex in their early years.

Our clinical experience suggests that resolves may be formed at or just before the twin's death, and become locked into the body and psyche of the remaining fetus. In an adult we would call these resolves decisions, and we find it more effective to work with them as if they were the outcome of conscious choice. They present as energetic attitudes that have become ingrained during the remainder of their time in the womb. The impact on later life made by the 'decisions' is so profound that the whole tenor of personality may be affected.

But were they made by the fetus? When death occurs in the early months the fetus has not developed the capacity to hear or see, let alone sense or remember experiences beyond the placenta. Yet the memories are precise, and clearly spelled out. It can only be the soul who remembers. Where there are twins in the womb their souls form a relationship that seems to begin from the moment of conception, if not before. Traumas follow from the twin vanishing, or when a twin is stillborn, and lie more between the two souls than in the psyche of the human. In some cases the surviving soul will 'hold on' to the one that would have disappeared, actually attaching an impression of its energy to the life of the fetus that lives.

The consequences manifest as an unfulfillment and longing in the surviving twin, without any sense of where these feelings come from. One person dreaded she may have taken a larger share of nutrients so her twin starved, and compensated by overeating and becoming a very large woman. Another felt the pain of the loss intensely in her heart, felt that if she had loved more her companion would not have died, and closed down her own heart. The outcome through life was to be constantly on a spiritual search without being able to share her love with herself, while feeling unworthy and self-critical.

These issues are almost intractable under normal therapy — the origin is so hidden that it hardly matters how long the counseling would be, it is unlikely to be uncovered. As the 'event' took place during the baby's creation, the impact is totally imbued into the cellular structure of the bones and muscles. Once understood consciously the disturbance can dissipate slowly with self-awareness and vigilance.

One client wrote:

> After a series of sandplays I realized one of the reasons I was scared of the dark was that when my male twin died I was left in the dark feeling alone and abandoned. I had always felt an eerie feeling behind me especially in the dark like someone was there, watching me. Later on, I discovered that when my twin died his sac collapsed onto my back where it stuck until it was absorbed into the placenta. My sadness at losing him turned to horror as his remains clung to my back. This created my fear of what was behind me: It was in fact my beloved, my lost twin.

In this example both identical male twins survived. The one who was our client I will call George, the other Sam. George was constantly out of step with himself, as if he was being run by two fundamental drives that cancelled each other out. One drive was the romantic dreamer, the other the practical fixer. These two qualities could have worked together, but in his case the dreamer would screw up the practical, while the practical would undermine every dream.

It turned out that the two souls had made an 'arrangement' in the womb so that Sam would stay and not depart. At conception George's soul was the dreaming soul, Sam's the practical. George offered to do everything for Sam to keep him around. The outcome in later life was that Sam would step back to let George attempt the practical things and then feel annoyed when he did, while George felt impelled to solve problems when his nature was urging him to just relax and fantasize. Both boys were filled with a resentment that they could not define. After the process George found that these two sides of his 'soul-nature' worked in greater harmony, without the uncomfortableness that had lain between them, and gradually his life changed in tune with that.

The very night after the process Sam, who had not been in contact for the past six years, telephoned George from the United States. He just had to make contact through the subtle telephone of the Field.

If any of this seems far-fetched, consider that George had two women in his life. The first was a practical down-to-earth person, while the second was dreamy and impractical. The first longed to help people while the second needed to be helped. Are these not core aspects of the two souls that were so confounded in the womb?

The manner of our birth changes soul

We need to recognize we are in prison, if we are to use what is available to escape.

—Georges Gurdjieff

The birth adds further issues to those of soul, as does any powerful external action.[370] Much has been written on this as its importance is gradually being recognized, especially at a time when a large number of children are being born by cesarean surgery.[371] It will be interesting to follow the next generation of young people born this way, for one of the imprints from early birth through surgery is to remove a sense that life needs to be worked for or that the mystic oneness experienced in the womb need ever evaporate — a sense that receives a rude jolt when faced with the maelstrom of the ambitious world we live in.

And there are further themes around the manner of presentation, whether the baby was strangled by its own umbilical chord, was it slapped on arrival, and so on. The issues are extremely complex, but of the greatest importance in affecting the soul-essence of the child. Imprinting from this time is forever.

Sue had a twin called Sally. She had become a therapist had undertaken considerable personal development. She had gone out of her way to investigate whom she was and how people 'worked.' Sally, in contrast, was in the army and was quite uninterested in any self-questioning. The two were like chalk and cheese.

In therapy Sue had reconnected with her time in the womb and believed that she had pushed Sally out of the way so she could be the firstborn. Though this seemed inconsistent with the receptive nature that had made her an effective therapist, she had come to believe it. The growing guilt had become a dominant influence in her life. It turned out that the belief was wrong, but in a most surprising way. She had been working on an irrelevant issue for a long time, which had not been to her benefit.

In a rebirth process as she was emerging from a 'womb' that had been carefully made from pillows, I made the 'mistake' of calling her Sally rather than Sue. At that moment of heightened awareness she suddenly realized that she was not the first to be born, but that it had been Sally who was first and that she had, by error, been given the name her mother had decided to give the first. Where in fact she should have had the name of Sally, she became Sue and thereafter the family had saddled her with their belief that she had been first. It was a family misconception, rather than a mistake made in the hospital, but had huge consequences.

The session changed her relationship with her twin. It also removed her block to writing essays. Before that session Sue's writing had been labored and confused. No matter how hard she tried, language and thoughts struggled out in knots as if the confused order in the naming at birth was being reflected in the ordering of her adult ideas and grammar. From the moment of this realization she wrote clearly argued and substantive essays, in perfect grammatical English.

Here is an event of the utmost importance for life that occurred at the moment of birth, when mother and nurse attached the wrong label onto Sue's wrist. This, and others like it, shows that we receive a high impact from the events during and just after birth.[372] Until I understood this I had always wondered why astrology chose the very minute of the birth, and no other, for their calculations. You would think that the moment of conception or of soul-connection would be the most important, but it is the second of the birth that matters, the child's emergence into the world.

Based on LSD experiments made in the 1950s, Stanislav Grof argued that the time in the womb is usually one of cosmic oneness most like our dreams of paradise, but that in the process of birth the baby is suddenly threatened in the most dramatic way.[373] Enormous inter-uterine pressures are suddenly applied to the unsuspecting fetus, while the road of escape may be blocked for hours or even days. He showed that this leads to the creation of powerful psychic structures that can have a profound influence on our views of the world.

For example, too much pressure may lead to the belief that we have to push to succeed, or that we have to surrender to events in case the outer pressure gets too much. A long hard birth that Grof called a 'no-exit' birth, may imprint the belief that it does not matter how much we try, we can't by the nature of things succeed. A cesarean that brings the child out before its time without having to make any effort can create the belief either that no effort is needed to achieve a goal, or that if an effort is made someone else will screw it up. Inducted and forceps deliveries often leave the child confused, not knowing when or how they should act.[374]

These early events usually come as rude shocks, in complete contrast to the easy wonder of their nurturing and companionship in the womb.

The waters broke some days early for one client, and she was dying in the womb, clutching and pulling at the umbilical cord for more sustenance to keep her going. In therapy her hands were grasping in the air, and when asked what she wanted to hold said, "it felt like a rope or cable." By the time she was born her terror was so deeply imprinted that even in her thirties when we first worked with her, her baby-like features dominated her looks. Even with a forthright personality the imprint pushed her into just those relationships that would exclusively provide her with nurturing and demand little in return. An infant part of her, like the inner child in Bradshaw's sense,[375] remained a baby trying to claw her way back into the womb to find the sustenance she had lost while being born.

From the Void to emptiness: soul is replaced by ego

The 'I am' consciousness is responsible for the creation of the organs through which our sense of individuality is enjoyed.

—Patanjali Sutra

No matter how born, most babies retain a sense of the cosmic spaciousness that was theirs in the womb. Events pass into awareness, are experienced and then pass out again like the droplets of a stationary cloud. We can see it in the way events and feelings are absorbed, reacted to, and pass away in the moment. Infants will be laughing passionately in one instant, and will cry their hearts out in the next. Nothing is held onto.

The very young permanently function in alpha mode rather than the beta mode of adult consciousness. This mode is the state of altered consciousness that comes in deep meditation. Children are far more intimately connected with the Field and their souls than adults. They receive more information, see auras and devas, and readily respond to the true, if hidden, feelings of others. At times children have picked up experiences that adults may interpret as past-life, but which may have been simply what they encounter while trawling the Field.[376]

During the first months baby remains partly merged with mother. But gradually baby recognizes that mother is not always there, the breast is not in his mouth when needed, and that missing a warm touch joins a thousand other denials that become his lot. Crying for food and love is received in a number of ways by the parents. The way baby is treated here will have the most profound impact. If mother insists on obedience and times breast-feeding by the clock, and leaves baby to cry alone in his room, the infant gradually recognizes a choice between the instinctual need to be fed and the obedience needed to obtain mother's love. From this comes a perceptible movement away from wholeness with soul in the full spaciousness of the Void to a withdrawal into isolation. The separation between us and the whole has begun.

The natural completeness of the Void is no longer perceived as a fullness, but as a hollowness. We redefine the fullness of the Void as emptiness. This is uncomfortable, and needs to be filled. Emptiness tints the joys of life with an unpleasant feeling of lack and even meaninglessness. As we begin to separate from the Field it becomes not the *experience* of space, but the *feeling* of emptiness.

In the process we are losing ourselves, but this time not from the cosmic all (as did the soul-field) nor from the mother-womb (as did the newborn) but from our own essence. We deny our true nature in order to buy acceptance. This produces a deep well of sadness, an existential grief that lies within us all, a sorrow for what we have lost.

The child fears this place. It is too sad to be recalled, too riddled with the feeling of what we were once really like. It feels like an ineradicable sorrow for which there is no solace. Emptiness, not fullness, becomes the ground of being. Here lies the origin of desire, and with it the most common source of human suffering. We become afraid of nothingness, and redefine sensations of desire as needs, and will is directed toward its satisfaction. Hence the popularity of magazines that support dreams of eternal love and the perfect marriage, of home and family.

Bit by bit the neural paths in the brain will deepen their tracks along whatever tracks the baby is using to compensate for the loss of wholeness, and of soul. This is how habitual behavior commences, and with it attachment to that behavior, to the point that in years to come the adult will tell you that these behaviors define him. Therapeutically, the huge loss the shift from fullness to emptiness brought about in life is a defining moment.

One defining moment was when Charlie felt constantly attacked, without understanding the sources, and was therefore overcautious in his life. Sandplay showed that grandmother's criticism of his mother, both verbal and energetic, was taken on by the little infant as a direct abuse of him. As the baby was still merged with mother, when mother was under attack, so was baby. Abuse was passed on instantly to the baby as if it had been directed at him. This was shown in his sandplay.

Fig. 42—Sandplay of the baby on the left taking on an attack aimed at mummy. Mummy is both the little frog hiding behind the barricade, and the goose softly looking down at her baby. Granny is, of course, all the terrifying creatures on the right.

The fearsome creatures on the right were recognized as being grandmother, and the little baby sitting on the rocks on the left was, of course, Charlie. His mother was tucked in behind the rocks, dancing in some irrelevant manner out of sight. Being merged with mother, he believed he was under attack. As mother was too scared to protect him, little Charlie was drawn to protect her himself. Over time this desire grew into the courage to stand up against others, but underneath lay the little baby who was scared of all confrontation. From the sandplay Charlie then realized that the conflict between fear and love (fear of granny's wrath and love of mother) had made him feel empty. He felt as if his soul had abandoned him.

From a myriad of these experiences we build defenses against being hurt. The ego, that we believe defines us — but is in fact a fabrication, an illusion — then develops into the behavior we call personality. We take on political issues, or addictions or we behave as superheroes. We stop looking within and seek a solution from without. It seems necessary for survival, but we come to lose something very precious, and often spend the rest of our lives in an unconscious search for what has been lost. This means we become surveyors or environmentalists or opera singers or criminals, or whatever role best fits the distorted response. A shorthand description of the process under the development of personality is set out in Appendix 2.

The outcome is the egoic energetic formations that from then on determine and define the behavior we call personality. We take on political issues, or addictions or we behave as superheroes. Actions are directed outside. We stop looking within and seek a solution from without. This means we become surveyors or environmentalists or opera singers or criminals, or whatever role best fits the distorted response. A shorthand description of how personality develops is set out in Appendix 2.

We have found in therapy that as clients explore deeper into themselves, the feeling of emptiness and soullessness hides underneath most of the surface issues. When examined, we find that the sensation of soul and that of the fullness of the Void are actually *one and the same feeling*. This is the feeling of what one really is beyond the pressing demands of the personal ego.

—|10|—

THE NATURE OF SOUL

Coming back or not: reincarnation

It is even as though there were a single intention behind it all, which always makes some kind of sense, though none of us knows what the sense might be, or has lived the life that he quite intended.

—Patanjali Sutra

The concept of past lives that are not completed with death but continue to influence the present is found in most cultures. It was even accepted among Christians until Saint Augustine in the fifth century. Much carefully controlled research now shows that past lives do affect the present.[377]

Ian Stevenson published the results of 2,000 cases from ten cultures, mainly children, as they would be less likely to be altered by parents' opinions. In most cases he found supportive evidence, including some with life histories that corresponded with the children's memories. They would usually remember from when they could first talk at about three, and would stop around five, about the same time as they stopped talking about their birth memories.[378] David Cheek has done similar work using hypnotherapy and itemized people who "had known their mothers before this lifetime."[379]

David Chamberlain reports a young girl, Sarah, who said, "I'm *not* a baby. I'm old. I'm not my age. I've known them. I don't understand why they keep acting like they have known me for this short time. I'm really frustrated. I am *not* supposed to be the baby; I'm supposed to be in charge... It's a crazy world."[380]

One famous story concerns William James and his friend John Hyslop. They had promised one another that whoever died first would find a way to leave a message for the other. Some years after James's death, a letter arrived for Hyslop from Ireland saying that a spirit called William James had (in a planchette séance) asked them to contact Hyslop to ask him if he remembered some red pajamas. At first this meant nothing to Hyslop, until he remembered they had been in France together and as their luggage had not yet arrived, he went out to buy pajamas for himself, and could only find a lurid red pair. For days afterward James teased him about their color. In the years that followed the incident had been completely forgotten.

It is very clear from work with our clients that souls do reincarnate, and that the particular energetic formations that soul brings into a life come from the accumulation of past events and experiences. The realm of soul collects and integrates the experiences of many incarnations. These are the preconditions of our lives carried into this incarnation from within the Field. But do they come to learn from their experiences in this life, or is this our interpretation-cum-projection?

As we are all part of the Field, totally connected to everything else, when the soul came on the journey of incarnation it was drawn to the vibrations of the parents who most closely 'matched' its nature, or whatever was connectable in the play between all the fields involved. Some like to say that 'soul chooses the parents,' and this is correct only in the way that water 'chooses' to run downhill. It is the match of energies between the family and the soul as they are constellated at that moment that 'chooses.'

When the soul energy returns, we cannot claim that its experience is 'our' past life. The personality that evolved in the earlier time evaporated when the soul returned to the Field. While down here soul would have 'taken on' some of the vibration from the events of this life, but after death it is no more the earlier person than a cricket ball is the cow that provided the leather. The field of the individual soul returns to the Source, and the new soul is one more spawn from the Source.

The way in which reincarnation happens differs from culture to culture. The Hindu tradition understands that Brahma is the creative principle and that all individuals and all dimensions of existence are just products of the endless transformations of the Brahman, which is another word for the Field. Any attachment to any manifestation of any field is considered an illusion, including past-life experiences.[381]

The Tibetans teach that on dying the soul moves into the white light followed by a three-day period of dark unconsciousness. As consciousness returns the soul may not know it is dead. It may be in shock that it neither casts a shadow nor finds its image in a mirror. They teach that if during life the soul had not resolved this past terror, it bounces back into life in whatever way conforms to its karma.[382] It is rather like Western stories of near-death experiences, but without the stage of compassion.

As this is not the experience of our clients nor of other Western studies, it would seem that the Tibetan view creates the experience. If we expect terror it will be waiting for us, if we expect to meet friends and guides they will be there.[383]

We have come to know this energetic form that we call soul through the inner searching of our clients. This has become clearer to us over the years, and the examples I give here are the tip of an enormous iceberg. In this example you can feel the core of the process and how only through the soul work could we support the client to reach a resolution.

Early on Melissa saw herself being born. She was a fighter, and was shocked to discover she didn't care if she hurt her mother in the process, but worse, actually want to hurt because of the pain she was in.

Then came the magical moment when she noticed she was not actually in the baby's body but was observing from on high. She wrote later, "My being, my soul was watching this process dispassionately. My spirit had not wanted to be in that womb. I thought I probably have been observing my whole life, not participating in it, just letting it happen to me, however it suited others."

Melissa's soul then made a conscious decision to enter this baby's body, and described it not as herself, but as her soul. It was a profoundly moving experience to hear her say, "I see myself as a light coming down through the baby's fontanel, bright, beautiful, sinewy tendrils of energy. I am deliberately streaming…(pause) as energy…through into my baby brain… Infusing myself through the cells and fibres, and breathing, breathing into it. I am spending time at the base of her neck (it's where I have tightness and pain today)…(pause, sighs)… It's a narrow place to get through, and once through am able to continue through all the meridians of her body."

Afterward Melissa felt regenerated, "like my soul and my body were ready to go forth and take on the world, and that the sum of one and one was more than two. This was a very powerful process for me. I felt light, newly alive, and powerful." As with the published examples by Wade, Chamberlain, and others, the sense of absolute reality in her experience, and the depth of her feelings and language all carried the flavor of soul that we have come to know so well.

Karma accumulates in the soul

In our drive for novelty, our curiosity, and our compulsion to investigate and to push beyond boundaries, we are evolution itself, expanding into new openings.

—Joseph Chilton Pearce[384]

Karma is the sum total of all the imprints of life experiences and actions onto the energy field of each soul. It is the sum of all previous incarnations, both positive and negative, and includes our shadows. These patterns are carried into later generations. A change in our energies, especially after trauma, will affect soul, for soul is in process, and is as pliable and flexible as a field. Jung wrote, "I feel very strongly that I am under the influence of questions which were left incomplete and unanswered by my parents and grandparents and more distant ancestors. It often seems as if there was an impersonal karma within a family, which is passed on from parents to children, that I had to answer questions which fate had posed to my forefathers, things which previous ages had left unfinished."[385]

Souls are our form-field while we are evolving in the womb and beyond. Wade, Chamberlain, and Newton show that soul remembers the events of this life from before conception, and previous lives that are less easily accessed. It observes and records consciously.

Gladys was a woman with a well-ordered background and no serious childhood traumas. Money had never been a problem. Yet she had no joy in her life. It felt like that when the rest of the world laughed, she could only smile. When we supported her to investigate her deeper feelings she came across a profound pool of grief that seemed to have no cause. The fact that it was always there without cause was deeply disturbing. It felt like someone in the family had suddenly died, but all of her close relatives were still alive.

She then realized that her mother must have had the same grief. At first we thought it was an energetic form Gladys had picked up in the womb from some trauma of her mother's. As she felt more deeply into her mother's energy she realized it was not hers either. This was an ancient unexpressed grief carried down from some much earlier generation.

She was then flooded with images of dying and mutilated men in the 1914 war. With a shock Gladys realized that her great-grandmother had lost two sons at Paschendale. In obedience to the demands of those times her feelings had been suppressed, and so the intensity of her loss became a karmic matter. The grief did not go away, but was carried on to their daughters and their daughter's daughters for three or more generations.

When this grief was unearthed in therapy almost a century later these women found that in clearing it for themselves they had profoundly affected other members of their families — even across the world. We have found this more among our female clients than among men.

Souls may at times make a second attempt at entering a family when once thwarted, recharging the family karma as it does so. A very young client had already had three abortions, destroyed two relationships and felt increasingly useless about her future. At the same time she retained the deep spirituality that had accompanied her throughout her adolescence. She also carried anger against her mother. Not that either of these things are particularly rare in the community, but what was important in her case was that the vibrations of anger also lay in her soul. Her soul voice said, "I have always been against the mother." We prompted her to discover what had happened, and she said, "It was very bad. Someone has died."

Inner searching disclosed that her soul had accompanied the first conception of her mother twelve years earlier, and that this baby had been aborted. The soul had reincarnated carrying angst about the abortion. Her mother was very young when this happened, and had been so scared of having the baby that it would have been easy for her to feel vicious toward it. The soul imbued the vicious and angry vibrations of the mother and on its return into the daughter's body still carried this energy. It had been spreading mayhem and destruction in her seemingly gentle life ever since. This was imprinted on the soul's energetic form, along with the concept of termination.

So not only did she carry an imprinting of violence from that earlier time, but also a propensity for the same action as her mother, which was to terminate her own pregnancies. It was as if this soul-form could only act out on others what had been done to it, and thus perpetuated the vibrations of the anger and abandonment and revenge that came with the earlier abortion.

Sharing operates both ways. Having imbibed what we are, souls reflect us back onto us. We become constrained by our distant past, and unless we work on the soul level we will never understand it. If we live in an age of violence and resonate with it — through being drawn to certain films and stories — then our predilection is reinforced by the content we continuously put into our soul-form. The incomplete aspects of our lives are reflected in the same incompleteness within the soul's.

Just as there are levels of coherence and beauty in humans, so there are among souls. Maybe it is an odd thought, especially for Christians, to consider that the soul may not be pure, being close to God. However, there is duality in the Field just as there is down here. The greater the karma the heavier the feeling of the soul, and as we help it clear the negativity the lighter the vibrations become, moving into higher realms that connect more immediately with the fullness of the Field. Just as we gravitate toward people who are more coherent, with lighter vibrations, so souls will gravitate toward the higher souls we call saints.

One man was unable to feel his legs. It was like having a plate that blocked all feeling for anything below his abdomen. In process he went back to the trenches in Flanders in the war, and struggled with barbed wire wrapped around him and a wound near the groin, and then further back to a wreck at sea struggling to get his crushed legs to move his body out of danger. The whole process took less than twenty minutes, but at the end he could feel the strength in his legs and spent the rest of the day walking around in happiness, ecstatic at something newly found like a toddler.

My sense is that older souls are more complex, having accumulated a richer collation of experiences from many lives. It shows us that if we wish to leave a heritage for our children, the clearer our karma the more love will imbue the future generations on this planet. This is an obligation on us as important as providing our children with a good education and health, and seeing that they inherit a clean and unpolluted earth.

Souls are not on a journey

We live in duality because the soul cannot distinguish between the ego and the Field.

—Patanjali Sutra

When the soul returns to earth some say, "the soul still has things to learn." The evidence shows that this is not the way it is, for no soul in our clinical investigations has shown any consciousness of being on a journey. It is not a victim waiting for one of its carriers to 'wake up.' It is just being itself.

It is we who are not being ourselves, but from our emptiness that brings yearning and our desires we project our needs onto soul. This is why we say they have been 'sent' to this world in order to 'learn,' whereas their coming is simply an inevitable aspect of the way the Field manifests. It may set us free to realize that there is no grand purpose in everything, nor plan, nor any will to learn nor to improve. There is only that total intercooperation that I would call essential love.

We project onto soul the idea that it is 'wounded' because our personal aspirations are not being fulfilled. It is correct that whatever in soul is at odds with itself is exactly what keeps it at its vibrational level in the Field: this is our inheritance. From our perspective the very issues that keep soul from being more coherent with the Field are precisely those that we are most in need of transforming in ourselves. For example, if a soul carries the vibration of being tremulously withdrawn, then withdrawal will manifest in us, and we will project that manifestation onto others so that our personal life will be full of situations that encourage withdrawal. Thus a field of reticence creates a person that 'needs to' shrink back, and this inducts in the environment situations that will trigger that response.

But soul itself has no impulse to change its vibration. Nothing in any of our sessions has shown that soul requires anything at all. Most of Michael Newton's clients seem caught in this trap of expectation.

He used hypnosis to access his client's soul memories. He describes souls learning between lives, and conscious management-like conferences being held between them. How much of this information is true, and how much has been tainted by our needs and desires? Information obtained through hypnosis is filtered through our egos. Newton recognized this when he wrote, "People tend to structure their frame of reference during a trance state with what their conscious mind sees and has experienced on earth. Each person translates abstract spiritual conditions into symbols that make sense to them."[386]

When our 'frame of reference' becomes more conscious we can more readily separate from our cultural opinions, as Newton found with those clients he recognized as 'advanced souls.' Their descriptions of the reality of the soul-world were closer to those of our clients. They were the only ones to accurately describe their experiences happening within a "non-space that is timeless."[387] I find their information closer to our own findings.

Interactions between souls appear more like a dance between clouds than anything as specific as learning. Play may be a better word than learn, with its suggestion of obligation and lack. There is never a sense in the soul of self-blame; there is no inner critic. There is just an acceptance at a very deep level that how they are is how it is. With that attitude they follow their nature, which is to incarnate, to have encounters, to mingle, and to accumulate experiences. However, a loving life leaves an imprint in the soul of openness, flowing oneness and sensitivity while a violent one leaves vibrations that are more jagged and torn. We can change the vibrations of soul by living a spiritual life, and the energy of our lives become part of our soul's vibratory pattern. This merges into its pre-existing karma, and surfaces as an impulse of love in the next generation.

Lovingness in this life does not always make for an easy journey next time. When the newborn recognizes the sadness and lack of self-worth so often carried by its parents, love turns into a passion to bring relief to their suffering. As infants realize this there is such an outpouring of compassion that they may take on the burden of a parent, hoping to take the pain from them.

The difficulty with such a degree of love is that the children may end up taking on the pain of that parent as if it were their own. Gloria watched her father wielding his anger like a weapon. She wrote, "It was like a great sword that I would try to hold and take from him. I would offer my joy and love in exchange for the hurts that created his rage. It was unfair, but I kept on trying even though I often got damaged in the process. I fought off my brother, as I believed (in the urgency of my need to heal Daddy) that only I could give him the slightest peace. And when I could see that my attempts were futile and my father had turned his anger on me once too often, I changed tack, buried his pain inside me, and tried to heal him by doing everything he wanted in the way he wanted it. I was about 3½ years old then. This approach did not end pleasantly."

This is Christ Consciousness that takes on the burdens of others, and with little children this is done with such sincerity that it requires a great deal of their energy. When they inevitably perceive how unaware the parent is and how intractable the trauma, there is great sorrow. Their love has failed.

The sorrow then feeds back into soul, and adds an ingredient of pain and grief to the karma of love. The actions we take in life to assuage the pain create more karma. This affects the next life that may contain more patterns of protection than love that will be expressed through a very different personality. If this life is a violent one, revulsion may develop that begets love once more. On every variation that we can imagine over many lives every movement flows into every other in an endlessly interconnected journey without purpose. In this there are no judgments, only a dispassionate weaving flow.

No emotions, no judgment, no suffering

Everything arises in mutual relation to everything else, so you can't blame anybody for anything.

—Joseph Campbell

Each of us could judge a soul by calling its karma bad or good or compassionate or stupid, and so on. But would soul join in our judgment? It would only if the Field possessed a moral code and adhered to it as if it were a law of nature. We find no evidence for this at all. Soul seems to have no attitude to its way of being, and no emotional content. It just is.

Again and again we have been shown that soul does not carry emotional baggage. The energy is cool and observant no matter how intense the level of karma that is being carried. It is only at some moment during the first trimester as the emotional center in the embryo is developed that soul may at times begin to participate in the emotions of the new child. As we have said of the whole Field, there is no feeling for the moral or emotional issues that bedevil humans. I have the impression that our emotional aspect, which has evolved through millions of years of survival in what are often hostile environments, has hunkered down with an easy going soul. The soul then takes on the consequences of being with this emotional body, not in an emotional way, but just by imbibing the vibrations that accompany the consequences of our actions, and thus carries karma.

It would seem that the more complex the field system of a species the more likely it is to develop the one essential quality that has been more highly developed in civilized humans, self-awareness. This is that quality within an organism's field that is able to separate within the unity of that field and look back on itself. Energy Psychology demonstrates that the soul is a self-aware field with a refined consciousness, but "souls may become so buried by human emotions in bodies which are unstable, that by the time of death they are contaminated spirits. If we become obsessed by our physical bodies, or carried along on an emotional roller coaster in life, the soul can be subverted by its outer self."[388]

For many people it is satisfying to their egos to believe that souls are inherently good. Though we find in our work that no soul seeks to be either good or evil, they can still carry the vibrations that cause people to do evil. People may wreck havoc from the harsh things that have happened to them, even if soul does not support it. But once we start on a harsh path the soul takes on our beliefs and contradictions. How we act and believe and think is all received into soul in the same way as we project them into the Field. This has been confirmed by David Chamberlain who found that souls that lay outside the womb during pregnancy describe their experiences in a rather matter-of-fact manner, while those that have been resident in the womb share more closely in human emotional reactions.[389] There is an observant consciousness in soul, as if it comes from the frontal cortex without any attachment to the limbic emotional brain.

Then how is it that we humans have purpose and morality? There may be other species like us in the universe, but as far as we know we are the only one in the Field that has a capacity for conscious self-criticism. The reason may be sought in our origins. We evolved from animals and have physically and instinctually many qualities of earlier species embedded in us. Animals have to respond to fear, to lust and hunger if they are to survive. During evolution these developed into an emotional body, with feedback loops for learning, from which feelings could be analyzed and acted on. Those that survived developed a supervisor to oversee emotional choices, whether to fight or flee, for example. As animals became more complex, subtler levels of feeling developed, including care and greed, guilt and pleasure, and more. These may reside in our foundations, but they are not in soul's.

In addition we are tribal creatures. Like many animals we have grown to enjoy packs and pods and prides. We have learned that it is contagiously fun to operate together, whether on the dance floor, in a band, or in a quilting bee. The price is to suppress our purely selfish needs such as anger and lust in order to enjoy the pleasures of the group. This is a very powerful motivation.

Human tribal codes and the morality that accompanied them have been projected onto the Field. Our god-projection is lumbered with a morality to be good and kind to whichever group prays to it, and we are usually shocked when our good god has gone to sleep and forgotten us. The evidence shows that neither the Field nor any projection we put onto it has the capacity to care.

Soul-fields don't contain the critical function of our left brain. Any vibration that is discordant would not be analyzed, dwelt on or in any way *acted on*. Instead there would simply be subtle readjustments in all the fields entangled with that vibration. Though we would *deduce* that this energetic entity is not in right order, and is an area of discordance, there would be no judgment in the Field, only amendments. Being in the presence of beings that just are is a blessing.

The perfect unity between all fields suggests that the higher animals may, through their vibrations and thoughts, be able to alter more solid entities such as trees, and even the earth itself? What of climate and tectonic events, or even forces such as gravity? Janet Dallett tells how she and her children decided to perform a traditional rain dance in the forest, and developed such fervor and passion that they continued for more than an hour, a fervor encouraged by the long dry spell in their area. When they stopped it immediately rained, not everywhere, but just over their campfire, which was immediately extinguished. She wrote, "I was stunned. I had entered the ritual naïvely, expecting nothing. I did not believe that dancing could cause rain, nor do I believe it now. Yet something in my psyche insists that the rain dance and the rain were not separate, independent events."[390]

She wrote that statistically it is equally likely that the rain caused the dance as that the dance caused the rain, or some third element caused both, or that she could have intuitively 'smelled' an imminent rainstorm that stimulated her to dance. But there is a third, that "when an archetype is activated, it tends to manifest in the physical realm as well as the psychological" through a perceptible field of psychic energy, and that we are so intimately interconnected on the vibrational level that within every field every sort of attraction and outcome is possible. This is a most exciting potential for humanity if we can grasp it.

Lynne McTaggart is running an international experiment to see whether the combined attention of large groups can alter the physical world.[391] She is using an attentive mindfulness, in which people are asked to participate without attachment. This is exactly the procedure we use in therapy at the Centre to bring souls' vibrations into alignment with our higher intentions.

As the soul has neither an agenda nor any longing to be either more, or less, in the Field, it is completely unconcerned with its own path — as does every aspect of the Field. On its own, soul has neither desires nor needs. Souls display no sense of suffering, for they lie outside the wheel of desire. It is we who have those desires, and thus it is we who suffer. Our reaction to suffering can be to withdraw into ourselves and in our despair separate ourselves from soul.

Separation from soul

I play the game that cannot be won but only played, looking for my place in the field.

—Bagger Vance

Normally the energetic field of a soul occupies the whole of us, though we may experience its center someplace just outside the body. Souls are normally intimately connected with us, but may separate from us from trauma or misdirection of our lives. The outcome is invariably disastrous. One client placed in the sandtray the figure of a little boy wearing a raincoat. He was looking at a pool full of loving animals, but was prevented by a notice that said: "No entry."

Fig. 43 — Sandplay of "no entry."

It connected him with a two-year old memory of running into his parents' bedroom while they were making love. His mother was angry at being caught, and her shock, plus some guilt, took over and in anger she physically threw him out of the room and locked the door. The little boy was totally devastated. Now all seemed empty and gray as if he had no home anywhere: his sanctuary had been desecrated. He felt he could never again enter the hallowed halls of their bedroom and dream to slip into the sheets between them. It was truly an instant of utter emptiness. At the same moment he could feel that his soul slipped away. He succumbed in himself to an unbearable barrenness, and spent the next thirty years longing for his soul, or for god, or for some such level of acceptance that was not dependent on the uncertainties of mum or dad.

Through too much sadness we can create a distance between us and the joy of soul. To the extent that we have separated ourselves from soul in childhood, the soul seems to withdraw into a quiescent state that we sense as a silent waiting, as if on hold until we reconnect. Just as 'soulful' refers to someone with a true depth of feeling or inner richness, losing one's soul means, "to lose contact with the inner depth and richness of being human."[392] But the loss is never total, for there are degrees of alienation, and intimacy can be re-established.

Humans may long for connection with soul, for it offers an inner place of being-ness and rightness. Some degree of longing is universal, and often expressed with the passion of Saint Augustine crying "O God, thou hast made us for thyself, and our hands are restless until they rest in thee." Not being able to permanently cross the veil, our occasional glimpses are so radiant and numinous that we long for a more permanent connection. Such longing is very common.

It is strengthened by the simple yearning to be loved by our parents. Just to be loved for being here, not conditionally, but totally. We are born as beautiful beings that respond so easily to care. When forcibly 'civilized,' surrounded by do's and don'ts and instructions of how we ought to behave rather than being loved and enfolded for being who we are, a sense of separation gradually occurs. We are no longer with our parents in the womb, nor merged with them in the months that follow, but are increasingly estranged, put out to fend for ourselves, and forced to solve the problems of relationship and lack of full acceptance with the help of only our own resources. Our coherence is affected, and natural connectedness with the Field and soul is diminished.

Martin, like many of us, could remember seeing auras as an infant. He saw his parents' soul-forms hovering around, but his mum's was usually somewhere else while she was doing the household chores: a soul mislaid. He tried to bring it back, giving it the kiss of life, all to no avail. Then Martin realized with horror that if his mother could drop her soul by the wayside, so could he. He described trying to rejuvenate his mother by chewing, like on a nipple. His attempts to bring her soul back became increasingly desperate as he began biting and shaking to shock it into reawakening. Biting and desperation became linked, and when he was four he bit chunks out of an armrest and broke a tooth on the dashboard of the car.

An adult's desire for soul may be triggered on recognizing that we have tried to 'go it alone.' The presence of longing in us begins by wanting touch and play and acceptance from parents, and then grows as the sorrow gets greater to include soul and through soul for the full enfolding of the Field that is ultimately a projection for our Great Parent in the sky that we call our longing for God. As Andrew Harvey cautioned in his passionate commentary on Rumi, "You have to become the 'prey of God.' If you are obsessed with all the details of your life, this will veil your path. The path is light itself, transcending all biography."[393]

Souls lean toward this union. I prefer to use a word like 'lean' rather than 'desire' as the souls we have met do not have anything remotely close to what we would call will. There is no sign that soul wants to be changed nor that soul longs for deliverance. Words like 'longing' and 'deliverance' are emotional human terms projected onto soul. Yet there is a natural inclination throughout the universe to return to wholeness and a fuller consciousness. We have found that soul does lean toward knowing the whole of creation and is aware that it is to some extent divided from it by its own veil. Soul is as 'stuck' in partial-unity as we are. Being conscious that we have been separated is as much soul's lot as ours. The difference is that soul lies on the timeless side of the veil, while we are on this, and knowing that we are stuck is not the same as intending to change it. Intent belongs to us, not to soul.

As we all have souls, some must be older than others. After all, the number of humans from which we all descend who were still alive at the end of the last ice age, anywhere on our planet, may not have counted more than 4,000 adults.[394] How did they grow into billions? Do souls split and divide? Do they spawn? I have the impression that there is great flexibility among souls, even to creating more than one life at a time. Souls of identical twins split, as we have seen.

The souls of one married couple had woven an energetic dance for centuries, a dance that was so entwined that their souls actually merged in alternative lifetimes and became one, and then split in two in a later life from the accumulation of karma.

One soul (and it did not matter whether it occupied a male or a female body) had a vibrational form that opened to absorb the other, softly like an amoeba. The other would open to be enfolded, but resisted being absorbed and digested. It maintained its identity by resisting what it 'desired' at the start. One wanted to ingest, a process that it could not control once it had begun, while the other wanted to be enfolded without being annihilated. There was a sense they each knew they could not have both, but that having willingly moved into the trap both were aware that neither could expect joy from the union.

When combined, the merged pair would manifest as a person who squeezed the joy, richness, and vulnerability out of other people. Whether a man or a woman, it suffocated all exuberance and aliveness from those around. The combination of the absorber and the absorbed operating in one body was incredibly powerful. It had projected what we would call a hatred of god, leaving a disturbance in the Field. In crossing over, the karmic consequences were so devastating and intense that the souls would naturally split apart in the next life.

In this life each soul carried not only their separate tendencies for engulfment and captivation, but in addition the karma from the previous life. These energetic impulses were continued through interlocking entrapment, where one soul snuffed out the energy of the other. It was significant that the latter was gradually succumbing to a wasting muscular disease without a name, while the former had trained as a doctor with an unconscious prescience of what was to come. The punishments and satisfactions from their union of opposites were mutual.

What prevented movement in the energetic fields was the awesome paradox that for the soul to recognize oneness with joy implied separation in which the connection between the two souls would be diminished, or even lost. This had prevented all change over eons, and may still today. The question for our clients was could they turn their souls from entrapment and the wish to be enfolded into a simpler love, so that an independent caring could be inducted into their souls' energy systems to replace the earlier extremes.

Creation of opposite fields

No good deed escapes punishment; no bad deed escapes its reward.

—Anonymous

In every moment in which judgments are created another field is born that encapsulates its opposite. The link between the fields then maintains the coherence of each in a dualistic union of opposites. In this game one aspect will predominate over the other, so when manifested in a person these energies will induct their attitudes and beliefs to one side or the other.

Some opposing fields can play havoc on this plane. For example, the twelfth-century Christian sect called the Cathars believed that by becoming good they would increase the overall level of goodness in the world, and thus overcome the badness around them. They interpreted the actions of the Old Testament Jehovah as evil. As Hillman writes, Jehovah "was a war god given to terrifying, destructive moods, inflicting plagues, floods, and slaughter on his people with little provocation."[395] They had a large following before they were exterminated in the thirteenth century, and one is tempted to ask whether the ferocity of their enemies was greater because of their goodness.

The constellations of these yin-yang fields stand in the way of enlightenment by keeping soul, and us with it, away from the emotional torrent of existence. The more contradictions there are the more the frothing mountain stream that is life becomes sluggish, slower, and more laden with debris as it approaches the ocean. In Tibetan imagery this is exemplified in the *dorjé* that is also called the double-diamond thunderbolt. As in the illustration, it is symmetrical around a diamond-like form or sphere at the center, with pointed needles thrusting through outward-facing crowns at each end. This is John Lilly's center of the cyclone, that absolutely still point around which all the turmoil and movement of existence broils and shifts.[396]

Fig. 44 — The dorjé is the Tibetan symbol for duality,
with two crowns pierced by a shaft of lightning. It is sometimes
called the double-diamond thunderbolt.

Having contradictory vibrations is as inevitable among souls as it is with us. After all, it is precisely this lack of coherence that keeps soul from being deeper in the Field. Here are some examples:

Sometimes we hide figures under the sand and ask clients to pick one without looking. We trust that through synchronicity they will pick exactly the most appropriate. Elaine chose a smart-looking and provocative adolescent she disparagingly called a Barbie doll, and a black panther with great teeth that made her decidedly uncomfortable. Both were shadow sides of her personality: the rejected sexual and the rejected aggressor. Yet she bleached her hair blonde and wore tight skirts not unlike the doll, and was a forceful if not dominating person. These two shadow parts were still being displayed though under control. After working on this she suddenly placed the girl on the panther's back and exclaimed, "this is how they ride together!"

Anne picked an eagle with one wing held up and the other hanging down. She said, "the eagle has a broken wing." She felt she could not fly straight, but was forced by the broken wing to sheer sideways all the time. In fact, she did this a lot in life, starting a process and then being diverted onto something else before she had completed it. Jenny chose an Indian calling into the sky that made her cry. She felt for the longing in the caller, and endless hopelessness of calling and calling and never being heard. It felt like the longing of soul for God, yet Jenny had no interest in God or any form of religion. She had rejected God in much the same way as her soul seems to have felt rejected by God.

Soul may contain mixed-up energies, such as lust and pride and self-abasement that, when incarnated, can create all sorts of unpleasant outcomes. They will carry on the most complex dances, seldom more apparent than between therapists and their clients.

Suzanne had a leaning toward the bliss of higher states while also being emotionally rigid. These two forces acted against each other to produce a feeling of being fractured into many parts. This combination seemed karmic, as the 'natural' leaning toward bliss was countered by a pulling-back in the soul-field. As with all fields, one firmly held quality 'creates' its opposite, so that being immobilized and being in longing were for her different sides of the one state.

As a therapist she would draw clients with similar soul-states to her. One was a man who was contemplating suicide as he was being drawn more to the splitting fractured side, while diminishing that part that wished to be anchored. She helped him over the months to adjust an acceptance of structure that diminished the desire to die.

Fig. 45 — Drawing created by a therapist trying to understand her relationship with her client.

She made a drawing to understand her difficulties with this client, difficulties that she felt reflected her own issues. The drawing has two overlapping circles. The concept of rigid control was depicted on the right, and of potential growth on the left. In the overlapping zone lay a rich and attractive organic livingness.

The boundaries that marked the 'feelings' of client and therapist also defined their behavior. Neither was able to access the center for both were absorbed by the conflict on each side. She could not help him beyond this insight as it mirrored her own.

She felt that when chaos threatened — the state we could also label freedom — they would each in their own way hang on to the rings around the circles that framed their opposing fields. From the energetic point of view there could be no resolution because the original opposites in the soul-field remained untouched. The soul maintained the tendencies that manifested in the behavior of both of them, locked in a circumscribed dance.

In time Suzanne and her client came to a mutual point of rest that allowed them to be at the center of their personal cyclones, but not yet at the center of any grander holistic center that could survey

a greater field beyond their personal ones. The extremes of the conflict had been assuaged in both so they rest at peace in themselves,
and in this their personal therapy is complete, at least on this issue.
To move toward a deeper level of enlightenment the presence of
that energetic conflict in their souls would have to be dissolved.

Grouping of soul-fields

Every passion can be a doorway to intimacy.

—Hilary James

Soul-forms are more than individual incarnations. Their energies join with wider communities of souls operating toward commonly held impulses. Just as the people of a country have attitudes
and beliefs that flow into and become a cultural field, rich in colors and forms and traditions, groups of souls with similarities are
aligned into larger units. If the people of a great city have a common
spirit, such as Sydney or New York or London or Paris, we feel it as
a collective agglomeration. We know when we visit a new place or
join a new community such as gays or filmmakers or greenies that
we enter into a new mood-zone that seems to arise from the common field of all their souls.

This is normal in families, and in long-term relationships. At
times the cohesion of a group of souls may become extremely
intense. One client would sit with her hand over her mouth unable
to breathe easily and found it hard, even in her fifties, to speak
above a whisper. She had asthma, had almost drowned in adolescence, and had been in an accident that affected her breathing. She
had had therapy from which she concluded it all came from childhood incest. That treatment had been only partially successful.

In processing she discovered her soul's experience of being
gassed in the Nazi ovens as a little Jewish girl. Carried into this
life, the shock was imprinted into her body, so that she would stop
breathing just in case there was more gas. She was reborn immediately after the war to a German family who had taken in and hidden
a relative who had worked at one of the extermination camps. This
was the man who had put her into the oven in the earlier life, and it
was the same man who sexually abused her at about the age she was

when she had died in the camp. The intense connectedness between them was being played out in more than one lifetime.

We can now understand why years of therapy had only scratched the surface. As well as the traumatic human story there was a deep interconnected vibrational trauma in which a number of souls were maintaining a common resonance in each other's company over more than one lifetime. The many soul-fields that were involved greatly complicated the issues that each carried.

At these times the soul is doing what a field does naturally, interconnecting with all other fields so that an easy fit occurs and each field, of whatever persuasion and direction, is in perfect flow with all the others around it. A soul's entry is like adding a dye into a stream of moving water: it settles comfortably, spreading out, merging, breaking into parts, reforming, and so on. In this process no *intent* is required; only fellowship — though in human terms the outcome may not be what we would call fellowship.

Souls are naturally drawn into groups of matching vibrations. In the Field every moment and every movement is totally in tune with every other, timelessly. Even the most rigid forms have a 'place to go' among greater constellations of like fields. This may be the explanation for Newton's clients recalling under hypnosis that they belonged to a particular group of like fields.[397]

Thinking back to the synchronicity in Lincoln's and Kennedy's deaths (page 25) is it possible that something similar was happening? — a wild idea, perhaps — but was Lincoln's soul reincarnated in Kennedy? All the fields that vibrated from the first shooting were still ricocheting around America and the presidential environment, in histories, personal memories, and in the unconscious of the security details. In a way, they may have moved as a cluster, all entwined with one another and gearing up for a replay exactly 100 years later. At least six souls were involved: president, wife, secretary, vice president, assassin, and cortege organizer. Was anything learned or changed in the soul's stories over this time? Or, as seems more likely, should we look for a replay in the future with a well-intentioned leader who will make powerful enemies and act it out all over again? Or will one of these souls along the way accompany someone who can guide it to a new level of consciousness, and break the cycle?

Some vibrations accumulate such intensity that Jung classified them among the archetypes. The Mother and the Patriarch derive from a billion family situations and dramas endlessly repeated until their projection into the Field manifests as a real force on this plane. Monkeys, lions, and most higher animals display similar gender differences, so the human brand of this archetype comes from much more ancient stock. It has been suggested that each of us aligns with a particular archetype,[398] but this means only that trends in humans reflect the accumulated trends in the Field. Were we to identify totally with the energetic system of an archetype its power would take us over, and we would become, in Jung's word, 'inflated.' Moslem and Christian fundamentalists show us the dangers in that.

On the lighter side, the Fool in the Tarot deck is the one who "goes on trusting. His trust is so pure that nobody can corrupt it."[399] The Fool trusts his intuition is in harmony with all that surrounds him. It is the archetype of the adventuring innocent who is always true to himself. This came up for one of my clients, Stan.

Stan was often spontaneous in life, and quite intuitive about it, yet the outcome would usually turn out to be injurious. You knew he was true in his actions, but too often they rebounded in an unsought way. He was fascinated by the end of things and possible armageddons, yet would become frantic when he broke things himself. There was something in this of his mother, who was not particularly intuitive but was spontaneously thoughtless in a way that the child found destructive. In therapy it looked like he was just carrying her node of callous indifference. But it was deeper than that.

The Fool aspect in Stan's soul had been attracted to that same aspect in his mother's — one of the reasons for his soul joining that family. It had in previous lives lashed out thoughtlessly, delighting in the brazen violence of a corsair. That wild lifetime had left an imprint of one who loved the mayhem and disaster of piracy with his whole being. That animal vitality continued into this life, though cloaked in a clerical and reclusive exterior that kept the wild side in the background.

Stan's fear of his mother's destructiveness lay like a pall over his Fool. It veiled soul so it could operate only through his fear of her. Thus both soul and Stan became projections of the mother. It was like double mirrors that reflected both ways with mother occupying the middle space. The fear was so great that the soul's influence over Stan was distorted, as was Stan's understanding of his own purpose in life.

As a result, whenever Stan was able to connect with his soul he could not stop himself from becoming entangled with the anarchic confusion in his mother, and thus expressing his soul as if it was her. The spontaneous Fool archetype could only express itself through the mother's projection. Independence was not possible until the distortions of that projection could be lifted. This process is so common that Jung could write that men project their soul qualities onto their mother, sister, and wife, and *vice versa* for women.

We find that the concept of soulmates in which souls have been joined in many incarnations, though strongly felt by some, is extremely rare. In most cases these people are tuning in to a fellow soul with similar qualities, and the two similarities dance together. The feeling of mutual 'knowing' is intense, but not necessarily evidence of past closeness.

Only through service can we change soul

I cannot find God unless I renounce this useless activity, and I cannot renounce this activity unless I let go of the illusion it defends. And I cannot get rid of an illusion unless I recognize it for an illusion.

—Thomas Merton

It is clear that souls carry a great deal of the stuff that makes us what we are. Being self-aware we may become dissatisfied with ourselves, and then our journey to alter our souls has begun. One of the greatest Arab mystics, Hakim Sanai, advised that an essential step on our spiritual journey was "to purify your soul from evil and fortify it with discrimination."[400] He knew this was our job, and was not within soul's capabilities. He understood that if we wanted enlightenment we needed to attend to our soul's issues as well as our own. In this sense, it is a human requirement rather than the Field's, which would have no desire either way. Like the dolphin, soul has no wish to change, as it does not have our capacity to do so.

Loaded with karmic material, we could say that soul comes with attitude, though we must be careful not to project onto soul our human partiality for turning everything into a moral issue. Coming with attitude just means that it has a vibrationary field that affects us in particular ways.

We said earlier that soul does not have a journey, for that implies that it would have a sense that it should be other than it is. Therefore, there is no journey for soul unless we make it so. The question is not "What does soul need to change?" but rather, "What are the major items in our own list that soul helped to create in the first place, and that soul continues to hold in place, and that we want to change in both of us?" This is our choice.

It is undoubtedly difficult to think of changing soul when we are in the same situation, but we have found that this is the most rewarding path. One way the soul's field can change is through a close interaction with their human 'host' on this plane. It is through incarnating that soul has unintentionally created its own mode of transformation. When we are conscious and make deliberate attempts to change our personal lives, to make them simpler and more loving — through meditation, therapy, good deeds, prayer and so on — then our energy becomes transformed and affects soul, just as our negative thoughts once did. When we deliberately include a conscious connection with soul the transformation for both is greater.

The fields within the Field do not change of themselves, just as flowing air cannot change its direction without some external impulse. For soul we are that impulse. This is our role. Because we are grounded in a material body we are able to create changes in the fields closest to us. It seems, in a strange way, that without the mundane world there would be no foundation on which soul can gain the purchase it needs to transform, just as we need to stand on the solid earth in order to walk or lift things.

Soul will change as we change, but the inertia from the old stuff slows the process down. All religions provide codes of good behavior — the ten commandments, the eight noble truths, and so on — for the very good reason that they create energetic fields that return these qualities to us. However, when we consciously support soul to clear its karmic entanglements as we clear our own personal matters a closer relationship develops beyond soul with the Field, and this brings with it the deepest qualities of compassion.

Indeed, the most transforming moment in therapy comes when we recognize the soul's nature, and make the momentous decision to support our soul to clear the karma it is carrying. This can affect the whole of our lives from then on. It is not an easy task, for we have to transform our own issues that were in part created by this same karma, so that we can release our soul from its karma.

It can be the most beautiful moment in our own realignment when we suddenly recognize that we are no longer alone. The decision to work with soul brings with it a major realignment in our priorities and the way we lead our lives. We experience in soul a companion that responds to consciousness. As we encourage soul to know itself we raise its consciousness as we raise ours by clearing our stuff. Gradually this enables it to integrate with the Field at a higher level, taking us with it. In this work we undertake to become no less than the good servant to the soul's transformation.

The good servant is like Hanuman in the Hindu epic, the Ramayana. Hanuman walks behind the god Rama, nurturing and supporting him, but when the enemy is at the gate he forces Rama to wake up and defend the palace. He guides Rama without dominating him. He knows a lot of things better than Rama, but is not himself capable of being god. This is the perfect analogy for the relationship between us and soul.

On the selfish side, becoming the servant of soul has a huge payback. The change in the alignment of our lives is always for the better. We are most positively affected when ego takes a backseat, and we become partners with soul. The alignment of both the ego as the good servant with the soul as higher companion has proven the most fruitful relationship in our therapy. We become active with our companion, no longer a lonely victim. This will usually align with our daemon, or destiny — the determining drive that comes from deep inside that some call fate. In this way the soul's particular bent, around which its pattern for transformation is aligned, also becomes ours.

Being in service encourages the most important human virtue: Humility. Without the humility of being the servant we have only our egos to rely on, and then we don't seem to be able to transform much further. By reconnecting with soul, or deepening our existing connection, we come to feel its presence in every part of us until it is so at home that we hardly notice it. The communion that follows helps us to recognize what we need to change in soul so that we can go on our own journey. Our soul-field becomes the core of our lives, and holds our deepest values. It brings joy and transparency, and the desire to share goodness all the days of our lives, as the psalm says.

We find that as personal issues are resolved we acquire a growing simplicity, for the dramas drop away. The fears in the ego and the contradictions in the personality become less. The ego in fact takes a backseat to soul, which is the truth in what Rumi wrote to his own, "When were you ever made less by dying?" As the coherence between us and soul becomes greater we approach our Buddha-nature.

11

RETURN TO EDEN

*Love is what's in the room with you at Christmas
if you stop opening presents and listen.*

—A six-year-old

I t is only in samadhi, or in the deepest meditation, that we really
fold into the Field. Most of the time we sip at the 'edges.' Of
course, I do not literally mean an edge, but a state more like
that of a spectator at a game of cricket who sits somewhat back
from the action, is able to glimpse something of the game but is
unable to note the facial expressions, the weave of the clothing or
the smell of grass and sweat. In touching an edge there is a slight
rendering of the veil, while most remains unknown. The edge is not
a part: the Field is indivisible. The edge is just a beginning, a *soupçon*,
as it were.

As the religions of the East have long upheld, the material world
is Maya, an illusion, and although we may think we are physical
beings moving through a physical world, this too is an illusion. It is
only our desires that support the illusion that this is the only reality. It is a desire not to change our deepest conditioning, of how we
interpret what our senses give us, of our conditioned ambitions to
be a mother or artist or whatever, and so on forever. These are all
'desires of the mind' that stand in the way of enlightenment.

The authority contained in the energetic level, and the enormous sense of numinous well-being one experiences when 'in touch'
is precisely why the great religious teachers keep telling us that
the physical world is 'illusory' and that the only reality resides in
the energetic realm. One of the oldest statements is contained in
the Yoga Sutra of Patanjali that appear under many of the chapter

heads in this book. They are at least 3,000 years old.[401] For so many generations "the greatest number of the subtler speculative minds and the great religious teachers have, in their various fashions, been engaged in"[402] meditation and prayer to reach this place, and tell us that we are already at one with all there is.

It is particularly poignant that most of our prescientific understanding of the Field comes from enlightened men and women who were able to see through our projections. Buddha defined the process of ongoing creation most clearly as *codependent arising*. That is, that all is emerging out of the Field and falling back in again, arising and outfolding and in the same instant infolding and returning.

What is our goal if not our enlightenment?

Beyond the senses are the objects, beyond the objects is the mind, beyond the mind the intellect, beyond the intellect the Atman, beyond the Atman the nonmanifest, beyond the nonmanifest the Spirit, and beyond the Spirit there is nothing, this is the end, it is Pure Consciousness.

—The Upanishads

Enlightenment is being able to go through what is often called the 'Veil of Perception' in order to experience both realities — the 'real' world of matter and sensual existence, and the 'illusory' world of energy — and to do so simultaneously, to shift back and forth in each world in every second. Enlightenment is not a toggle switch, either you are in or you are not. It is a gradual process of increasingly being able to sense beyond our five senses.

In my earlier book, *Notes to Transformation*, I readily admitted my ignorance, yet attempted to draw a map of the sacred journey.[403] It has proved useful, but I had to put it aside once I recognized that the numinous reality of the Field leaves the mind behind. Nevertheless signs and directions can be useful, and libraries are full of attempts to provide them.

The most succinct description of the journey I have ever read is that of the great twelfth-century Arab teacher, Hakim Sanai. In the *Hadiqa* he gives a short roadmap. It is worth intense study. Though I have added my personal invocation to some, these are stages that must be *experienced* rather then talked about. Here is what he wrote:

"If you ask me, Oh my brother, which are the signs of the path, I would answer you very clearly and without ambiguity. The Path is to look at the Truth and to break with lies, to turn your face to the living universe, to despise worldly rewards, to spring your mind free from any ambition of glory and fame, to stoop to His service, to purify your soul from evil and fortify it with discrimination, to leave the house of those who talk too much and go to the one where people are silent, and to travel from God's manifestations to God's attributes and from there to His knowledge. Then, at that moment, you will have crossed the world of mysteries and arrived at the door of poverty. When you are poverty's friend, your deep soul will have become a penitent heart. Then, God will extract poverty from your heart, and when poverty is gone from there, God will stay in your heart forever."[404]

I am hugely moved every time I read this. I try to do so aloud, as the sounds deepen the experience. I am in some doubt at even attempting to try a slowing-down sequence in absorbable bits, for I am still on the journey and far from being in Being-ness. Nevertheless, the words are like the Buddha's noble truths that support us to start learning what one is in truth and living it, in stepping aside from even the subtlest ambitions in worldly matters, to become servant to the soul's transformation and actively support the soul to be as pure as possible. This, though, is only the start. He goes on to explain that after seeking silence rather than the dramas of life, we:

"Travel from God's manifestations

from attachments to our egoic beliefs that there is anything permanent in the explicate realm, the realm in which we manifest our daily destiny

to God's attributes

to our original soul qualities that we were born with, to higher levels of the spirit including archetypes and all collective consciousness, to our original face

and from there to His knowledge.

249

to receive the intuition and wisdom that descends through the heart from the wholeness of the Field that has nothing to do with information, but carries the wisdom of the whole

Then, at that moment,

these wonderful words: "at that moment." Instantaneously. Now. No waiting.

you will have crossed the world of mysteries and

and!

arrived at the door of poverty.

The most powerful command! So hard to really comprehend this level of modesty, of being in total service to the divine and to the soul's transformation, of having nothing, not even the desire for the love for God

When you are poverty's friend,

when you do nothing for your egoic self, but revel in the experiences of knowing there is nothing to do yet watching it all happening as it unfolds

your deep soul will have become a penitent heart.

Then, God will extract poverty from your heart, and when poverty is gone from there,

God will stay in your heart forever."

Forever!

What clarity for a vision! And within the concepts of the Great Field, how true and logical and complete. Hakim Sanai offers a recipe, as so many have before and after, for obtaining access to the other side of the veil. We knew it in the womb, we have glimpsed it again and again as a child and one hopes in our later teens, and then find we have to struggle for the rest of our lives for a permanent intimacy. Yet, as the following quotations show, there is then no struggle:

God's nothingness fills the entire world; his something is nowhere.

—Meister Eckhart

Even though you tie a thousand knots, the string remains one.

—Jalal-ud-Din Rumi

Beingness is in nothingness in the mode of nothingness, and nothingness is in being in the form of being.

— Azreil of Gerona

The Tao flows through all things, inside and outside, and returns to the origin of things.

— Lao Tzu

This is what all the higher religious texts tell us, that there is no distinction between the real world and the unseen. The unseen is the nondual world without time that is the Field. The mystic state and being in the Field are one and the same thing. This is where there are no distinctions, no separations. It goes beyond the duality of our experience, beyond the definition of 'us' and 'them' and all the desires that come with that.

The richness offered in all the ancient texts is so similar that Aldous Huxley called it the perennial philosophy.[405] Just as the understanding is everywhere the same, so is the method: all aimed to help us go beyond the dualistic operation of the mind to the coherent singularity of the ground of our being.

It means that all opposites are the same, all contradictions are identical, all definitions are in the moment. It means that everything rests within the universal Ground of Being. It means there is absolutely no separation between observer and observed. It feels like we rest at a midpoint between the contradictions of life.

Ken Wilber, in using the word Spirit where I would use Field, wrote: "The nondual traditions are uncompromising: there is only Spirit, there is only God, there is only Emptiness in all its radiant wonder. All the good and all the evil, the very best and the very worst, the upright and the degenerate — each and all are radically perfect manifestations of Spirit precisely as they are. There is nothing but Spirit in all directions, and not a grain of sand, not a speck of dust, is more or less Spirit than any other."[406]

This beautiful vision contains the essence of our human potential. It is a statement of ultimate coherence in which no part of us and nothing within the Field is out of tune. We are all in the dance, and its movements are full of the compassionate love of all-pervasive rightness. Under these conditions life becomes extremely simple.

Can therapy help us get there?

Who are you to tell God when to come or when to go? You cannot tell him anything. He will arrive in His own good time. All you have to do is wait and keep the house clean.

—Bhagwan Shree Rajneesh

'Keeping the house clean' is what most spiritual teachers offer in practices and rituals including meditation and monastic retreats. Most involve long periods of discipline to still the mind and deal with the personal and energetic issues as they arise. These principles work, or we would no longer have teachers or gurus, though it is a fact that the journey is such an individual one that the methods that suited one person may not work with another. This is why few great teachers have pupils of the same quality and depth.

There is also a 'short route' offered in our times. It does not bypass other disciplines, but makes it a lot easier to get through the barriers of personal 'stuff' that hold most of us back on the journey. Various types of personal therapy are able to clear traumas more effectively than the stilling procedures of the ashram or the meditation hall. They address the problems directly, and so leaves one clear to go deeper with less accompanying baggage.

There is a profound difference between talking therapy, like counseling or behavioral modification, and transpersonal psychology that aims for the subtler and more hidden issues. When the work is allowed to go deeply into the energy fields and the soul, the coherence that results from therapy produces a quantum leap into our essence. Gallo has popularized the term Energy Psychology to cover all therapy that goes beyond the five senses and that works with fields of energy.[407] In practice there is no single method used by all practitioners, and an enormous range of modalities.[408]

I will describe the strategic approach we have developed at the Crucible Centre. There are two tributaries to the work. They might be defined in a simplistic way as removing egoic attachments and aligning our life's purpose with that of soul — of detachment and service. The two streams are examined side by side until they are each so clear they are able to flow together into the sea. There are no rules to this process for, as you would understand, each of us moves along our streams at our own pace and in our own individual ways.

The work begins by dealing with the hot traumas that worry us most so we can start developing a witnessing consciousness. The witness is our detached inner observer. When we see life from the witness we can separate from the intensity of our daily dramas and our hurts and pains. This is vital as the emotional body too easily interferes with the clarity we should be able to live by. The early stage aims to create such a balance in the psyche that we no longer manifest the traumas and dramas that most of us get caught up in. With the help of the witness we get less 'juice' from them.[409]

This quietens the mind. Though the physical nature of the brain is the source of our genius, its two hemispheres create its structural incapacity for oneness. The difference in the way each hemisphere operates creates, by its nature, the sense of incompleteness that breeds desire. It is a major task to come to the center between them, that calm space that lies in neither.

While dealing with the parental issues we sensitize ourselves to energy and soul. Gradually the wisdom of the heart finds a balance with the intellect of the brain. We connect with our souls in a deepening intimacy that brings us gradually into our true nature. Working at the energetic the more intractable issues can be cleared up, such as vanishing twins and the karma carried by the soul.

Among the teachings of Buddha there is one injunction that sums up the entire process of inner healing: it is that *all desire brings suffering*. This phrase is simple and true, especially in the more subtle work. Most contemplative religious practices emphasize the importance of letting go the demands of the ego.[410] The Christian mystic Eckhart wrote, "Whatever we find ourselves attached to we must abandon."[411] The Patanjali Sutra states: "Nonattachment is freedom from longing for all desires, either earthly or traditional, either here or hereafter." The way the mind holds onto its thoughts and beliefs is the basic resistance in therapy.

As we lose our attachment to parental issues we discover that desires are much more subtle than we may have imagined. The next step is to detach from being identified with any of them. This becomes easier as we become more conscious. Whether in the ashram or the monastery, the aim has been the same, though not always consciously expressed: to wither the belief that we are defined by our needs and thoughts.

Gradually the endless thinking and planning and mindless commentaries fade away. It is a beautiful moment when we recognize that the old dramas are passing through like a mist without us having any desire to hang on to them. This shows there is less attachment, thoughts are less dominant, and we are becoming more coherent. Jung called this state individuation, and Maharishi called is the first stage in enlightenment.

From then on any actions we undertake for some good cause can provide us with the perfect opportunities to hone our ability to remain detached.[412] When we are asked to save the earth, or to succor the poor and dying, or whatever great task we take up, we need to act with all our heart and all our energy but — the biggest 'but' of all — without being attached to the outcome.[413] The *Bhagavad Gita* states, "Be not attached to the fruits of your actions."

This does not mean we don't feel, respond, get excited, and have our hearts pounding. It does not mean we don't have moral values or ethics. But we remain unattached to the outcome. It does not eliminate fear or passion, but it does mean that fear need not degenerate into guilt or anxiety. We are strong enough in ourselves to stand up for what we are without having to manipulate for survival. If our actions turn out to be against the flow we can adjust, and let go, and create no karma through conflict. Opinions and preferences remain, though without judgment.

Then a deep inner stillness develops — a sure sign of coherence. Gradually there is a fundamental shift in attitude. As we witness our desires in order to lessen attachment to them we begin, through connection with soul, to follow the spiritual path of Hanuman, of being the Good Servant to the soul's transformation, which is like saying we are serving the truth of who we are.

Work with soul offers the most precious level of healing, for it realigns our life so we are not out for our gain, but for the transformation of our soul, and through that for the greater betterment of mankind. Through this commitment we create subtle alterations in the Field itself. Not only do we see our origin over lifetimes, but we also see ourselves within the great dance of life, we acknowledge that death has no sting, and begin to understand how we are co-creators of our lives moment to moment. Gradually we acquire the great virtues of humility, compassion, and above all, gratitude. What more can we ask for?

It is a remarkable moment to realize at this point that life can become very simple. The simpler life may, at least at first, appear rather dull. It certainly has been more interesting to be excited about a drama. This in turn brings us into such an alignment with soul that the song of life is beautifully harmonious. Less struggle and fullness is a fair exchange for less drama and uncertainty.

At this level of simplicity we notice that there is a natural morality. We do not have to compel ourselves to be unselfish or caring: We just are. If the other presents a game that is unpleasant or unjust we no longer have to play the drama game. It is like being the water in a stream that works its way around dams and snags, but is never untrue to its nature. The coherence this brings subtly changes the way we respond so we discriminate rather than react. It is moving from being under the control of the lower brains to knowing ourselves from the higher realm of the forebrain.

Peak experiences: meeting the Field unexpectedly

It was as if I were in ecstasy. I felt as though I were floating in space, as though I were safe in the womb of the universe — in a tremendous void but filled with the highest possible feeling of happiness. 'This is bliss,' I thought. 'This cannot be described: it is too beautiful.'

—Carl Jung[414]

From the beginning people with very different beliefs about God have described a reality that is both immanent and transcendent at the same time — transcendent, because it transcends the normally accepted limits of our five senses. They do not describe these states as being utterly strange, but rather they are unexpectedly familiar, like a secret place already known. They write statements like, "I have come home again," or "this is who I really am." Beyond the feeling of reconnecting with something lost but remembered, there are frequent references to the experience having included some supernormal understanding and insight, even into the past and future. There may be clairvoyance, extraordinary insights into all layers of heaven and hell, and even the capacity to speak other languages, yet it feels very commonplace at the same time, "each being fundamentally linked with ordinary human nature."[415]

Toward the end of his life Jung wrote about his experience of "the ecstasy of a nontemporal state in which present, past, and future are one. Everything that happens in time had been brought together into a concrete whole. One is woven into an indescribable whole and yet observes it with complete objectivity."[416] This was, in Hannah's words, "his experience of the miracle of grace, decisive for his whole life, and he knew for ever afterward the vital necessity of fulfilling the will of this divine power."[417] The experience is more intense than any ordinary moment, and is so much more real than everyday events that we know it is true — nothing else competes.

In two surveys conducted in Chicago they found that over fifty percent reported that at some time in their lives they had had intense, overwhelming or indescribable experiences beyond the ordinary. In these 'altered states of consciousness' time stood still, and they were left feeling joyful and uplifted. "Visionary experience is an eruption of what the medieval mystics called the unitive vision. An image or event seizes one through the imaginative faculty with such power that one really knows and experiences the unifying truth of the self. One sees, for a brief time, a glimpse of the true unity, beauty, and meaning of life."[418] It leaves us feeling immense gratitude for every aspect of life, a natural humbleness in the face of the enormity of everything.

It is not surprising that peak experiences lead people to dedicate their lives to reconnecting with the fullness of the Field, and sharing its unsharable wonder in all sorts of enigmatic ways. "Every numinous content possesses a fascination, a richness beyond the power of consciousness to apprehend and organize, a charge of energy surpassing consciousness. Hence an encounter with it always leads to an upheaval of the total personality."[419]

For a few people the experience may arrive with such intensity that the psyche is overpowered. Doctors may treat the sensations as if they were psychotic, and try to still the upheaval with drugs.

This is a huge mistake. Many people work with these Spiritual Emergencies, so-called because spirit is emerging from within the shell of the person.[420] The hardest thing about such rare and extreme events is that the person is usually totally unprepared, and may be so shocked by the experience that they make it a life's mission to understand it. Almost inevitably, they will long to experience that sense of grace again.

The Christian idea that grace is dispensed by a deity is as foreign to these peak experiences as it is to Zen and Buddhism. Grace, like compassion, is always and everywhere present, everlastingly available, and endlessly responsive to our aspirations if we only dissolve the veil. "The function of grace is to condition men's homecoming to the center...it is the very attraction of the center itself which provides the incentive to start on the way and the energy to face and overcome its many obstacles. Grace is the welcoming hand when man finds himself standing at long last on the brink of the great divide where all familiar landmarks have disappeared."[421]

It corresponds to a whole dimension of spiritual experience that is acknowledged by all religions. It is a process by which intuitive knowing, self-transcending love, and other extraordinary capacities emerge from within. These seem to be freely given rather than earned, spontaneously revealed rather than attained through any egoic effort.

Abraham Maslow coined the phrase 'peak experience.' He showed that transcendent experiences occur universally, and yet cannot be shared, as the experience is unique to each person.[422] Maslow preferred this phrase because he wished to secularize the encounter as a natural event that was available without organized ritual, though a religious context could help one to understand it. From it arises a natural sacredness that comes of its own volition. It remains with us forever, "becoming a state of mind achievable in almost any activity of life, if raised to a suitable level of perfection."[423] It is something we should be encouraging (if that were possible) so that those who "have never had them or who repress or suppress them" might have a route for their spiritual longings.[424] This is the ultimate purpose of Energy Psychology.

If it's a mission, it's impossible

Nonexistence is eagerly bubbling up in the expectation of being given existence.

—Jalal-ud-Din Rumi

Peak experiences usually push us into the desire to know this realm more deeply. The desire to want to work hard for a more permanent enlightenment and inner peace is natural. Ken Wilber has discussed this most clearly, and called it the Great Search.[425] I am very grateful for his clarity, and will use some of his phrases in this part.

But there is a trap here: working at getting enlightened actually gets in the way of getting it. This presumes that something in us needs to be changed, and is just one more desire. Most self-development movements are caught in this delicious trap. It is the trap of wanting the unwantable, grasping at the ungraspable. Just as the mind cleverly transforms the energetic vibrations in the cones of the eye into a world of objects, so the mind transforms our natural coherence with the Field into a belief that we have to do something in order to connect with it.

The concept of the Great Search, in fact, prevents us from crossing the veil, because it presumes that we have lost something. In truth, losing any part of the Field is impossible. Attachment to the aim initiates the very mechanism that pushes the aim away. Attachment promises to find tomorrow that which exists only in the timeless now. Attachment clutches at the future so fervently that the present always passes us by — very quickly — and god's smiling face with it.

We have created the idea that we are empty, which means that we need to be filled. One illusion, called loss, has spawned a host of others, called desires. These drive everything in our lives. They are attachments. Whereas if they were replaced by a simple Being-ness we would already be at our right level of coherence in the Field. This means we are much closer to 'being there' than we were when we were striving our best to get there through hard work, dedicated meditation, or long-suffering therapy.

Wanting it, by its nature, undoes the purpose! The concept of having to be dedicated simply reinforces the mistaken assumption that we are not already in the Field, and that we need to overcome that which is lacking in order to partake of that which is full. But there is no thing lacking, and there is no thing more full. There is only the ever-present flow of the Great Field. Therefore, seeking of any sort, determination of any sort, even attainment of any sort, has to be called profoundly useless.

However, should we then simply cease looking? Definitely, if we could. But the effort to stop looking for something that is such an essential human desire is itself more of the same effort. That would be pointless as the belief that we have to try and the act of trying are two consequences of the same thing — the attachment to the idea that we are not already full. This means we should relax, keep it simple, and stay awake. As the saying goes, "Merely chop wood and carry water."

So, why do any spiritual practices? Is this not just another example of the trying, and as such destined to fail? This is the most exquisite paradox of all, the most exquisite double bind that engages us in the sneakiest fashion that Zen calls "selling water by the river." We know that effort is needed, and equally we know that such effort is futile. So what do we do?

Paradox again, we just keep on doing what we are doing, while keeping the bow of the canoe facing downstream, without adding energies like ambition that just induct their opposites and hold us in place, and without any attachment to the outcome. I write this book because there are demands in me that, without thought, get me up at five every morning and impel me to turn on my laptop. I write with care and to the best of my ability, but I step back from having any attachment to the outcome — or, at least I try to. I have looked for a publisher without needing to have it published, and found Elite Books through a chance meeting with a great Swiss sandplay therapist, Ruth Ammann. It is not the same as being laid back. It is subtly different. It is doing without being forced to, with the passion of a child who lives his life in only the moment that that life is being lived.

This does not mean we should not clear up any mess we are still carrying. The canoe gets stuck in the riverbanks if we don't do this. Steering in fast-moving waters requires us to be very attentive to how we are in each moment, and free to make inner adjustments as necessary. We still need to get rid of the old entanglements and parental hangups. The more we are in tune with the flow of the water the less 'steering' we have to do.

This way, there is nothing 'we' can do to stop ourselves, because the 'we' and the play of life are just two names for the same state. Therefore remain with an effortless gentleness with yourself. Give yourself space to simply be. *If there is any sense of effort it is a distraction.* We may attain, or we may not, either is equal. Don't obstruct any natural evolution, just surrender to the Field and we will find the grace that comes through being servant to soul.

We are the consciousness of the Earth

The state of unity becomes possible when the qualities of matter no longer exercise any hold over the Self, and the pure spiritual consciousness withdraws into the One.

—Patanjali Sutra

The mystic is one of those people, existing in all religions, who understands themselves in the light of the direct experience of God.

—Robert Johnson

The ideas and evidence presented here lead to two inescapable conclusions: that everything in the universe is simultaneously physical and energetic, including the human psyche, and that every movement in one realm affects every part of every other realm. Matter and energy form a seamless and indivisible whole woven within the interactive flow of the Field. The energy in everything is affected by the entire range of energetic forms that exist.

Spiritual suffering today is deep-seated. The remoteness and immorality of Western culture is projected onto the world so that as we disparage the energetic presences of nature — be they fairies or angels or devas or pixies — we lose respect for their living presence in the environment. By polluting the earth we are changing the relationship between the Field and humanity. The connections are becoming less. Those powers in the Field that in the past resonated with every form on this planet are gradually withdrawing from the Earth. The mutual projections are diminishing.

This only increases our suffering as we humans are finding ourselves more and more on our own. We have to live in our own steel and concrete environment without support or integration. A deep and painful separation is occurring, as painful as birth or death. All our lives would be transformed were we to really take this in at the very depth of ourselves, for we could no longer feel we were alone, but inevitably part of the whole. Indeed, it is our belief in our separateness that is the greatest barrier to the survival of our species on this planet.

The natural state of life is to be so coherent that we are in tune with all the fields around us. We are born into this state, and as we lose it the psyche is disturbed, and with it our energy field. This disturbance is experienced as suffering that then impels us to disturb further all that we come in contact with.

The paradigm that most people in the world have accepted is that this is a material universe of separate objects that affect one another through direct contact. It underlies every assumption in education and scientific discussion, and when questioned will often raise eyebrows, if not temper. The 'separate-matter' paradigm, after the experimental work of the past twenty-five years, can no longer pose the only 'correct' view of the world. Neither the universe nor we humans are merely an assembly of mechanical bits, nor are our organs, including the brain, operated and maintained only by chemicals and genes.

What modern research is showing, and many of us have believed unconsciously, is that these views are too limited to explain the complexity and wonder of our world. They have formed the bedrock of physics and biology, and all our wondrous technology and our unprecedented standard of living. We have much to thank science for. However, the other side to this coin is illustrated by the unbelievably crass way in which we treat the planet and pollute the environment on which we depend — a daily stream of self-destruction not found in any other society nor any other species in history.

Globalization has produced a new social order without a holistic myth to explain, support, and direct it. Efficiency has become more important than morality. A new global myth is required, a new view of the planet and the purpose of life that has the authority to inspire and is so true it cannot be ignored. Joseph Campbell has argued, "We have to get back into accord with the wisdom of nature and realize again our brotherhood with the water and the sea. If you will think of ourselves as coming out of the earth, rather than having been thrown in here from somewhere else, you will see that we are the Earth, we are the consciousness of the Earth. You will see we are the eyes of the Earth, we are the voice of the Earth."[426]

This is what the ancients knew. All Eastern religions and sacred philosophies teach us that this is exactly the nature of reality, and they are correct in referring to our 'normal' and civilized vision as an illusion. Once we accept the possibility that all our perceptions are illusory virtual projections, we can lift the filtering and distortions of our images from the sordid desecration around us.

The simplicity this vision offers for our comprehension of existence is quite astounding. All distinctions drop away and we are left with the most satisfying concept: that we are all one in the Field, and that whatever we are and wherever our souls, life and the environment grow or fade together.

The universe exists in a vast present that includes all points of space and all moments of time in a single instant. In the Great Field, life and energy, our personal aims and the galaxies beyond exist as equally present and now. Sentient beings proceeding through countless lifetimes in different forms in infinitely many universes of infinitely many worlds — the vast unfolding of consciousness on an unimaginably large canvas. It is no paradox that soul, in being the juice by which we are nourished, is our guarantee of ordinariness.

APPENDIX I

Possible Scenario for the Creation of Matter Out of the Great Field

Purely by thinking through the nature of the Great Field as shown by experiments and clinical research, I tentatively suggest the following process by which the totality of the Field became the diversity and wonder of manifestation. The short one-sentence version is given first, and then this is split into steps. The descriptions are brutally short and may require a number of readings, but through being short one can maintain the interdependency and necessity for each step.

Short version: *movement* causes *resistance* that manifests an *identity* by asymmetrical *duality* that is *sustained* by the *coherence* of its mathematics. Only consciousness creates the illusion of *separateness*.

1. The unitary nature of the Great Field is self-disturbed by its intrinsic nature so that constituent but separate fields form and unform in its continuous flow.

2. All *movement of an individual field* through the Field causes the tiniest *resistance* that triggers the first step in manifestation. No freely flowing vibration is totally free, but is 'dampened' by the totality of vibrations in the Field. Resistance to movement slows energy down, thus 'inventing' time.

3. Resistance is in its nature an opposition that, in the next moment, implies choice that becomes more complex and less random as systems develop through endless repetition. *Duality* would then be the most fundamental state of

creation that in its simplest form is represented by attraction and repulsion. One has to induct the other for balance.

4. Through such repetition firmly coherent fields develop in play with each other at the simplest and most fundamental level, thus creating the *laws* that direct further evolution.

5. Symmetry should be the outcome of balanced duality, but never is. A very slight unpredictable imbalance generates in time that holding or clumping that produces a particular *identity* with its own type of field. As in identical twins, one is often slightly more extroverted than the other.

6. Each identity is defined by, and its permanence in the Field is *sustained by*, the coherence of its mathematics. Coherence resists change. One could say it is 'attached' to its particular mathematical model and will 'resist' attempts to change it. Thus, mud remains mud and does not loop further to become rock until another process joins in.

7. The model becomes more complex as the number of fields in a system increases, and permanence is maintained as long as there is *coherence*, which is the nature of any sovereign part of the field. Matter is never divided from the holographic nature of the Field, so that organisms are able to function as definable species.

8. When an identity ceases to be homogeneous its fields are no longer coherent and there is dis-ease, autonomy breaks down, survival may be affected and entropy ensues.

9. In higher organisms consciousness around identity, needs, will, and desires create illusions in the mind of *separateness*, and this creates the veil. The internal contradictions that follow reduce coherence. The reaction is *resistance to movement itself*. The circle is complete.

All of this reminds me of the Buddhist phrase of codependence arising.

APPENDIX II

Summary of the Psyche that Has Been Applied to the Great Field

The Field is an integral partner in the creation of personality, with all its potential, imagination, traumas, and violence. Our years of therapeutic and energy work at the Crucible Center have shown that personality is created by the following items, more or less in this order. Their relation to the Field will be clear from the earlier discussion.

1. Our primary formative factor is an energetic form we call soul. Each person's soul is a unique aspect of the Field and carries its own patterns that empower the newborn. These patterns usually include both positive and negative aspects.

2. The patterns of soul are combined with qualities acquired while in the womb and from genetic inheritance, that some call essence, and this mix forms the Ground of our Being, or Self. The natural spontaneous child is true to the Self.

3. Among all the influences on us from conception to death, the period of our creation in the womb seems to be the most important, followed by the experiences during and immediately after the birth.

4. Through connection with soul, babies are bathed in the Void of the Great Field. Thus they have an awareness of the vibrations around them, and being able to see the auras of other people are able to know them at the depth of their being.

5. We define love as being totally responsive to everything in all the fields around us. In this way we receive from life everything we energetically put out for, and thus love is the core of the universe.

6. As children see that the adults around them live in pain, grief, and tension the infant's natural response is to provide what they seem to need, and to support and heal them. Adults interpret this as unconscious love whereas in fact it is highly conscious compassion.

7. From this state of love the infant, and the child, makes decisions of how to support and nurture these unhappy adults, and do so from the natural wisdom that comes from their intuitive contact with the Field.

8. Seldom does an adult change in response to the child's support. This leaves a terrible sense of failure, and often rebounds in a sense of personal worthlessness.

9. The Self is rapidly modified by these decisions, and from the next level of decisions that are made in response to people's reactions to the earlier decisions. Decisions on how to behave and what to believe are usually made with some level of consciousness, and can therefore be remembered.

10. When a decision provides a benefit, either in love returned or in greater safety, it is reinforced until it becomes firmly fixed into the psyche as an energetic node. These will have specific locations inside and outside the body, and will continue to direct life long after their usefulness is over.

11. All accumulations of energy held in the psyche induct their opposites, which themselves turn into further accumulations.

12. As each belief or decision has changed or limited the Self, any natural creativity and curiosity that lay in the opposites will usually end up buried in the shadow. As most decisions involve replacing our real selves with something more 'civilized' we can see that a process of Self-annihilation has begun.

13. The pain of Self-annihilation is so great that we hide what we have done to just get on with life. The benefit of hiding is that we keep all these powerful feelings permanently out of sight and settle for half a life.

14. Most beliefs contradict or are negated by other beliefs, for they each arise in response to specific situations and are seldom part of any well-considered plan for survival. Being out of sync with each other they form enormous vibratory imbalances in the human energy field.

15. Situations and social requirements change as childhood moves on, and what was done from love will usually become a burden, counter-productive or plainly out-of-date. Yet by eleven of twelve changes in the structure of the brain ensure they remain fixed in place, which creates further imbalances.

16. Together these create an inner tension that becomes so habitual it feels like the essence of ourselves. Tension being a negative feeling, we hold on to it and develop a tremendous resistance to letting it go.

17. The most common pin that locks these beliefs and nodes in place is the grief that comes from having so permanently changed ourselves for love of another. This goes hand in hand with a deep yearning for the Self we have abandoned, along with its original connections with the Field.

18. The greatest healing comes when we reverse this process, re-establish contact with the essential Self, and let go of the childhood decisions that still limit us. Then we realize that love, forgiveness, and trust can lead to the highest value of all, gratitude. Intense inner joy follows. Sadly, this comes only after much inner work.

This list is a shorthand history, but I trust it is worth rereading. In it I have attempted to summarize one of the most complex tasks of our age. In the nitty-gritty of therapy we have to reverse this process, tackle some aspects from the middle, and often wait for the hardness in the personality to soften. This is not a book on the techniques of transpersonal therapy, nor is it a manual of all the varieties of human happiness and suffering — for this we need other books. It is enough to establish the nature of the Great Field and the place of our soul in it.

Permissions
& Acknowledgments

Many illustrations are copyright-free, and I am grateful to the following for permission to use illustrations: Figure 1 from the INT Photometric H-Alpha Survey of the Northern Galactic Plane, prepared by Nick Wright, University College London, on behalf of the IPHAS Collaboration; iStockphoto for Figures 2, 7, 10, 11, 12, 22, 23, 30, 34, and 38; Fotolia for 13 and 31; Chiam Tejman for Figures 19 and 20 from his site www.grandunifiedtheory.org; Cambridge University Press for 6, from D'Arcy Wentworth Thompson, *On Growth and Form*, 1996; Rudolf Steiner Press Ltd for 8, 9, 14, 16, and 17 from Theodor Schwenk, *Sensitive Chaos: The creation of flowing forms in water and air*, 1965, London; Figure 44 from a client. All other illustrations are the author's.

ENDNOTES

1. Harvey, Andrew, *The Way of Passion: A Celebration of Rumi,* Berkeley, 1994, **.

2. Jung, Carl, *Memories, Dreams, Reflections,* New York, 1963, 293 and 321.

3. Commoner, Barry, *The Closing Circle: Nature, Man, Technology,* New York, 1971.

4. McTaggart, Lynne, *The Field: The quest for the secret force of the universe,* St Ives, 2001.

5. Sheldrake, Rupert, *The Sense of Being Stared At, and Other Aspects of the Extended Mind,* London, 2003, 201.

6. Wilber, Ken, *Integral Psychology: Consciousness, Spirit, Psychology, Therapy,* Boston, 2000, 61.

7. Keynes Jr., Ken, *The Hundredth Monkey and other Paradigms of the Paranormal,* Loughton, 1991.

8. Jung, Carl, *Synchronicity: An acausal connecting principle,* London, 1962.

9. Sheldrake, Rupert, *Morphic Resonance and the Presence of the Past: The habits of nature,* Rochester, 1988, xii–xiv.

10. Sheldrake (see n.9), 97.

11. Sheldrake (see n.9), xix.

12. *The Guardian,* Nov, 2004.

13. Sheldrake (see n.9), 97.

14. Lipton, Bruce, "Insight into Cellular 'Consciousness,'" *Bridges,* xii, 2001, 5.

15. Tsong, T., "Deciphering the language of cells," *Trends in Biochemical Sciences,* xiv, 89–92, 1989.

16. Editorial, *Science,* 284, 1999, 79–109.

17. Dennett, Daniel, *Consciousness Explained,* Boston, 1991, 123.

18. Sheldrake (see n.5), 333.
19. Talbot, Michael, *The Holographic Universe, A remarkable new theory of reality*, London, 1991.
20. Langer, Susanne, *Philosophy in a New Key*, Cambridge, 1942, 21.
21. McTaggart (see n.4), 85–86.
22. Ruth, Bernard, and Fritz-Albert Popp, "Experimentelle Untersuchungen zur ultraschwachen," *Archiv fur Geschwulstforschung*, xliv, 295–306, 1974.
23. Ho, Mae-Wan, *et al.*, "Energy and Information Transfer in Biological Systems: How physics could enrich Biological Understanding," *Proceedings of the International Workshop, Acireale, Catania*, 2002.
24. Lipton, Bruce, *Fractal Biology: The science of innate intelligence*, Santa Cruz, 1998.
25. Benveniste, Jacques, *et al*, "The molecular signal is not functional in the absence of 'informed' water," *FASEB Journal*, vol. 13, Abs. 163, 1999.
26. Schiff, Michel, *The Memory of Water: Homeopathy and the battle of ideas in the new science*, London, 2001, 4.
27. Benveniste, Jacques, *et al*, "L'agitation de solutions hautement diluées n'induit pas d'activité biologique spécifique," *Comptes-Rendus de l'Académie des Sciences de Paris*, cccxii, 461–466, 1991.
28. Oyama, S, *The Ontogeny of Information*, Cambridge, 1985, 1–2.
28. Benveniste, Jacques, *et al*, "Highly dilute antigen increases coronary flow of isolated heart from immunized guinea-pigs," *FASEB Journal*, vi, A1610, 1992, 6.
30. Schiff (see n. 26).
31. *The Lancet*, 1994, 1585.
32. Davenas, E, *et al*, "Human basophil degranulation triggered by very dilute antiserum against IgF," *Nature*, cccxxxiii, 816–18, 1988.
33. Benveniste, Jacques, "Understanding digital biology," www,digibio,com/cgi-bin/node,pl?nd=n3, 1998.
34. Schiff (see n.26), 116.
35. Emoto, Masaru, *The Hidden Messages in Water*, Tokyo, 2004.
36. McTaggart (see n.4), 81.
37. Grad, Bernard, "Some biological effects of 'laying on of hands': a review of experiments with animals and plants," *Journal of the American Society for Psychical Research*, lix, 95–127, 1965.
38. Philbrick, Helen, and Richard Gregg, *Companion Plants & How To Use Them*, Old Greenwich, 1966.
39. Riotte, Louise, *Carrots Love Tomatoes: Secrets of companion planting for successful gardening*, Pownal, 1998.
40. Pert, Candace, *Molecules of Emotion, the science behind mind-body medicine*, New York, 1999, 187.

41. Grosinger, Richard, *Embryos, Galaxies and Sentient Beings*, Berkeley, 2003, 41+.

42. Pert (see n.40), 184–5.

43. Pert (see n.40), 171.

44. Pert (see n.40), 187.

45. Lipton (see n.14), 5.

46. Tsong (see n.15).

47. Davies, Paul, and John Gribbin, *The Matter Myth: Dramatic discoveries that challenge our understanding of physical reality*, New York, 1991.

48. Briggs, John, and David Peat, *Turbulent Mirror: An illustrated guide to chaos through the science of wholeness*, New York, 1989, 127.

49. Lipton, Bruce, *The Biology of Belief: Unleashing the power of consciousness, matter and miracles*, Santa Rosa, 2005, 38.

50. Sheldrake, Rupert, *A New Science of Life*, London, 1987.

51. Pearson, H, "Geneticists play the numbers game in vain," *Nature*, vol. 423, 576, 2003.

52. Lipton (see n.14), 3.

53. Lipton, Bruce, "The Human Genome Project: A cosmic joke that has the scientists rolling in the aisle," 2002, www.brucelipton.com/article/?pg=2.

54. Baltimore, David, "Our Genome Unveiled," *Nature*, vol. 409, 816, 2001.

55. For example, Ridley, Matt, "What makes you what you are," *Time Magazine*, 56–63, June 2, 2003.

56. Ridley, Matt, "What makes you what you are," *Time Magazine*, 56–63, June 2, 2003.

57. Mattick, John, *et al*, "Ultraconserved elements in the human genome," *Science*, May 2004.

58. Nijhout, H., "Metaphore and the role of genes in development," *Bioessays*, xii, 441+, 1990.

59. Waterland, R., "Transpersonal Elements; Targets for early nutritional effects on epigenetic gene regulation," *Molecular and Cell Biology*, xxiii, 5293–5300, 2003.

60. Pennisi, Edward, "Researchers Trade Insights About Gene Swapping," *Science*, Vol. 305, 334–335, 2004.

61. Lipton (see n.49), 45.

62. Heritage, John, "The fate of transgenes in the human gut," *Nature Biotechnology*, xxii, 170+, 2004; Milius, Stan, "When genes escape, does it matter to crops and weeds?", *Science News*, 164, 232+, 2004.

63. Bohm, David, "A New Theory of the Relationship of Mind and Matter," *Philosophical Psychology*, iii, 271–286, 1990, 272.

64. Bohm (see n.63), 274-5.

65. Lipton (see n.49), 102.

66. Heisenberg, Werner, *Physics and Philosophy*, New York, 1938.

67. Hiesenberg (see n.66).
68. Jahn, Robert, and Brenda Dunne, *The Margins of Reality: The Role of Consciousness in the Physical World*, San Diego, 1987.
69. Talbot, Michael, *Mysticism and the New Physics*, New York, 1981, 5.
70. McTaggart (see n. 4), 21.
71. *Nature*, Feb. 26, 1998.
72. Wheeler, John, *Geons, Black Holes, and Quantum Foam: A life in physics*, New York, 2000.
73. Zohar, Danah, *The Quantum Self: Human nature and consciousness defined by the new physics*, London, 1990, 31-34.
74. Starfield, B., "Is US health really the best in the world?" *Journal of the American Medical Association*, cclxxxiv, 483–485, 2000; Null, G., *et al, Death by Medicine*, Nutrition Institute of America, New York, 2003; Lipton (see n. 49),108.
75. Laszlo, Ervin, *The Interconnected Universe: Conceptual foundations of transdisciplinary unified theory*, Singapore, 1995.
76. Swimme, Brian, *The Hidden Heart of the Cosmos: Humanity and the new story*, New York, 1996, 93.
77. Haisch, Bennie, *et al*, "Beyond E=mc²: A first glimpse of a universe without mass," *Science*, 26+, 1994, 30-31.
78. Stefanov, Andre *et al*, "Quantum Correlations with Spacelike Separated Beam Splitters in Motion: Experimental Test of Multisimultaneity", *Physical Review Letters*, 88, 2002, 120404.
79. Bouwmeester, Dirk, *et al*, "Experimental quantum teleportation," *Nature (London)*, vol. 390, 1997, 575.
80. Blatt, Reiner, University of Innsbruck, reported in BBC News, June 16, 2004.
81. Schmidt, Helmut, "A proposed measure for psi-induced bunching of randomly spaced events," *Journal of Parapsychology*, vol. 64, 301–316, 2000.
82. Radin, Dean, and D. Ferrari, "Effects of consciousness on the fall of dice: a meta-analysis," *Journal of Scientific Exploration*, vol. 5, 61–83, 1991.
83. Braud, William, "Wellness implications of retroactive influence: Exploring an outrageous hypothesis," *Alternative Therapies in Health and Medicine*, vol. 6, 37–48, 2000.
84. Braud (see n. 83).
85. McTaggart (see n.4), 22-23.
86. Talbot (see n. 19), 39
87. Bohm, David, *Causality and Chance in Modern Physics*, London, 1957.
88. Talbot (see n. 19), 41
89. Einstein, Albert, *et al*, *Physics Review*, xlvii, 777, 1935.
90. Bell, John, *Speakable and Unspeakable in Quantum Mechanics: Collected papers on quantum philosophy*, Cambridge, 2004.

91. Bohm, David, *Wholeness and the Implicate Order*, London, 1980.
92. Aspect, Alain, *et al*, *Physics Review Letters*, il, 1804, 1982.
93. Bohm (see n. 63).
94. Bohm (see n. 91).
95. Bohm (see n. 91), 305–6.
96. Bohm (see n. 91), 11.
97. Bohm (see n. 63).
98. Talbot (see n. 19), 47.
99. Bohm (see n. 63), 279.
100. Bohm, David, and Basil Hiley, *The Undivided Universe*, London, 1995.
101. Peat, David, *Superstrings and the Search for the Theory of Everything*, London, 1988.
102. Capra, Fritsjof, *The Tao of Physics: An exploration of the parallels between modern physics and Eastern mysticism*, London, 1989.
103. Finkelstein, David, "All is Flux," *Quantum Implications: Essays in honor of David Bohm*, eds, Basil Hiley and David Peat, 289–294, London, 1987.
104. McLuhan, Marshall, *The Gutenberg Galaxy; The making of typographic man*, Toronto, 1962.
105. Quoted in Talbot (see n.19), 271.
106. Talbot (see n. 19), 43.
107. Wade, Jenny, *Changes of Mind, A holonomic theory of the evolution of consciousness*, New York, 1996, 201.
108. Haisch, Bernie, "Brilliant disguise: light, matter and the zero-point field," *Science and Spirit*, x, 30+, 1999.
109. Jung, Carl, *Modern Man in Search of a Soul*, San Diego, 1933, 17.
110. Wilber, Ken, *Eye to Eye: The quest for the new paradigm*, Boston, 1996, 154.
111. Gelder (Kunz), Dora van, *The Real World of Fairies*, Wheaton, 1977.
112. Gelder (see n. 111), 74 and 2.
113. Cairns, John, "Origin of Mutants," *Nature*, 1988.
114. Thompson, D'Arcy, *On Growth and Form*, Cambridge, 1969.
115. Thompson (see n. 114), 11, 321.
116. Ridley (see n. 56), 60.
117. Hoffman, Joseph, *The Life and Death of the Cell*, New York, 1958.
118. Goodall, Jane, *My Life with Chimpanzees*, London, 1996.
119. Pert (see n. 40).
120. Pert (see n. 40), 143
121. Kendel, Eric, *et al.*, *Principles of Neural Science*, New York, 2000.
122. Grof, Stanislav, *The Adventure of Self-Discovery*, New York, 1988.
123. Lilly, John, *The Center of the Cyclone: An autobiography of inner space*, London, 1972, 197.
124. Myss, Caroline, *Anatomy of Spirit: The seven stages of power and healing*, London, 1997, 40.

125. Rothschild, Babette, *The Body Remembers: The Psychophysiology of Trauma and Trauma Treatment*, New York, 2000.
126. Thorpe, W., *Learning and Instinct in Animals*, London, 1963.
127. Sicher, Frederick, *et al*, "A randomized double-blind study of the effect of distant healing on a population with advanced AIDS: report of a small-scale study," *Western Journal of Medicine*, vlxviii, 356–63, 1998.
128. McTaggart (see n.4), ch. 10.
129. Chopra, Deepak, *Quantum Healing: Exploring the Frontiers of Mind/body Medicine*, New York, 1989, 127.
130. Sheldrake (see n.5), 274.
131. Gerber, Richard, *Vibrational Medicine: The Handbook of Subtle-energy Therapies*, San Francisco, 1988.
132. Reiter, H., and D. Gabor, *Zellteilung und Strahlung: Sonderheft der Wissenschaftlichen Veröffentlichungen aus dem Siemens-konzern*, Berlin, 1928.
133. Burr, Harold, *Blueprint for Immortality: Electric Patterns of Life Discovered in Scientific Break-through*, New York, 1972.
134. Leadbeater, Charles, *Man Visible and Invisible*, Chicago, 1971.
135. Brennan, Barbara, *Hands of Light, A Guide to Healing Through the Human Energy Field*, New York, 1993.
136. Spermann, Hans, *Embryonic Development and Induction*, New Haven, 1938; Weis, Paul, *Principles of Development*, New York, 1939; Gurwitsch, Alexander, "Uber den Begriff des embryonalen Feldes," *Archiv fur Entwicklungmechanik*, li, 383+, 1922.
137. Weis (see n. 136), 291.
138. Gelder (Kunz), Dora van, *The Spiritual Aspects of The Healing Arts*, New York, 1985.
139. Schwenk, Theodor, *Sensitive Chaos: The Creation of Flowing Forms in Water and Air*, London, 1965.
140. Burr, Harold, and Harold Saxton, *The Fields of Life: Our Links with the Universe*, New York, 1973, 62.
141. Riotte, Louise, *Carrots Love Tomatoes : Secrets of Companion Planting for Successful Gardening*, New York, 1998.
142. Thom, René, *Structural Stability and Morphogenesis*, Reading, MA, 1975; *Mathematical Models of Morphogenesis*, Chichester, 1983.
143. Schwenk (see n.139), 34-35.
144. Benveniste (see n.33).
145. Greenberg, Gary, "Is it Prozac? Or Placebo?" *Mother Jones*, 76–81, 2003.
146. Kirsch, Irving, T, Moore, *et al*, "The Emperor's New Drugs: An analysis of antidepressant medication data submitted to the U,S, Food and Drug Administration," *Prevention and Treatment — American Psychological Association*, article 23, v 2002.

147. Fröhlich, Herbert, "Evidence for Bose condensation-like excitation of coherent modes in biological systems," *Physical Letters*, li, 21, 1975, 21.

148. Stapp, Henry, "Light as the foundation of Being," *Quantum Implications: Essays in Honor of David Bohm*, eds., Basil Hiley and David Peat, London, 1987, 260.

149. Novak, Michael, *The Joy of Sport*, New York, 1976, 164

150. Giudice, Emilio del, and Giuliano Preparata, "Water as a free electron dipole laser," *Physics Review Letters*, lxi, 1085–88, 1988.

151. McTaggart (see n. 4), 88-93.

152. Schiff (see n. 26), 15.

153. Nelson, R, D, "The physical basis of intentional healing systems," *PEAR Technical Note 99001*, 1999.

154. Grinberg-Zylberbaum, J., and J., Ramos, "Patterns of interhemisphere correlations during human communication," *International Journal of Neuroscience*, xxxvi, 41–53, 1987.

155. McTaggart (see n. 4).

156. Braud, William *et al.*, "Reactions to an unseen gaze," *Journal of Parapsychology*, lvii, 391–409, 1993; Shelldrake (see n. 5).

157. McTaggart (see n. 4), 180.

158. Dossey, Larry, *Reinventing Medicine: Beyond mind-body to a new era of healing*, San Francisco, 1999.

159. Yamamoto, Mikio, *et al.*, "Study on analyzing methods of human body functions using various simultaneous measurements," *Journal of International Society of Life Information Science*, xviii, 61–97, 2000.

160. Hegel, J., *et al.*, "Effects of group practice of Transcendental Meditation Program on preventing violent crime in Washington, D,C,: Results of the National Demonstration Project," *Social Indicators Research*, xlvii, 153+, 1994.

161. Dillbeck, M, "The Transcendental Meditation Program and crime-rate change in a sample of 48 cities," *Journal of Crime and Justice*, iv, 25–45, 1981.

162. Mandelbrot, Benoit, *Fractals and Chaos*, Hamburg, 2004; see also Mandelbrot, Benoit, *The Fractal Geometry of Nature*, New York, 1982.

163. Schwenk (see n. 139).

164. Lipton (see n. 24).

165. Thompson (see n. 114), 17.

166. Hamming, R, "The unreasonable effectiveness of mathematics," *American Mathematics Monthly*, lxxxvii, 1980, 81.

167. Peitgen, Heinz-Otto, *The Beauty of Fractals: Images of complex dynamical systems*, New York, 1986, 75.

168. Gleick, James, *Chaos: Making a new science*, Bungay, 1987, 293.

169. Goldberger, Ary *et al.*, "Some Observations on the Question: Is ventricular fibrillation chaos?" *American Medical Journal*, 338, 1988.

170. Zohar (see n. 73).
171. Gleick (see n. 168).
172. James, John, *The Contractors of Chartres*, Wyong, 1978.
173. Lipton (see n. 14).
174. Tejman, Chiam, in www,grandunifiedtheory,org,il.
175. Tejman, Chiam, *Grand Unified Wave Theory*, Haifa, 2001.
176. Wilber, Ken, *The Eye of Spirit: An Integral Vision for a World Gone Slightly Mad*, Boston, 1998.
177. Lorenz, Edward, "Predictability: Does the flap of a butterfly's wing in Brazil set off a tornado in Texas?" address to the American Association for the Advancement of Science, 1979.
178. Pearce, Joseph Chilton, *The Biology of Transcendence: A Blueprint of the Human Spirit*, Rochester, 2002, 28.
179. Goldberg, Elkhonon, *The Executive Brain: Frontal Lobes and the Civilized Mind*, New York, 2001.
180. Carter, Rita, *Mapping the Mind*, London, 1998, 71.
181. Pearce (see n. 178), 32.
182. Pribram, Karl, *Brain and Perception: Holonomy and Structure in Figural Processing*, New Jersey, 1991.
183. Grof, Stanislav, *Realms of the Human Unconscious*, New York, 1976.
184. Talbot (see n. 69)
185. Davies, Paul, *About Time: Einstein's unfinished revolution*, London, 1995, 278.
186. Bohm (see n. 63), 284.
187. Talbot (see n. 19), 50
188. Freeman, Walter, *How Brains Make Up their Minds*, New York, 1999, 117.
189. Pribram (see n.182)
190. Fodor, Jerry, *The Mind Doesn't Work that Way*, Boston, 2001.
191. Prideaux, Jeff, "Comparison between Karl Pribram's 'Holographic Brain Theory' and more conventional models of neuronal computation," *Virginia Commonwealth University*, www.acsa2000.net/bcngroup/jponkp/#chap5
192. McCraty, Rollin, *Heart-Brain Neurodynamics: The Making of Emotions*, HeartMath Institute, 2002.
193. Armour, John, and J. Ardell, eds., *Neurocardiology*, New York, 1994.
194. Pert (see n. 40).
195. McArthur, David, and Bruce McArthur, *The Intelligent Heart*, Virginia Beach, 1997.
196. Rein, Glen, and Rollin McCraty, "Structural changes in water and DNA associated with new physiologically measurable states," *Journal of Scientific Exploration*, viii, 438–439, 1994.
197. McCraty, Rollin, *The Energetic Heart: Bioelectromagnetic Interactions Within and Between People*, Boulder Creek, 2003.

198. Cooper, Robert, and Ayman Sawaf, *Executive EQ: Emotional intelligence in business*, London, 1997.
199. Pearce (see n.178), 66.
200. Pearce (see n.178), 60.
201. HeartMath Centre, www.heartmath.org/research/research-publications.html.
202. Ring, Kenneth, *Life at Death*, New York, 1980, 247.
203. Belo, Jane, and Margaret Mead, *Children and Ritual in Bali*, New York, 2001.
204. Pribram (see n. 182), ch 9.
205. McLean, Paul, *The Triune Brain in Evolution*, New York, 1990.
206. Carter (see n. 180), 182.
207. Pearce (see n. 178).
208. Johnson, Robert, *Transformation: Understanding the three levels of masculine consciousness*, San Francisco, 1991, 104–5.
209. Laszlo (see n. 75).
210. Goldberg (see n. 179).
211. Schore, Allan, *Affect Regulation and the Origin of the Self: The Neurobiology of Emotional Development*, Hillsdale, 1994, 252.
212. Pearce (see n. 178), 49–52.
213. Pearce, Joseph Chilton, *Evolution's End*, New York, 1992, 146.
214. Schore (see n. 211).
215. Pearce (see n. 178), 48.
216. Pearce (see n. 178), 48.
217. Storr, Anthony, *Human Aggression*, New York, 1968.
218. Pearce (see n. 178), 61.
219. Bailey, Alice, *The Yoga Sutra of Patanjali*, trans., Djwhal Kuhl, London, 1927.
220. McTaggart (see n. 4), 159–163.
221. Myss (see n. 124), 39.
222. Peat, David, *Synchronicity: The Bridge Between Mind and Matter*, New York, 1987, 235.
223. McCraty, Rollin, *et al.*, "Electrophysiological Evidence of Intuition: The surprising role of the heart," *Journal of Alternative and Complementary Medicine*, 2004.
224. Baud, William, *et al.*, "Attention focusing facilitated through remote mental interaction," *Journal for the American Society for Psychical Research*, 89, 1995, 103–15.
225. Rosenthal, R, "Combining results of independent studies," *Psychological Studies*, lxxxv, 185–93, 1978.
226. Laszlo (see n. 75), 101.
227. Backster, Cleve, "Evidence of a Primary Perception in Plant Life," *International Journal of Parapsychology*, x, 139–52, 1967.
228. Pearce (see n. 178), 88.

229. Grof, Stanislav, *The Cosmic Game: Explorations of the frontiers of human consciousness*, New York, 1998, 113.
230. Sheldrake (see n. 9), xvii.
231. Abram, David, "A More-than-Human World," *An Invitation to Evolutionary Philosophy*, ed. Anthony Weston, New York, 17–42, 1999.
232. Bohm (see n. 63), 280.
233. Quoted in Talbot (see n. 19), 271.
234. Bradbury, Ray, *Bradbury Stories: One Hundred of his Most Celebrated Tales*, San Francisco, 2003.
235. Moody, Raymond, and Paul Perry, *The Light Beyond*, New York, 1988, 103–7.
236. Talbot (see n. 19), 249.
237. Moody, Raymond, *Life after Life*, New York, 1975.
238. Farrant, Graham, "Cellular Consciousness," *Aesthema*, vii, 28–39, 1986.
239. Rothschild (see n. 125).
240. James, John, *Notes to Transformation*, Leura, 1994, 12–13.
241. John of Salisbury, *Metalogicon*, Bk II, ch. 17.
242. Jung, Carl, *Archetypes and the Collective Unconscious*, London, 1961.
243. Jung (see n. 242).
244. Wilber (see n. 6).
245. Davies, Paul, *The Mind of God: Science and the search for ultimate meaning*, London, 1992.
246. Tuchman, Barbara, *The Guns of August*, London, 1994.
247. Lovelock, James, *The Revenge of Gaia*, London, 2006.
248. Grof, Stanislav, and Hal Bennett, *The Holotropic Mind: Three Levels of Human Consciousness and How They Shape Our Lives*, San Francisco, 1990.
249. Wilber (see n. 176), 264+.
250. Lovelock, James, *Gaia: A New Look at Life on Earth*, Oxford, 1982.
251. Grinberg-Zylberbaum (see n. 154).
252. Moody (see n. 237).
253. Ornish, Dean, *Love and survival: The Scientific Basis for the Healing Power of Intimacy*, New York quoting Gary Schwartz, Director of the Human Systems Laboratory, 1998, 190.
254. Wheeler (see n. 72).
255. Dossey, Larry, *Be Careful What You Pray For…You Might Just Get It: What we can do about the unintentional effect of our thoughts, prayers and wishes*, San Francisco, 1998.
256. Roberts, Jane, *Seth Speaks: The Eternal Validity of the Soul*, Englewood Cliffs, 1972
257. Dass, Ram, and Mirabai Bush, *Compassion in Action*, New York, 1992.

258. Straugh, Ralph, *The Reality Illusion,* New York, 1983.

259. Pearce (see n. 178).

260. Cromwell, David, "Zen and the Art of Theories of Everything," *New Humanist,* cxiii, 1998.

261. Franz, Marie-Luise von, *Archetypal Dimensions of the Psyche,* Boston, 1999.

262. Jung (see n. 2), 414.

263. Jung (see n. 2), 293 and 321.

264. Jung, Carl, *Man and his Symbols,* London, 1978, 73.

265. Jung, Carl, *Answer to Job,* in *Collected Works,* xi, Princeton, 1973.

266. Jung (see n. 2).

267. Pearce (see n. 213).

268. Jung (see n. 2).

269. Everett, Hugh, "Many-universe interpretation of quantum theory," *Revolutionary Modern Physics,* xxix, 454, 1957, 454; also Witt, B. de, and N. Graham, *The Many-worlds Interpretation of Quantum Mechanics,* Princeton, 1973; Davies, Paul, "Multiverse or Design? Reflections on a 'Third Way,'" Talk Sydney, Nov, 2003.

270. Hartle, James, "Excess Baggage," *Particle Physics and the Universe: Essays in Honor of Gell-Mann,* Cambridge, 1991.

271. Davies (see n. 245), 159.

272. Stenger, Victor, *The Comprehensible Cosmos,* New York, 2006, 122; Goswami, Amit *et al.,* *The Self-Aware Universe: How Consciousness Creates the Material Universe,* New York, 1995.

273. Hawking, Stephen, *A Brief History of Time,* London, 1988, 141.

274. Hooft, Gerard 't, *In Search of the Ultimate Building Blocks,* Cambridge, 1997, 174.

275. Davies, Paul, *The Accidental Universe,* Cambridge, 1982.

276. Carter, Brandon, *Confrontation of Cosmological Theories and Observations,* Dortrecht, 1974.

277. Lovelock (see n. 250).

278. Wheeler (see n. 72).

279. McFadden, Johnjoe, *Quantum Evolution: The new science of life,* New York, 2001.

280. Bradbury (see n. 234).

281. White, John, and Stanley Krippner, "A New-Age fallacy," *Future Science,* 257–279, New York, 1977.

282. Brennan (see n. 135).

283. Sheldrake (see n. 5).

284. Braud, William, and Marilyn Schlitz, "Consciousness interactions with remote biological systems: Anomalous intentionality effects," *Subtle Energies,* ii, 1–46, 1991.

285. Ravitz, Leonard, and Edward Russell, *Electrodynamic Man: Electromagnetic Fields Measurements in Biology, Medicine, Hypnosis and Psychiatry,* San Francisco, 1995.

286. Popov, Vladimir, and Constantine Tsipis, *New Methods in Quantum Theory*, Stuttgart, 1996.

287. Quoted by Talbot (see n. 19), 47; see also Mindell, Arnold, *Quantum Mind: The Edge Between Physics and Psychology*, Portland, 2000.

288. Lipton (see n. 14).

289. Brennan (see n. 135).

290. Ho, Mae-Wan, "The Entangled Universe," *Yes! A Journal of Positive Futures*, 2000.

291. Josephson, Brian, and Fotini Palikari-Viras, "Biological utilization of quantum nonlocality," *Foundations of Physics*, xxi, 197+, 1991, 199.

292. Brennan (see n. 135).

293. Pribram (see n. 182).

294. Loye, David, *An Arrow Through Chaos: How we see into the future*, Rochester, 2000, 16–17.

295. McTaggart (see n. 4), ch. 5.

296. McTaggart (see n. 4), 117–19 et seq.

297. Schempp, Walter, *Magnetic Resonance Imaging: Mathematical Foundations and Applications*, London, 1988.

298. Pribram (see n. 182), ch 9.

299. Talbot (see n. 69), 5.

300. McTaggart (see n. 4), 109.

301. McTaggart (see n. 4), 119.

302. Bohm (see n. 63), 271.

303. Jahn, Robert, "A Modular Model of Mind/matter Manifestations," *PEAR Technical Notes*, 2001.

304. Jahn and Dunne, in McTaggart (see n. 4), 161, n. 44.

305. Johnson, Robert, *Inner Work, using dreams and active imagination for personal growth*, San Francisco, 1989, 30.

306. Patterson, Stephen and Marvin Meyer, *The "Scholars' Translation" of the Gospel of Thomas*, www.users.misericordia.edu/davies/thomas/Trans.htm, 37.24a–35.

307. James (see n. 240).

308. Berne, Eric, *Games People Play: The Basic Handbook of Transactional Analysis*, New York, 1996.

309. Johnson, Robert, *Owning Your Own Shadow: Understanding the Dark Side of the Psyche*, New York, 1992.

310. Jung (see n. 264).

311. Post, Lauren van der, *A Walk with a White Bushman*, London, 1986, 49.

312. Stone, Hal, and Sidra Stone, *Embracing Your Inner Critic: Turning Self-criticism into a Creative Asset*, New York, 1993.

313. Johnson (see n. 305), 30; see also Wolf, Fred, *The Spiritual Universe: How Quantum Physics Proves the Existence of the Soul*, New York, 1996.

314. Danesh, H, *The Psychology of Spirituality*, New Delhi, 1998, 42.

315. Griffin, Donald, *God and Religion in the Post-modern World*, New York, 1989.

316. Steiner, Rudolf, *Occult Science: An outline*, trans. George & Mary Adams, London, 1972, 53; Rank, Otto *et al.*, *Psychology and the Soul: A Study of the Origin, Conceptual Evolution, and Nature of the Soul*, Baltimore, 2003.

317. Bettelheim, Bruno, *Freud and Man's Soul*, Random, New York, 1984.

318. Hillman, James, *The Soul's Code: In Search of Character and Calling*, London, 1996; Moore, Thomas, *Care of the Soul: A Guide for Cultivating Depth and Sacredness in Everyday Life*, New York, 1992; Sardello, Robert, *Facing the World with Soul: The Reimagination of Modern Life*, New York, 1994.

319. Murphy, Michael, *The Future of the Body: Explorations into the Further Evolution of Human Nature*, New York, 1992, 185.

320. Rowan, John, *The Transpersonal: Psychotherapy and Counseling*, London, 1993, 99.

321. Ali Hameed Almaas, *The Inner Journey Home: Soul's Realization of the Unity of Reality*, Boston, 2004, 20.

322. Jung (see n.109), par. 85.

323. Bailey, Lee Worth, and Jenny Yates, *The Near-Death Experience: A Reader*, New York, 1996.

324. Jung (see n. 109).

325. Johnson (see n. 305), 30.

326. Moore, (see n. 318), xiii.

327. James, John, "Soul Clear, Soul Mysterious," *Living Now!*, liv, 2003, 4; Tarrant, John, *The Light Inside the Dark: Zen, Soul and the Spiritual Life*, Sydney, 1999.

328. Hilman (see n. 318).

329. Moore (see n. 318).

330. James (see n. 240), ch. 17.

331. Bailey and Yates (see n. 323).

332. Newton, Michael, *Journey of Souls: Case Studies of Life Between Lives*, Minnesota, 1998, 72.

333. Leadbeater, Charles, and Fritz Kunz, *The Personality of Rocks*, London, 1925.

334. Lovelock, (see n. 250).

335. Harvey, (see n. 1).

336. Hillman, (see n. 318), 27.

337. Vaughan, Frances, *Shadows of the Sacred*, Wheaton, 1995.

338. James (see n. 240), ch. 17.

339. Garvan, Marg, *Energetic Love: A Transpersonal Approach to Knowing Yourself*, Grad-Dip thesis, Hartley Vale, 2005, 6.

340. Ali Hameed Almaas, *The Void: Inner Spaciousness and Ego Structure*, California, 1992; Grof (see n. 229).

341. Grof (see n. 229), 30.
342. Grof, Stanislav, *Beyond the Brain: Birth, Death and Transcendence in Psychotherapy*, Albany, 1985.
343. Nelson, John, "Madness or Transcendence?" in *Transpersonal Psychotherapy*, ed. Seymour Boorstein, 305–328, New York, 1996, 309.
344. Ali Hameed Almaas, *Essence: The Diamond Approach to Inner Realization*, Maine, 1986, 81+.
345. Wade, Jenny, "Physically transcendent awareness: A comparison of the phenomenology of consciousness before birth and after death," *Journal of Near-Death Studies*, xvi(4), 249–275, 1997, 255.
346. Lilly (see n. 123).
347. Chamberlain, David, *Babies Remember Birth: And Other Extraordinary Scientific Discoveries about the Mind and Personality of your Newborn*, Los Angeles, 1988, 188; Verny, T., and John Kelly, *The Secret Life of the Unborn Child*, New York, 1981.
348. Sabom, Michael, *Recollections of Death: A Medical Investigation*, New York, 1982.
349. Chamberlain (see n. 347), 104.
350. Wade (see n. 345), 252.
351. Wade (see n. 345), 256–57.
352. Wade (see n. 345).
353. Wambach, Helen, *Life before Life*, Boston, 1982.
354. Chamberlain (see n. 347), 181.
355. Chamberlain, David, "Babies are conscious," *Untwinned: Perspectives on the Death of a Twin before Birth*, ed. Althea Hayton, St Albans, 2007, 121+.
356. Chamberlain, David, "The expanding boundaries of memory," *Pre- and Peri-natal Psychology Journal*, iv, 1990, 179; also Chamberlain, David, "Are telepathy, clairvoyance and 'hearing' possible in utero? Suggestive evidence as revealed during hypnotic age-regression studies in prenatal memory," *Pre- and Peri-natal Psychology Association of North America*, vii, 125–137, 1992.
357. Bouchard, Thomas, *et al.*, "Sources of human psychological differences: The Minnesota Study of Twins Reared Apart," *Science*, cv, 782–91, 1990.
358. Clark, William, and Michael Grunstein, *Are We Hard-wired? The Role of Genes in Human Behavior*, Oxford, 2000, ch. 3.
359. O'Brien, Meredith, *The Rescuing Hug: The Benefits of Co-Bedding Infant Twins*, on the web, 1996.
360. Chamberlain (see n. 347).
361. Hayton, Althea, ed. *Untwinned: Perspectives on the Death of a Twin before Birth*, St Albans, 2007; James (see n. 240).
362. Weinrib, Estelle, *Image of the Self: The Sandplay Therapy Process*, Massachusetts, 1983.

363. Dusen, W. van, "Wu Wei, No-Mind and the Fertile Void in Psychotherapy," *Psychologia: an International Journal of Psychology in the Orient*, i, 253–56, 1958.

364. Hayton (see n. 361).

365. James, John, "The vanishing twin syndrome, and the reality of the trauma the loss leaves behind," *Untwinned: Perspectives on the Death of a Twin before Birth*, ed. Althea Hayton, 184+, St Albans, 2007.

366. Sulak, L., and M. Dodson, "The vanishing twin: pathologic confirmation of an ultrasonographic phenomenon," *The American Journal of Obstetrics and Gynaecology*, lxviii, 811–15, 1986.; Landy, H., and L. Keith, "The vanishing twin: a review," *Journal of Human Reproduction (Update)*, iv, 177+, 1998.

367. James (see n. 240), ch. 3.

368. Chamberlain (see n. 355).

369. Leboyer, Frederick, *Birth without Violence*, London, 1975.

370. Grof (see n. 342).

371. Grof (see n. 122); James (see n. 240).

372. Bradshaw, John, *Homecoming: Reclaiming and Championing your Inner Child*, New York, 1992.

373. Laszlo (see n. 75), 102–3.

374. Shroder, Tom, *Old Souls: The Scientific Evidence for Past Lives*, New York, 1999.

375. Stevenson, Ian, *Cases of the Reincarnation Type*, Virginia, 1979.

376. Rossi, Ernest and David Cheek, *Mind-Body Therapy: Methods of Ideodynamic Healing in Hypnosis Cheek*, New York, 1992, 135.

377. Chamberlain (see n. 347), 191.

378. O'Grady, Annie, *Past Lifetimes: Keys for change*, Burra Creek, 1997, 19–40.

379. Rinpoche, Sogyal, *The Tibetan Book of Living and Dying*, Sydney, 1993.

380. Moody (see n. 237).

381. Pearce (see n. 178), 38.

382. Jung (see n. 2), 233.

383. Newton (see n. 332), 97.

384. Newton (see n. 332), 194.

385. Newton (see n. 332), 248.

386. Chamberlain (see n. 356).

387. Dallett, Janet, *The Not-yet Transformed God*, York Beach, 1998, 86+.

388. McTaggart, Lynne, *The Intention Experiment*, New York, 2007.

389. Almaas (see n. 321), 5.

390. Harvey (see n. 1), 265.

391. Lovelock (see n. 247).

392. Hillman, James, *The Force of Character: And the Lasting Life*, New York, 1999, 95.

393. Lilly (see n.123).

394. Newton (see n. 332), 37-.
395. Myss (see n. 124).
396. Rajneesh, Bhagwan, *Dang Dang Doko Dang*, Rajneeshpuram, 1997, ch 2.
397. Harvey (see n. 1), 163.
398. Bailey (see n. 219).
399. Lovejoy, Arthur, *The Great Chain of Being: A Study of the History of an Idea*, Harvard, 1970.
400. James (see n. 240), ch. 21.
401. Harvey (see n. 1), 163–64.
402. Huxley, Aldous, *Perennial Philosophy*, New York, 1945.
403. Wilber (see n. 176), 281
404. Gallo, Fred, *Energy Psychology in Psychotherapy: A Comprehensive Source Book*, New York, 2002.
405. Church, Dawson, *The Genie in your Genes: Epigenetic Medicine and the New Biology of Intention*, Santa Rosa, 2007, 215+.
406. James (see n. 240).
407. Freke, Timothy, and Peter Gandy, *Die Welt de Mystik*, Munich, 2001.
408. Forman, Robert, *Meister Eckhart: The Mystic and the Theologian*, Longmead, 1991, 78.
409. Ram Dass (see n. 257), 133+.
410. www.planetextinction.com
411. Jung (see n. 2), 293 and 321.
412. Murphy (see n. 319).
413. Jung (see n. 2), 295.
414. Hannah, Barbara, *Jung: His Life & Work: A Biographical Memoir*, Wilmet, 1999, 339.
415. Johnson (see n. 305), 216–17.
416. Neumann, Erich, "Mystical Man," *Analytical Psychology Club*, New York, Spring 1961, 15.
417. Grof, Stanislav, and Christina Grof, *The Stormy Search for the Self*, Los Angeles, 1991.
418. Pallis, M, "Is there room for grace in Buddhism?" *Sword of Gnosis*, 275–79, London, 1974.
419. Murphy (see n. 319), 41–42 and 386–526.
420. Maslow, Abraham, *The Farther Reaches of Human Nature*, Esalen, 1982, 170.
421. Maslow (see n. 420), 179.
422. Wilber (see n. 6).
423. Campbell, Joseph, *Myths to Live By*, New York, 1972.

INDEX